THE GEEK'S GUIDE TO SPACE

INSIDE GEMINI

David Woods and David M. Harland

Rosen YA
New York

This edition published in 2018 by
The Rosen Publishing Group, Inc.
29 East 21st Street
New York, NY 10010

Library of Congress Cataloging-in-Publication Data

Names: Woods, David, author. | Harland, David M, author.
Title: Inside the Gemini / David Woods and David M. Harland.
Description: New York : Rosen Publishing, 2018. | Series: The geek's guide to space | Audience: Grades 7–12. | Includes bibliographical references and index.
Identifiers: ISBN 9781499466973 (library bound)
Subjects: LCSH: Project Gemini (U.S.)—History—Juvenile literature.
Classification: LCC TL789.8.U6 W66 2018 | DDC 629.45'4—dc23

Manufactured in China

Originally published in English by Haynes Publishing under the title: *NASA Gemini 1965–1966 (All Missions, All Models): An Insight Into NASA's Gemini Spacecraft, the Precursor to Apollo and the Key to the Moon* © David Woods and David M. Harland 2015.

Acknowledgements

The authors would like to thank the following for their assistance in the production of this manual: Mike Jetzer of heroicrelics.org for helping to ferret out documents and pictures; Steve Garber and Colin Fries at the NASA History Division; Rob Getz of stellar-views.com for supplying scans from his collection; Gary Brossett for supplying images of the Titan II rocket and engines; Steve Jurvetson for making images from his Flickr collection available; Chuck Penson of the Titan Missile Museum; National Museum of the US Air Force; US Space & Rocket Center; Don Boelling for supplying engine schematics; Mark Gray of spacecraftfilms.com; Kevin Woods for creating the front cover illustration and assisting with the graphic demands of the book; and Anne Woods for supplying the coffee that kept the effort going.

Contents

6 Introduction

8 Gemini – history and development

Mercury 10
Apollo and the lunar goal 11
The mode decision 12
Lunar orbit rendezvous 12
Mercury Mark II 12
Titan II launch vehicle 13
Gemini becomes official 14
A spacecraft for pilots 15
Space race 15
Air Force Gemini 16
The Rogallo wing 18

20 Titan II launch vehicle

Vehicle description 25
First stage 25
LR-87-7 engine 26
Second stage 28
Flight 28

30 Gemini-Agena target vehicle

Agena for Gemini 33
GATV 34
Engine starting 36
Helium pressurization 36
Attitude control 36
Secondary propulsion system 36
Target docking adapter 37
Augmented target docking adapter 39

40 Spacecraft structure

Overview 41
Re-entry module 43
Spacecraft skin 47
Heatshield 48
Adapter module 49

52 Propulsion

Orbit attitude and maneuver system (OAMS) 55
De-orbit solid rockets 58
Re-entry control system (RCS) 60

62 Guidance and control

Radar 64
Inertial guidance system 68
Horizon scanner 70

72 Power and life support

Electrical system 74
Environmental control system (ECS) 77

80 Pyrotechnic systems

Slow burn or fast? 82
Earth landing/recovery 84
Ejection seats 87

90 Crew systems

Spacesuits 92
Cabin interior 96
Communications/tracking 97

100 Launch and endurance

"No liftoff!" 104
Flight duration 106

110 Orbital operations

A meeting in space 115
The perils of Gemini 8 119
The angry alligator 122
One mission, two Agenas 126
Rendezvous in one 130
Gemini 12 135

140 Spacewalking

Jetpacks for Gemini 146
Cernan's terror 147
"A motion of stately grace" 151
Gordon's trials 153
EVA licked 155

162 Returning to Earth

Gemini 3 off target 164
Ballistic re-entry 166
Navigation error 166
Nearing the ships 167

171 Conclusion

172 Appendix

174 Glossary

175 For More Information

177 For Further Reading

178 Index

Introduction

“Gemini, in its own historical context, was perhaps as important as Apollo because without Gemini, there would have been no Apollo.”

Eugene Cernan; Pilot Gemini 9, Commander Apollo 17

OPPOSITE **Gemini 7 coasts over the ocean, as photographed from Gemini 6. The meeting of these two spacecraft represented the first rendezvous in space, a demonstration of techniques that would be crucial to the upcoming Apollo program.** *(NASA)*

April 1961 was a very difficult month for John F. Kennedy, the recently elected president of the United States of America. On the twelfth, a Wednesday, his administration was severely tested when the Soviet Union once again took the lead in space by sending a human, Yuri Gagarin, into orbit. On the following Monday, CIA-backed Cuban exiles dismally botched an attempted invasion of Cuba. In the aftermath, Kennedy looked around for a gesture that might restore the United States' reputation.

The following month, on May 25, he challenged his country's engineers to achieve a manned lunar landing before the Sixties were over, an audacious goal that left many aghast. After all, only 20 days earlier, the US had gained just a few minutes of space flight experience when Alan Shepard took a short ride in the first Mercury spacecraft, a flight that didn't even achieve orbit.

With an already tight deadline, NASA struggled for over a year to figure out how best to accomplish this task. Once a plan had been agreed, it became starkly clear that getting to the Moon would demand a suite of skills that this budding spacefaring nation had yet to learn. Chief among these skills was rendezvous, the ability to bring two spacecraft into close vicinity even as they travel at great speed.

Rendezvous appeared to be a risky, dangerous thing to do, yet it was an essential element of the method NASA had settled upon to reach the Moon. They even called this technique *lunar orbit rendezvous* (LOR) because this capability defined the entire mission, right back to the size of the launch vehicle that would begin the trip. In particular, on leaving the lunar surface, LOR would require a crew to rendezvous with a mothership. Both ships would be travelling around the Moon at nearly 6,000km/hr and there would be little navigational support. Though many other skills would be needed – such as docking, long duration flight, spacewalking, and accurate landing – the highest priority was to learn how to rendezvous in space.

At the same time, the Mercury project was hitting its stride. This little conical spacecraft gave the US its first experience in manned space flight, but it had been designed in a hurry and had to be light. The Atlas rocket that placed it into orbit was meant to carry lightweight nuclear warheads, not passenger-carrying spacecraft. As a result, the capabilities of the one-man Mercury spacecraft were severely limited. It had no means to maneuver except to rotate. It could not alter its orbit, and once set to return to Earth it could not control where it would land.

Engineers learned much about spacecraft design from Mercury. Among its many shortcomings, it proved difficult to test or repair since its systems were stacked inside its pressure shell and were often inaccessible. As it began to fly, thoughts turned to its successor.

The new spacecraft, to be launched on the much more powerful Titan rocket, would be a two-man machine and it was formally instituted in December 1961 as a NASA program called Gemini. Its main purpose was to develop the skill of rendezvous, in many ways the key to the Moon. Along the way, there would be a raft of technological and managerial questions that would have to be addressed, and a series of near and actual disasters that NASA would have to come to terms with.

Gemini was the teacher and thanks to its lessons, we were able to reach the Moon in 1969.

Chapter One

Gemini – history and development

In a sense, the Gemini spacecraft is a bit like the Ford Model T car. To modern eyes, its engineering and technology seem relatively unsophisticated. Yet at the time, it represented an incredible leap in the state of the art from a machine that just about worked, to one that worked well enough to be useful. Whereas the pilots of the Mercury spacecraft had done little more than go along for the ride, with Gemini they could actually do something. Like the Model T, lessons learned in Gemini's design would profoundly influence subsequent spacecraft. And in a short space of time, more than a dozen would come off the production line at the McDonnell Aircraft Corporation.

OPPOSITE Artist's cutaway of the Gemini spacecraft. *(NASA)*

Mercury

McDonnell had already cut their teeth as spacecraft builders with the Mercury capsule. This small, one-man ship had been central to the United States' unsuccessful attempt to get a man in space before the Soviet Union. Within a fledgling NASA, it was conceived by a small team of former aircraft engineers known as the Space Task Group who were based at Langley Research Center in Hampton, Virginia. They would eventually relocate to Houston, Texas to form the Manned Spacecraft Center, the home of mission control for US human space flight.

Mercury was a crash program. It was instituted as the space race left the starting blocks and designed in a hurry by people who were still feeling their way into an entirely new medium for travel. Apart from technology borrowed from the nuclear missile programs, they had little to go on. But Mercury did prove that many of their initial hunches were correct. A heatshield at the blunt end of a conical capsule was a good way to get a human passenger through the very high temperatures associated with atmospheric re-entry. A parachute could provide a safe landing on Earth's surface. Small maneuvering thrusters were essential to control which way the spacecraft pointed; its so-called *attitude*. And the use of a single gas, oxygen, as a crewman's air supply would be sufficient for his needs.

As events transpired, Mercury was beaten into space by a Soviet spacecraft called Vostok that carried Yuri Gagarin on a single orbit of Earth on April 12 1961. Nevertheless, the Mercury project did eventually deliver six US astronauts to space successfully; two on short up-down ballistic flights and four on orbital missions of increasing duration. It ended on May 16 1963 when Gordon Cooper nursed his spacecraft far beyond its designed lifetime, flying 22 orbits to set an American endurance record of 34 hours.

But the technology for Mercury was immature and its execution rushed. To get into space, it rode rockets designed to deliver either short-range conventional explosives or the lightweight nuclear weapons of the US military. When these launchers were called upon to lift

LEFT The Mercury spacecraft with the launch escape tower on top and the retrograde package attached to its base by straps. *(NASA)*

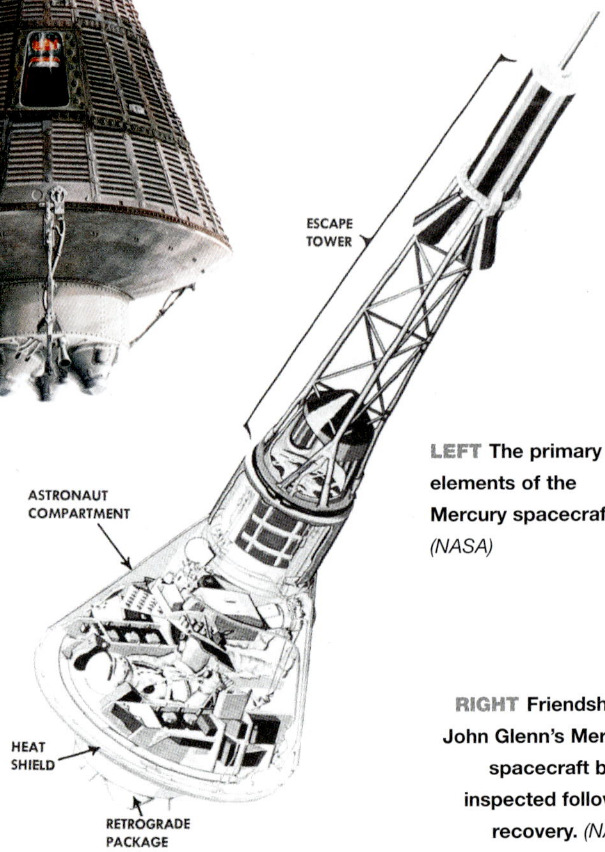

LEFT The primary elements of the Mercury spacecraft. *(NASA)*

RIGHT Friendship 7, John Glenn's Mercury spacecraft being inspected following recovery. *(NASA)*

FAR LEFT **Alan Shepard rides atop his Redstone rocket in the first manned Mercury spacecraft, Freedom 7, on May 5 1961.** *(NASA)*

LEFT **Gordon Cooper begins the final flight of the Mercury program in a spacecraft named Faith 7 launched atop an Atlas booster on May 15 1963.** *(NASA)*

a Mercury spacecraft, they were barely capable of the task, and then only by severely limiting the ship's mass. As a result, the spacecraft carried a tiny amount of propellant in order to align the ship for re-entry. None was available for in-space propulsion; the ship simply followed the orbit provided by its launcher until the time came to return to Earth. Electrical power came from storage batteries that were intrinsically heavy and therefore limited in capacity. Given that the spacecraft could do little but coast along, no equipment was provided for guidance, navigation and control.

Apollo and the lunar goal

Even before Mercury began to make heroes of NASA's first group of astronauts, the agency's aggressive "can-do" approach was reflected by its engineers, who conceived a sophisticated spacecraft to follow on from the limited Mercury. They called this new ship Apollo. It would be a three-man craft that was everything Mercury was not. With propulsion and guidance, it would be capable of going somewhere, though at the time there were only vague ideas about where that might be. Some sort of space station seemed the most likely destination, but some thought had been given to using Apollo to reach the Moon.

Then on May 25 1961, when President John F. Kennedy challenged his nation to achieve a lunar landing before the decade was out, NASA was ready to offer Apollo as the means to fulfil this goal. The prevalent idea was to mount the spacecraft on a landing stage and take it down to the surface. Apollo, however, would be a heavy spacecraft by virtue of its wraparound heatshield, its structural strength, and the sheer amount of equipment it would carry. To get it onto the Moon and off again implied an enormous lunar landing vehicle. Consequently, the task of getting that lot off Earth and on its way to the Moon demanded a launch vehicle of stupendous proportions.

Behind the scenes, some at NASA and its contractors had been thinking about the problem of rendezvous in space. They recognized that many tasks would require this skill; for example, when visiting the

BELOW **A comparison to scale of the Mercury, Gemini and Apollo spacecraft and their corresponding launch vehicles; Atlas, Titan II and Saturn V.** *(NASA)*

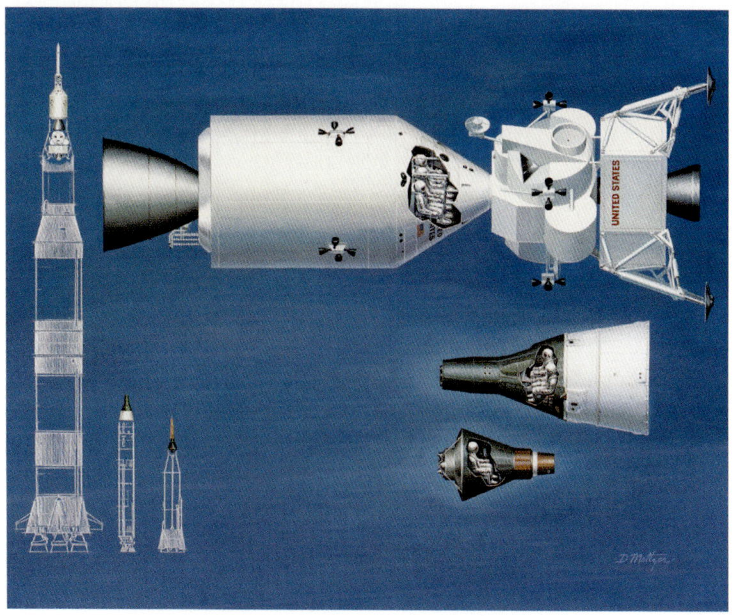

aforementioned space station. Many believed rendezvous would be fiendishly difficult to master, if not downright dangerous; a point of view that was hardly surprising given the lack of knowledge and experience, and the limited navigational aids available at that time. After all, it required that one spacecraft find another and come alongside as they were careering through space at extraordinarily high speeds.

Despite the doubters, the case for rendezvous began to dominate because NASA had to decide exactly how it was going to get to the Moon, the so-called mode decision, and rendezvous was crucial to at least one of the possible scenarios.

The mode decision

Rather than being a tightly controlled singular organization, NASA has always been a collection of field centers, each a fiefdom that battles for a degree of independence even as headquarters in Washington DC seeks to assert its authority. Two camps had arisen, each in distinct centers and each proposing a different means of going to the Moon. The dispute took over a year to resolve.

One camp, based around the Space Task Group, thought that the simplest plan was to use sheer brute force to go directly to the Moon, land, and return directly to Earth. Rendezvous would not be required for this *direct ascent* approach, but it would have entailed a launcher of staggering dimensions. This, along with other shortcomings which slowly came to light, began to make the direct concept look unworkable.

Another camp was centered on the Marshall Space Flight Center in Huntsville, Alabama, which hosted a team of German engineers led by Wernher von Braun. In early 1962 NASA had decided to develop the Saturn V launch vehicle for Apollo and the Marshall team were masterminding its development. They envisaged a two-part Moon-ship, each part of which would be inserted into orbit near Earth on its own Saturn V. After rendezvousing and linking up, they would set off for the Moon. Critics said that Marshall was attracted to this mode, known as *Earth orbit rendezvous* (EOR), primarily because it would require lots of rockets.

As these two camps fought, a third possibility came from a team that was studying rendezvous in detail and this would take the technique of rendezvous to new heights, quite literally.

Lunar orbit rendezvous

Zealously championed by Langley engineer John Houbolt, *lunar orbit rendezvous* (LOR) took the idea of rendezvous between two spacecraft all the way to the Moon, though many deemed it to be excessively risky and foolhardy. He and his team, however, had realized that by going into orbit around the Moon, there was no need to land the entire vehicle on the surface. The heavy section that had to bring the crew back to Earth could stay in lunar orbit as a mothership. That way, only the smallest possible craft would land and an even smaller one would leave the lunar surface, thereby saving substantial mass. The figures looked very promising. Mass saved at the Moon bestowed a far greater saving on the mass of the launch vehicle. This seemed to bring a complete landing mission within the capability of a single Saturn V.

Houbolt wrote, "Almost spontaneously, it became clear that [LOR] offered a chain reaction simplification on all back effects: development, testing, manufacturing, erection, countdown, flight operations, etc." Houbolt's dream not only demanded that NASA carry out rendezvous, viewed as a difficult and strange technique, but that they should do so, not close to the relative safety of Earth, but nearly 400,000km away in the lonely environs of the Moon. This terrified NASA's management.

Mercury Mark II

The direct approach to reaching the Moon was waning in popularity and NASA became increasingly aware that whatever mode was chosen, EOR or LOR, the agency would have to get to grips with rendezvous. This was a time when space flight technology moved very fast; when a five-year wait for Apollo was deemed far too long. Yet the basic and experimental Mercury spacecraft was unfit for the task. Something had to fill the gap and allow the intricacies of rendezvous to be practiced and perfected. To hasten the development time, NASA looked to an advanced version of Mercury that was already on the drawing boards.

Egged on by a NASA engineer, Canadian James Chamberlin, McDonnell had been considering upgrading Mercury to counter what he saw as its major shortcomings. He presented his initial ideas to NASA bosses on 17 March 1961 at a meeting about which he later recalled, "As far as I was concerned [that] was the initiation of Gemini." By starting with the Mercury design, he hoped "to use and build on experience, to gain and not start over again." His goal was to transform an experimental craft into a vehicle that a pilot could truly fly in space.

Mercury was proving to be problematic. Ground crews were struggling with the repercussions of its design. All of its equipment had been installed within its pressure hull, with the result that its various systems could only be accessed through its single hatch by one worker at a time. Worse, to cram it all in, every available space around the astronaut had been filled with gear, often in layers, which made the testing, checkout, and repair of the spacecraft horrendously difficult and time consuming. For what was initially dubbed Mercury Mark II, Chamberlin wanted to place equipment outside the pressure hull but within the spacecraft's exterior surface where it would be more accessible.

Another of Chamberlin's beefs with Mercury concerned the weight and complexity of the rocket-powered escape tower that sat on top of the spacecraft. This included the elaborate systems that would trigger it in an emergency. As an alternative, he pushed for an aircraft-style ejection seat, an arrangement which required a large door to permit a safe exit.

By mid-1961, more modifications were being presented to deal with Mercury's shortcomings. One was its lack of maneuverability when it re-entered Earth's atmosphere. Once set on a path back to the surface, a Mercury spacecraft had about as much ability to steer as had a cannonball. But by deliberately designing a spacecraft to be heavier on one side, McDonnell's engineers saw that its flight path through the air would be slightly skewed laterally, and this provided the pilot with a means to steer the craft.

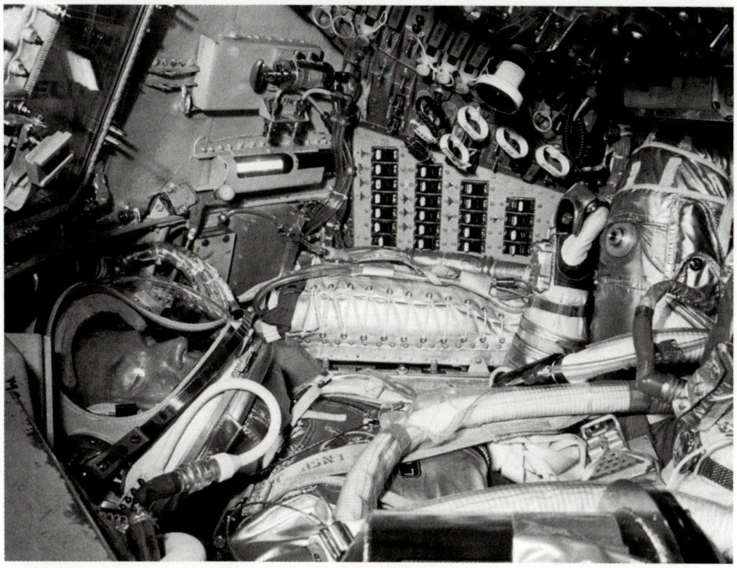

ABOVE Astronaut Gordon Cooper squeezed into the cramped confines of his Mercury spacecraft. *(NASA)*

Titan II launch vehicle

Perhaps the most influential decision in the development of Mercury Mark II was the choice of the Titan II rocket as its launch vehicle. Maxime Faget, the Space Task Group's chief spacecraft designer, had already suggested that more than one crewman would be required to carry out the workload of advanced space operations, such as rendezvous. And, he surmised, if an astronaut were to go spacewalking, surely

LEFT Friendship 7, Glenn's spacecraft with its heavy escape tower, undergoing preparation for launch. *(NASA)*

ABOVE A Gemini-Titan vehicle on Launch Complex 19 with its hinged erector tower being lowered. *(NASA)*

RIGHT A test launch from Vandenberg Air Force Base of the Titan II intercontinental ballistic missile, designed to carry the largest nuclear warhead in the US inventory. *(USAF)*

RIGHT Official emblem of the Gemini program. *(NASA)*

another would be needed to look after the ship. By employing a powerful launcher like Titan II, engineers gained sufficient performance to let them double the spacecraft's crew and greatly increase its overall capability.

Like the Atlas launch vehicle that put Mercury in orbit, Titan II had been designed to lob nuclear weapons across the planet. However, it had benefitted from improvements in rocket technology that made it capable of carrying America's largest and most powerful bombs. If it could be made safe enough for a human payload, it would allow the new spacecraft to be nearly twice as heavy as Mercury.

The choice of Titan II also favored the use of ejection seats. Though its propellants yielded prodigious power in its engines, they were felt to be less explosive in the event of a catastrophe when compared to conventional propellants. An ejection seat would have sufficient power to carry a pilot clear of a fireball.

Gemini becomes official

NASA had yet to fly a man in orbit, yet it was in keeping with the bold times that the advanced Mercury spacecraft officially became a program on December 22, 1961, to give the agency the rendezvous experience it needed prior to Apollo. The extraordinary momentum that was being generated by the space race is demonstrated by the fact that despite its interim nature, the scope of this new program was huge.

As well as creating a complex two-man spacecraft and carrying out safety work on the Titan II rocket to rate it for human flight, NASA had to provide something with which to undertake the rendezvous. Thus the program included funds to turn a small rocket stage called Agena into an unmanned spacecraft that would not only incorporate rendezvous and docking apparatus but would also have sufficient rocket power for substantial joint maneuvers.

As 1962 began, and with an award of a bottle of whisky, Alex Nagy at NASA headquarters gave the program a name, Gemini, that worked on many levels. Gemini is one of the constellations of the zodiac and represents the Twins, an astronomical metaphor

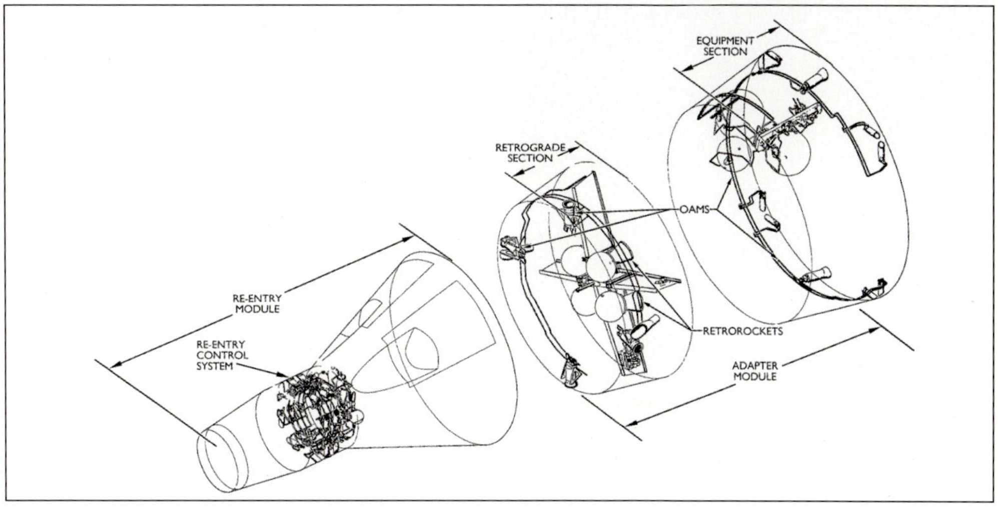

LEFT The primary elements of the Gemini spacecraft. *(NASA)*

appropriate for a two-seater spacecraft. Its astrological symbol is very similar to the Roman number II, reflecting that this was a Mark II development of Mercury (using a Titan II rocket) and so it easily lent itself to the program's official patch which also bore the two dominant stars from the constellation, Castor and Pollux.

A spacecraft for pilots

For the Gemini spacecraft, engineers from NASA and McDonnell started with what was familiar – namely, the Mercury capsule – and began to add the elements that would make it into a useful, maneuverable machine. The habitable section, now called the *re-entry module*, retained the same shape as Mercury, a truncated cone and blunt heatshield whose aerodynamics were understood; yet it was enlarged to accommodate two astronauts sitting side by side.

A cylindrical section at the top of the cone carried a set of thrusters, doubled up for redundancy, to let the pilot steer the spacecraft through the atmosphere. Known as the *re-entry control system* (RCS), it was only intended to be employed at the end of the mission. Another cylinder, slightly tapered, topped the lines of the ship. Called the *rendezvous & recovery* (R&R) section, it carried equipment required for these roles; radar, docking gear and parachutes being the major items.

Something akin to a service module was added behind the heatshield. Superficially, this was an adapter to accommodate the difference between the spacecraft's 228.6cm (90in) diameter at its base and the Titan II's diameter of 304.8cm (120in). But more than that, this *adapter module* housed a number of systems that transformed Gemini into the remarkable spacecraft it would become. The adapter itself split into two.

The larger *equipment section* had redundant sets of small maneuvering rockets to enable Gemini to change its orbit. Also installed was an enhanced electrical power system that pioneered the use of fuel cells rather than batteries to permit long duration flight.

The smaller part of the adapter was only brought into use near the end of the mission. After the equipment section had been jettisoned, this *retrograde section* provided a mount for four solid-fueled rocket motors that were fired against the spacecraft's motion in order to head home. Its job done, this section was jettisoned to uncover the heatshield of the re-entry module.

Space race

Gemini's early years were in the eye of a geopolitical maelstrom as two large multi-state blocs squared up to each other, each convinced that it knew the right way forward for humankind. The Soviet Union, along with surrounding states under its influence, had adopted various flavors of communism and socialism. The United States saw itself as the natural leader of those countries that embraced capitalism and democracy, and it was resolute

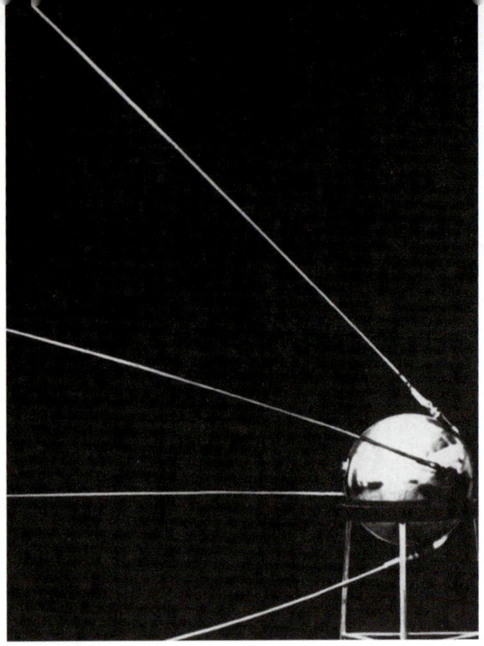

RIGHT The world's first artificial satellite, Sputnik, launched October 4 1957 by the Soviet Union. *(Getty Images)*

in its belief that its lead in science and technology was evidence of its superior system.

But during the 1950s the Soviets repeatedly battered American assumptions of superiority, first by testing nuclear weapons every bit as powerful as those of the US. Then on October 4 1957, they upped the ante by orbiting the first artificial satellite. A nuclear armed country that could place an object in orbit could deliver a bomb to essentially any place on the planet.

The effect on the US was electrifying. Forced to play catch-up, its military succeeded in placing a satellite in orbit on January 31, 1958. Then President Dwight Eisenhower created the *National Aeronautics and Space Administration* (NASA) to keep America's space flight developments in the civilian realm.

RIGHT Yuri Gagarin, the first human in space. *(Getty Images)*

But both sides knew that a man in space would deeply impress the world and both engaged in a breathless technological race to get someone up there safely. Yuri Gagarin took the honors for the Soviet Union on April 12 1961. The American response came on May 5 with Alan Shepard making a suborbital flight aboard the first manned Mercury.

Space firsts had become politically charged events and Gagarin's pioneering flight did much to provoke President Kennedy's Moon challenge just three weeks after Shepard's foray into space. Over the next two years, each Mercury mission was meticulously compared with the sparse facts that the secretive Soviet regime chose to reveal about its achievements. On paper, they appeared to be very far ahead with longer flights, the first woman in space, the first multi-man crew, and the first spacewalk.

One stunt in particular appeared to show that the Soviets had got to grips with rendezvous before a single Gemini had even been built. On August 11 1962, Andrian Nikolayev was launched into orbit. The following day Pavel Popovich was launched into an almost identical orbit. The Soviet press reported that the distance between the two Vostoks was slowly closing, implying that they were actively pursuing rendezvous. But it was a ruse. Though they came within a few kilometers of each other, only accurate launching and the dynamics arising from the slight differences in their orbits had allowed the otherwise passive ships to come close. Rendezvous was a skill yet to be mastered.

Air Force Gemini

Though NASA had been instituted as a civilian agency, it took great interest in what the US military could offer, not least because their big missiles could make excellent launch vehicles. Likewise, the military kept an eye on NASA as that agency got to grips with its own ambitions. In the initial heady years of the space race, when big ideas were easily floated, the Air Force believed it could benefit from a manned space station, primarily to carry out reconnaissance.

In 1962 the USAF proposed the *manned orbital development system* (MODS), a space station to be tended by Gemini spacecraft flown by Air Force crews. This earned the name Blue Gemini though it never officially became a program due to competing interest in the X-20, known as Dyna-Soar, which envisaged a winged glider/spacecraft that would be more maneuverable than Gemini. At one point, the Secretary of Defense, Robert McNamara suggested merging the needs of NASA with those of the Air Force, a move that was fiercely resisted by both parties.

After the cancellation of the X-20 at the end of 1963, Air Force interest in Gemini increased. By this time, their space station concept had evolved into the *manned orbiting laboratory* (MOL). This would be placed into orbit using the more powerful Titan III launch vehicle, with the crew riding on top in a modified spacecraft called Gemini B.

MOL was approved in August 1965 and would be built by the Douglas Aircraft Company to house a two-man crew for a 40-day sortie in a helium/oxygen atmosphere. Rather than having to spacewalk to gain access to the station, the crew would pass through a hatch cut into Gemini's heatshield. In all, 17 astronauts were recruited for the program in three groups.

Additionally the Air Force wanted to develop a package to allow astronauts to propel themselves away from MOL to visit other satellites. This *astronaut maneuvering unit* (AMU) was taken into space by NASA as part of its Gemini program, but circumstances ruled against it being tested.

The MOL program became a victim of the increasing maturity of the space flight business and developments in technology. It became increasingly apparent that reconnaissance could be better achieved with a new generation of unmanned satellites. When MOL was cancelled in June 1969, seven of its astronauts transferred to NASA.

Only one flight was ever made in the program. This occurred on November 3 1966, with a Titan III lofting the refurbished Gemini 2 spacecraft atop a mockup MOL created from a spare Titan II propellant tank. This demonstrated that a heatshield incorporating a hatch was able to survive re-entry.

ABOVE LEFT An artist's rendering of a Titan IIIM launching a Manned Orbiting Laboratory with an Air Force Gemini spacecraft on top. *(USAF/Courtesy of Rob Getz – stellar-views.com)*

ABOVE A 1960 concept illustration of a manned laboratory in orbit. *(NASA)*

LEFT The only launch of the MOL program was an unmanned test on November 3 1966. *(NASA/USAF)*

RIGHT **A wind tunnel test of the Rogallo wing on a Gemini scale model.** *(NASA)*

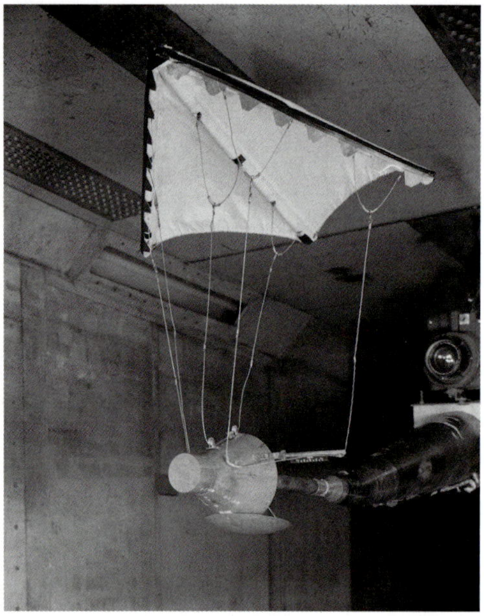

The Rogallo wing

It is one thing to place a spacecraft on top of a rocket and launch it into orbit 250km up. It is quite another to bring this pared-down, light-as-possible vehicle back down to Earth's surface without killing its crew at the point of impact. Mercury had established that parachutes were adequate for the final descent, at least for a landing on water. However, recovery at sea is expensive and anyway, the team designing Gemini had aviation backgrounds. Their instincts pulled them towards what they were familiar with: wings and controlled landings on runways. In the early days of the program, much thought was devoted to giving the spacecraft some form of wing.

The attachment of a deployable rigid wing to Gemini was always going to be excessively heavy and was never considered. Instead, every iteration of the engineers' outlines for the spacecraft's design included a radical method for giving the ship wings; the paraglider. To modern eyes, it appears that the Gemini spacecraft had been hung from a hang glider, and essentially, that was the plan.

Gertrude and Francis Rogallo were a married couple who flew kites for pleasure during the time that Francis worked at Langley as an aeronautical engineer in the years after the Second World War. One of their patented designs was a flexible affair that could be deployed like a parachute but then establish a shape reminiscent of a delta wing. It was known variously as a parawing or paraglider.

Few took their wing-shaped parachute seriously until the space race began, at which point many across NASA began to investigate the Rogallos' wing as a means of soft-landing a spacecraft on Earth. As Mercury Mark II morphed into Gemini, extensive work was carried out to assess how such a wing would deploy and be controlled. This included manned tests with a version called Parasev – what would nowadays be called a microlight – to see how pilots reacted to it. Many didn't like its handling qualities, with one saying it flew as if "controlled by a wet noodle."

The problems that surrounded the Rogallos' wing could not be ironed out fast enough for the breakneck pace of Gemini's development and in mid-1964, NASA cancelled further work, at least for manned space flight. The Rogallos continued to work on their wing designs for sport, resulting in its great popularity in the 1970s and '80s for hang gliding.

BELOW **Operational sequence for a Rogallo wing to set a Gemini spacecraft down on dry land.** *(NASA/ Courtesy of Mike Jetzer – heroicrelics.org)*

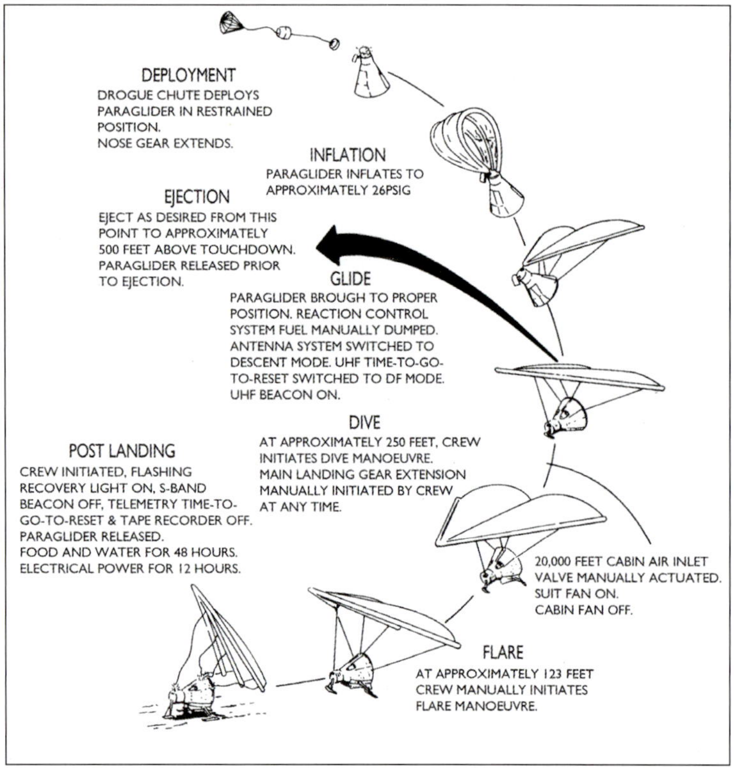

Orbits

Once upon a time in a Hollywood movie, flying in space was described as "falling with style." It's a good description because, for most of the time, a spacecraft coasts through space without its rocket engines blazing. Essentially, it is falling from place to place in much the same way that a stone thrown over a cliff is falling to the ground. Anyone and anything contained within the ship is likewise falling exactly in step with it and therefore appears to float inside, apparently weightless. This leads us to a way that we can understand concepts like weightlessness and the orbit. We can approach them from something we know intuitively; what happens when you fall.

So how does a stone thrown from a cliff lead to the idea of the orbit? Imagine that the stone is thrown horizontally as hard as we can muster. For these thought experiments, we have to ignore air resistance. Once the stone leaves the hand, it is perfectly obvious that it will fall in a curved path to the ground. The harder the throw, the further the stone travels as it falls before it reaches the bottom.

Now extend this scenario to one where we replace the stone with a cannonball and accelerate it to greater and greater horizontal speeds. We'll use an imaginary cannon mounted at the top of a high tower. We begin to notice that at very high speeds, the cannonball can travel far enough horizontally that the curved surface of Earth has fallen away somewhat below its path. So by the time it falls the height of the tower, it has yet to hit the ground and can therefore travel a greater distance before it does.

Now imagine we build our tower tall enough that it reaches the internationally agreed threshold of space, 100km. We place a really big but carefully measured charge in our cannon and set it off to send our cannonball to the truly astonishing speed of 28,260km/hr. Something strange occurs; as our cannonball falls towards the ground, the surface of Earth curves away in exact sympathy. The cannonball never gets to approach the ground and instead, it finds itself arcing around Earth at a constant altitude until, 86 minutes later, it has coasted all the way around the planet and returned to the tower. It has completed one orbit.

Replace the cannonball with a spacecraft like Gemini and the cannon with a launch vehicle like Titan II, and we have conventional orbital space flight. Gemini orbited at a higher altitude than our cannonball, about 250km, but in other respects the situation is the same. The spacecraft will remain in orbit until something acts to slow it down, be it air resistance from the extremely thin atmosphere at that altitude or the thrust from firing retrorocket engines to bring the crew home.

The force of gravity gradually weakens with increasing altitude and this profoundly affects how we establish a circular orbit at greater distances from Earth. As the pull towards Earth weakens, we require a slower horizontal speed to counteract it. Two things have changed. Not only is the speed around the planet slower, the orbit now traces out a larger circle around Earth. Both effects combine so that the time taken for a single orbit is much longer.

There are notable cases that show the changes very well. A satellite that takes pictures of Earth for mapping or reconnaissance purposes must orbit just above the atmosphere, at about the same height that Gemini flew. Its speed is 27,930km/hr and its orbit lasts 89 minutes.

If we place a satellite in an eastwards orbit exactly over the equator and at a precise altitude of 35,786km, it will travel at 11,052km/hr and take exactly 24 hours to complete one orbit. This special case is called a geostationary orbit because it will appear suspended at a single point in the sky. This is extremely useful for communications because antennae aimed at the satellite can be fixed in position. Satellite television broadcasting depends on the geostationary orbit.

By the time we reach the distance of the Moon, about 384,400km, Earth's gravity has weakened to the point that a circular orbit is maintained by travelling at only 3,600km/hr. The time taken to go around this huge circle is about 29 days, which is why the Moon requires about one month to orbit Earth.

Orbits around Earth or any other body are never exactly circular. Rather, they will always have some degree of ellipticity, making them oval in shape. Hence, every orbit has a point at which the altitude is lowest and another exactly opposite where it is highest. For orbits around Earth, these points are known as *perigee* and *apogee* respectively.

UNITED STATES

Chapter Two

Titan II launch vehicle

The end of the Second World War was punctuated by the devastation of two Japanese cities, Hiroshima and Nagasaki, each by a single nuclear weapon. Both devices were delivered to their targets by aircraft but as geopolitical tensions increased with the onset of the ensuing Cold War, military strategists realized that such weapons could be delivered much faster by rocket.

Early rockets of the Space Age

TOP LEFT A Redstone missile being prepared by the US Army for launch in May 1958. *(NASA)*

BOTTOM LEFT The Juno II was a civilian space launcher derived from the Jupiter missile. Though largely unsuccessful, this example managed to launch Explorer 7 to orbit on October 13, 1959. *(NASA)*

TOP RIGHT This early Air Force test of the Atlas missile on February 20, 1958 excluded the central sustainer engine normally seen on the booster. *(USAF)*

BOTTOM RIGHT The capable R-7 booster, seen here shortly prior to launch, gave the Soviet Union a crucial lead in the space race. *(Getty Images)*

RIGHT **An Atlas D booster during preparations for Gordon Cooper's flight aboard the Mercury spacecraft Faith 7. The walls of the Atlas were so thin that with a payload on top, the tanks had to be kept pressurized to maintain its structural strength.** *(NASA)*

Spurred on in a race for global supremacy, the two sides rapidly developed the rocket as a missile through the 1950s and '60s. Both began with the A-4/V-2, a liquid-fueled design with a range of 350km that Germany had used during the war. By the late 1950s, both had long-range rockets in their armories, the so-called *intercontinental ballistic missiles* (ICBM). Notable in the armory of the United States were the Redstone, the Jupiter/ Juno, and the Atlas missile, while the Soviet Union wielded the powerful R-7, nicknamed Semyorka.

It was thanks to the power of the liquid-fueled rocket that the space race kicked off in 1957 in an effort by east and west to display technical superiority to the wider world. It was believed that whoever held the "high ground" controlled Earth. In this new endeavor, both sides reached for their ICBMs to place artificial satellites into space rather than to lob bombs across continents.

However, the United States found itself at an unexpected disadvantage. Not only had it pioneered the design of nuclear weapons, it led the way in their refinement. In so doing, it had managed to produce warheads that were much lighter than those of the USSR for the same explosive yield. Consequently, early US rockets did not need to be as powerful as those designed in the Soviet Union.

This disparity in rocket power gave the USSR a huge head start when applied to space flight. Their R-7 proved to be sufficiently powerful yet adaptable to repeatedly deliver space firsts for its political masters; the first artificial satellite, the first man in orbit, and so on. The reply from the US relied on the Jupiter/Juno to place their first satellite in orbit, a Redstone to get a Mercury astronaut into space for a few minutes, and the Atlas to place such a spacecraft into a sustainable orbit.

However, the Atlas ICBM was barely powerful enough for its role in Mercury and could not be used as a launch vehicle for the much heavier Gemini. Even as an ICBM, it had drawbacks. It could not carry the heavier and more powerful warheads that the US military were designing. One of its propellants, liquid oxygen, was cryogenic – it had to be kept extremely cold to stay liquid and could not be stored in the missile which therefore could not be maintained ready to launch at a moment's notice.

In the long term, the Atlas rocket did see continued development, not as an ICBM but as a small launcher for unmanned spacecraft. As a measure of how far it has left its military past behind, its most recent derivatives use an engine of Russian design.

Aware of Atlas's drawbacks, the Air Force contracted the Martin Company to develop

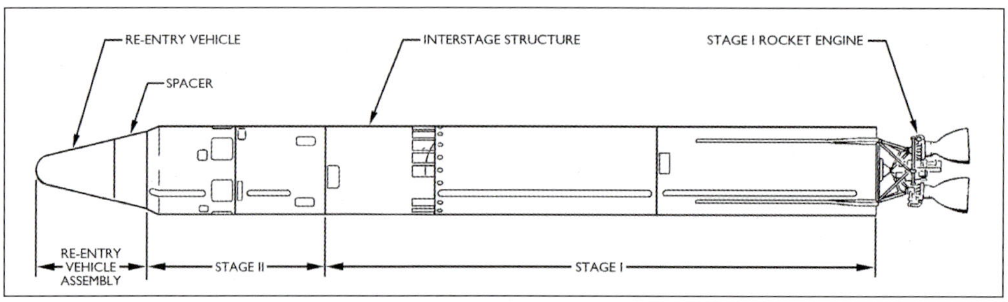

RIGHT **The primary elements of the Titan II ICBM.** *(USAF)*

another rocket as a standby in case the program hit unsurmountable difficulties. By virtue of its later birth, this new rocket, called Titan, could take advantage of continuing developments in the field. Its first version, Titan I, burned kerosene and liquid oxygen propellants (in common with Atlas) and it had a limited production run.

The Titan II saw a change to *hypergolic* propellants and its engines were adapted to these very different liquids. The fuel was Aerozine 50, a half-and-half mix of two very similar chemicals; hydrazine and *unsymmetrical dimethylhydrazine* (UDMH). This fuel yields slightly improved properties than hydrazine alone; it is denser, has a higher boiling point, and is more stable. The oxidizer was nitrogen tetroxide.

Not only would these propellants ignite on contact, thereby simplifying the vehicle's systems, both substances were storable liquids at room temperatures. This gave the Titan II a particular advantage in its role as an ICBM because the vehicle could sit in its silo for extended periods, years even, fully fueled and ready to launch within a mere 60 seconds.

Titan II was a two-stage rocket and a much more capable vehicle than the Atlas. As an ICBM, the military chose it to deliver the W-53, the most powerful thermonuclear warhead in the inventory. As a space vehicle it could place more than 3,000kg into orbit, double the payload mass of the Atlas and enough for the Gemini spacecraft. However, its conversion from ICBM to a rocket fit to carry humans proved troublesome.

Rocketry and Hypergolic Propellants

A rocket does not need combustion to work. The rocket principle is based on Isaac Newton's third law that for every action, there is an equal and opposite reaction. It merely requires that stuff is thrown out one end of a vehicle to make said vehicle move in the opposite direction. A water rocket works by squirting water out of a bottle under pressure. For a useful rocket what is needed is a lot of energy to do the throwing, and a neat way of obtaining that energy is through combustion. The process of burning generates a great deal of heat which causes the exhaust gas to expand tremendously. This expansion can be pointed in one direction.

Many rockets are "bipropellant" machines; that is, they burn two substances, collectively known as propellants, to generate the thrust that makes them go. One of those is a *fuel* and the other, the *oxidizer*, provides the oxygen that reacts with the fuel to release energy. (There are alternatives to oxygen but they are very rarely used.)

A common oxidizer is liquefied oxygen and this is usually burned with fuels like kerosene or liquefied hydrogen. One property of these propellant combinations is that they need a source of ignition to get the combustion started. This in turn requires an additional system to ensure that ignition occurs at the right time, every time.

As a way of improving the reliability of rocket engines, engineers sometimes use propellant combinations that are self-igniting; they merely have to come into contact with each other in order for the conflagration to begin. These combinations are described as being *hypergolic*.

The most common hypergolic fuel is hydrazine, a compound of nitrogen and hydrogen:

N_2H_4

Hydrazine is a nasty chemical when brought into contact with humans, since it is highly toxic and corrosive. But it is liquid at room temperature and, compared to propellants that have to be kept at extreme cold, it can be stored for long periods. For a hypergolic reaction, hydrazine is most often burned with nitrogen tetroxide:

N_2O_4

This substance is also storable for long periods at room temperatures.

With little more than high pressure supply tanks and a set of redundant valves to control the flow of propellants to a combustion chamber, you have a highly reliable and controllable long-term rocket system.

This assurance of ignition and the ability to be stored for long periods has led to this propellant combination becoming almost ubiquitous in space flight. It powered the Apollo spacecraft with which we went to the Moon and has been used on the Space Shuttle, other manned spacecraft, and most of our satellites and deep space probes.

ABOVE The primary intended use for the Titan II missile was to be stored in a silo ready for launch at a moment's notice. *(Titan Missile Museum/ Courtesy of Chuck Penson)*

BELOW View upwards of a Titan II missile stored in a silo. *(Photo by Jurvetson (flickr))*

Right from the first launch of the vehicle on 16 March 1962, Titan II was found to be particularly prone to an unpleasant characteristic that has always plagued rocket engineers, *pogo*. Named after the pogo stick, a popular toy that uses a large spring to allow someone to bounce along, it is the tendency of a rocket, particularly a liquid-fueled rocket, to shake lengthways.

Pogo is an interaction between the vehicle's natural mechanical resonance, the small variations in thrust that are always present in a rocket engine, and the dynamics of the fluid propellants as they pass through ducts to the engines. If these characteristics feed back on themselves they can create vibrations which shake the rocket back and forth. If uncontrolled, pogo has the ability to shake a human passenger senseless.

Initial attempts to address pogo failed. In fact they made it worse, increasing the magnitude of the vibrations from ±2.5*g* to a bone-shattering ±5*g*; this on a launch vehicle that NASA insisted should subject a human payload to no greater than ±0.25*g*. However, Titan II was not NASA's launch vehicle. It was an Air Force project and with subsequent modifications and test flights, the military decided that at ±0.6*g*, pogo had been adequately suppressed for its intended role of carrying nuclear warheads.

Another problem that affected the vehicle was combustion instability. Tests on the second stage engine indicated that it was dynamically unstable. Ground tests had established that the shock endured upon starting could be sufficient to put it in a mode where it would tear itself apart, an unacceptable condition for a human-rated vehicle. On some flight tests, the second stage engine significantly underperformed. A cure was effected by adding baffles around the injectors within the combustion chamber.

Over time, the Air Force began to consider Gemini as a useful vehicle for their military space aspirations and hence, like NASA, they became interested in human-rating the Titan II in the expectation that a version of the spacecraft would operate in conjunction with their MOL space station. As it became a serious prospect, they reached an accommodation with the civilian space agency that permitted the necessary further development of the launch vehicle. When a Titan II test flight on November 1 1963 showed pogo vibrations of only ±0.11*g*, it was decided that the modifications it incorporated – namely a collection of standpipes and accumulators – should be applied to those vehicles assigned to launch the Gemini spacecraft.

Only once did pogo become a problem during the manned program, when the first stage of Gemini 5 suffered severe oscillations for 13 seconds towards the end of its burn. The vibrations came as a surprise and gave the crew an unpleasant ride, peaking at ±0.38*g* while superimposed on the 3.3*g* acceleration at that phase of the ascent. An investigation found that a delay of the launch had meant that a nitrogen-filled standpipe in the oxidizer feed had been improperly recharged during the second countdown and had received only 10%

of the volume of gas required. This nitrogen was to damp out pressure fluctuations in the fluid flow. The pogo faded several seconds before the first stage shut down, and the staging was nominal.

Other modifications made to the vehicle to human-rate it were to add a *malfunction detection system* (MDS) to trigger aborts when necessary, another to provide backup flight control, and a method for the crew to shut off an engine if required. An additional section of skin was added to the vehicle to hold the spacecraft clear of the top dome of the second stage's oxidizer tank. The small rocket systems which provided additional control to the missile version were removed.

A major change concerned the guidance system. The military Titan II had an inertial guidance system that consisted of a gyroscopically stabilized platform with accelerometers. This was a common means of rocket guidance and was also used on many spacecraft. However, it was felt that it would be too expensive to rate this inertial system for human flight, and instead, NASA chose a radio control system whereby, in essence, the path of the rocket was guided from the ground.

Vehicle description

The Titan II used as the *Gemini launch vehicle* (GLV) was 27.7m tall excluding the spacecraft, which added another 5.8m. Its main body was mostly a semi-monocoque structure, meaning the skin contributed a portion of its structural strength. It was fabricated from aluminium alloy type 2014-T6 and this was anodized to form a protective layer of oxide on its surface.

To keep the weight down, the thickness of the vehicle's skin was carefully controlled by the use of chemical milling, where metal is removed not by cutting it with tools but by etching it away chemically. For aluminium, the etchant was usually sodium hydroxide, a powerful alkali. Where most strength was required, the skin was 4.3mm thick, reducing to 1.27mm for the least loaded sections. Conduits were provided along the external surface of the rocket to carry any required cabling that had to bypass the tank.

An interesting difference between the earlier Atlas and the Titan II was that the tank walls of an Atlas were so thin, they had to be kept pressurized like a soda can, even when empty, to stop the weight of the payload from crushing the vehicle. The Titan's tank walls possessed enough strength not to require such pressurization.

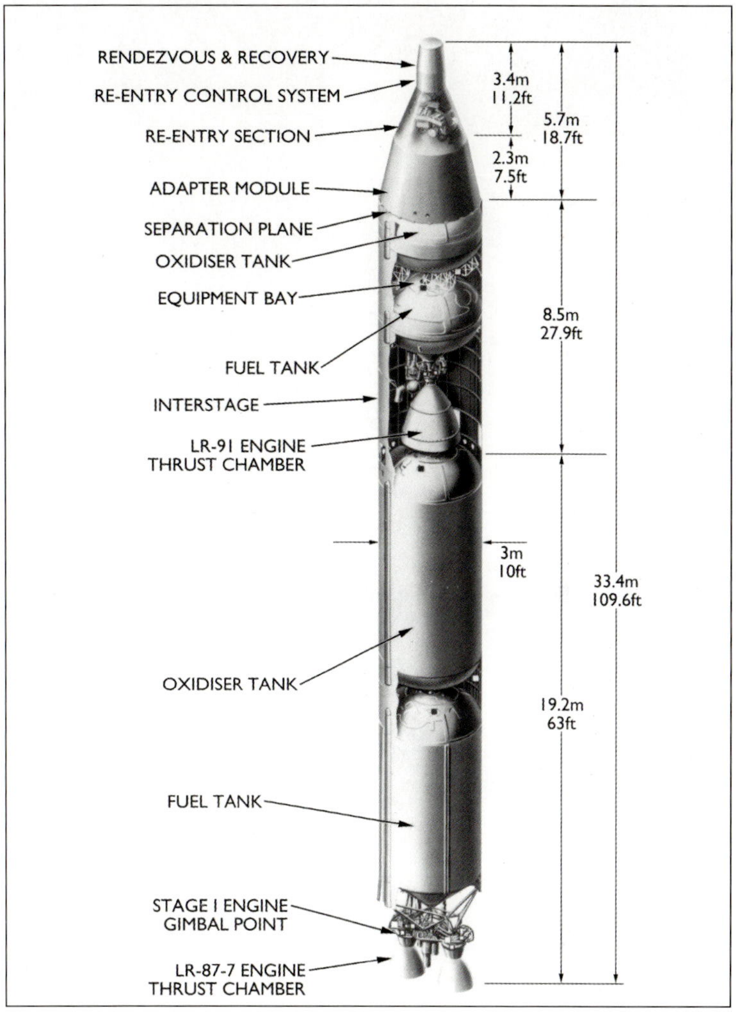

ABOVE Gemini-Titan vehicle dimensions. *(NASA/Courtesy of Rob Getz – stellar-views.com)*

First stage

The vehicle's first stage was 19.2m (63ft) long and 3m (10ft) in diameter, most of which consisted of two huge tanks with a total capacity of over 90,000 liters whose walls formed much of the outer skin. These tanks had domed ends to withstand the internal pressures. A cylindrical section between them maintained the stage's aerodynamic lines.

The upper tank contained nitrogen tetroxide oxidizer and the lower tank held Aerozine 50

ABOVE LR-87-5 engine mounted on the end of a Titan II airframe. *(Courtesy of Gary Brossett)*

fuel. Oxidizer reached the engine by being fed down through the center of the fuel tank via a large duct. Directly below the fuel tank, a conical thrust structure supported the LR-87-7 engine and, along with the engine frame, transmitted the thrust to the vehicle's cylindrical skin.

A cylindrical section, the *interstage*, was mounted at the top to support the upper stage and to provide clearance for its LR-91 engine nozzle. This section included an arrangement of open ports to allow the exhaust of this engine to escape during its start-up sequence while the stages were still attached.

LR-87-7 engine

The Aerojet LR-87 engine family was unusual for liquid rocket engines because the one basic design was adjusted to allow it to burn three different propellant combinations. For the

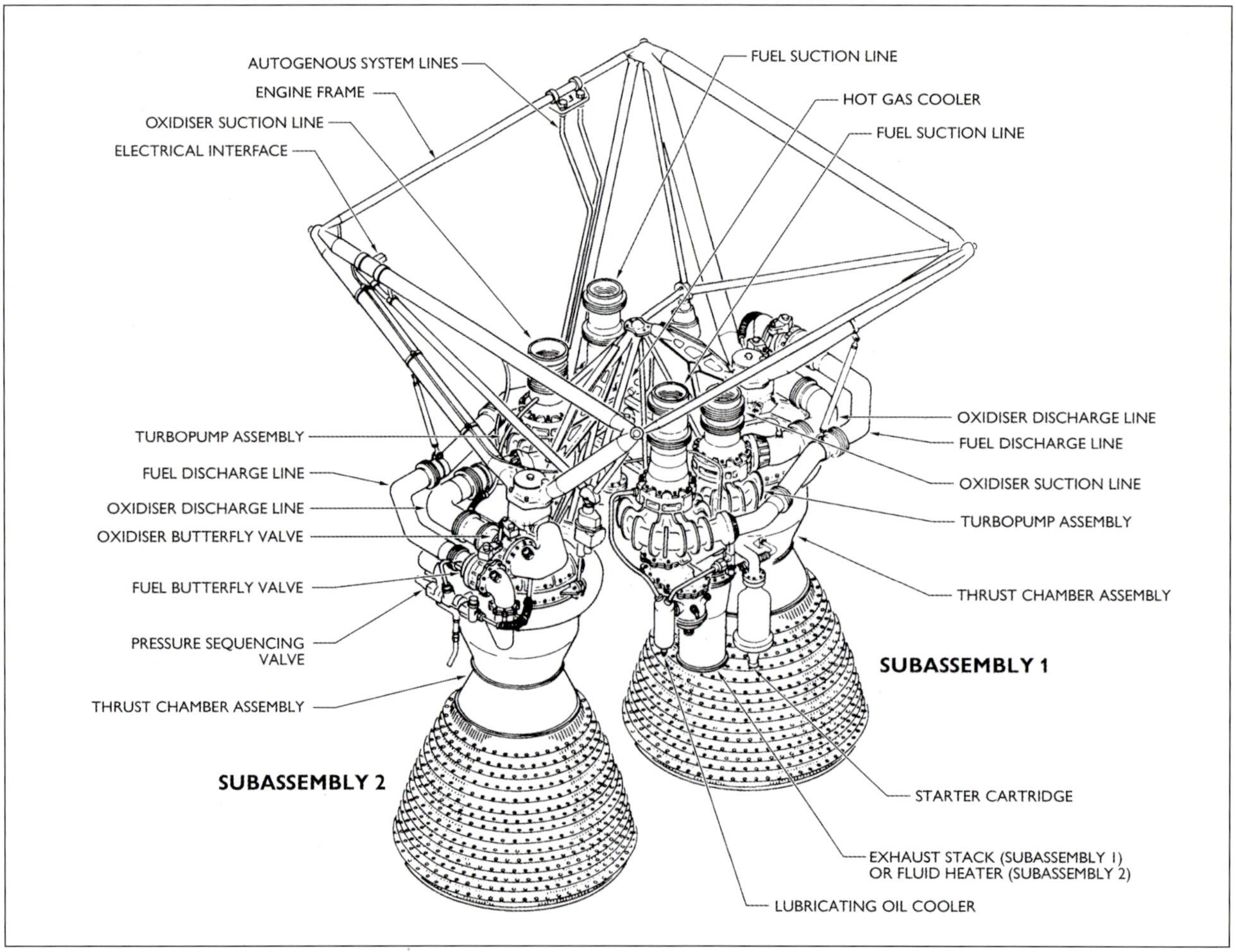

BELOW Diagram of the LR-87-5 engine, essentially identical to the -7 version used in the Gemini-Titan launch vehicle first stage. *(USAF/Courtesy of Don Boelling – titan2icbm.org)*

RIGHT The thrust chamber walls of the engine were protected by being fabricated from a network of piping. Fuel flowed through these pipes on its way to the injector plate, seen here at the far end of the combustion chambers. This view of a LR-87-5 engine also shows the exhaust ports for the turbopumps. *(Photo by Jurvetson (flickr))*

Titan I missile, the LR-87-3 burned kerosene with extremely cold liquid oxygen. In the -5 version, the engine was modified for hydrazine and nitrogen tetroxide propellants that would be used in the Titan II. The company that produced it, Aerojet, also created a version that would burn the cryogenic fuel, liquid hydrogen. In order to satisfy the human-rating requirements of the Gemini-Titan vehicle, the -5 version was modified by reducing its thrust slightly. This became the LR-87-7 version.

BELOW Schematic of the LR-87 engine in operation. In each subassembly, a gas generator drives turbopumps to force propellant into the thrust chamber. The second subassembly is used to generate additional gas to pressurize the tanks.
(USAF/Courtesy of Don Boelling – titan2icbm.org/Kevin Woods)

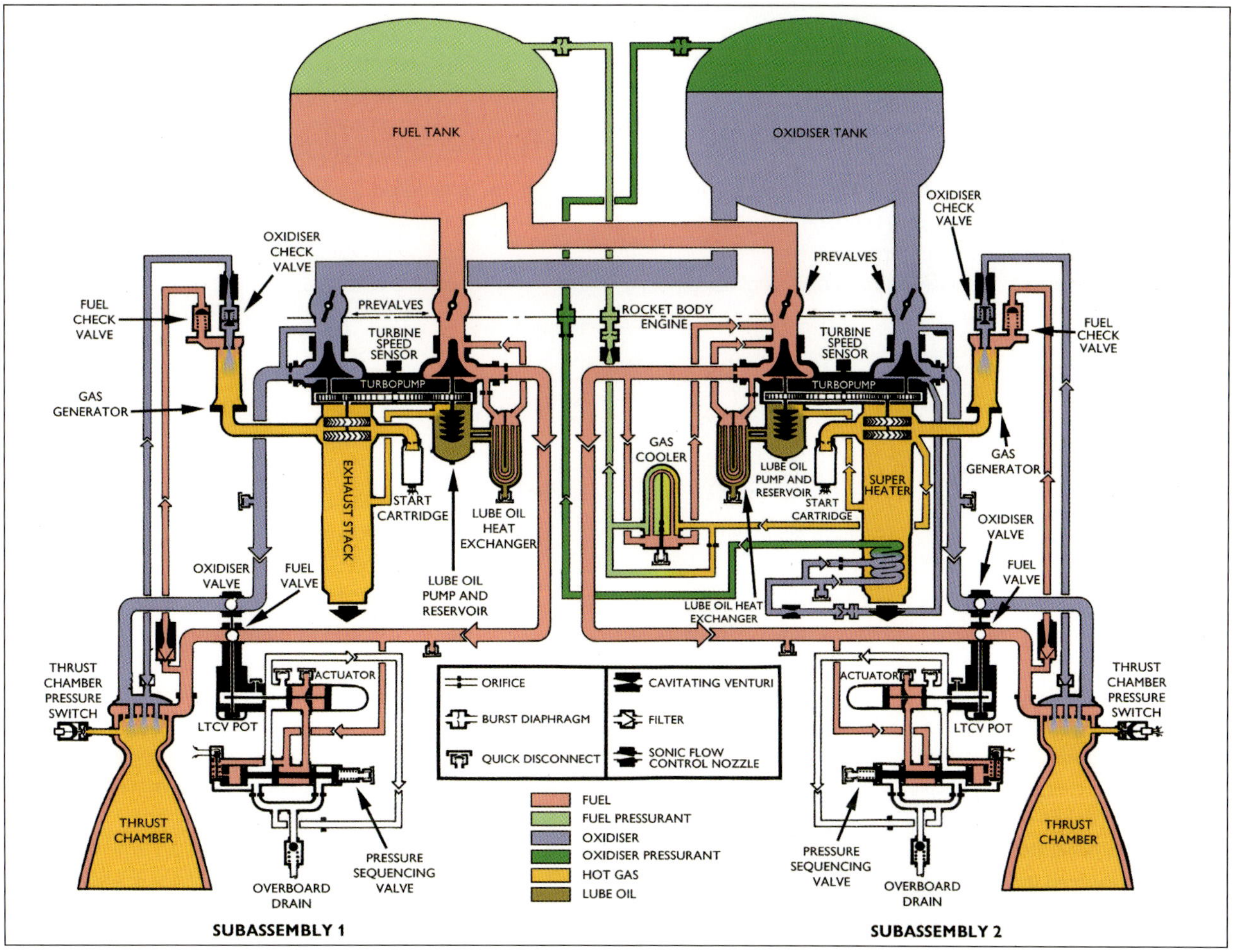

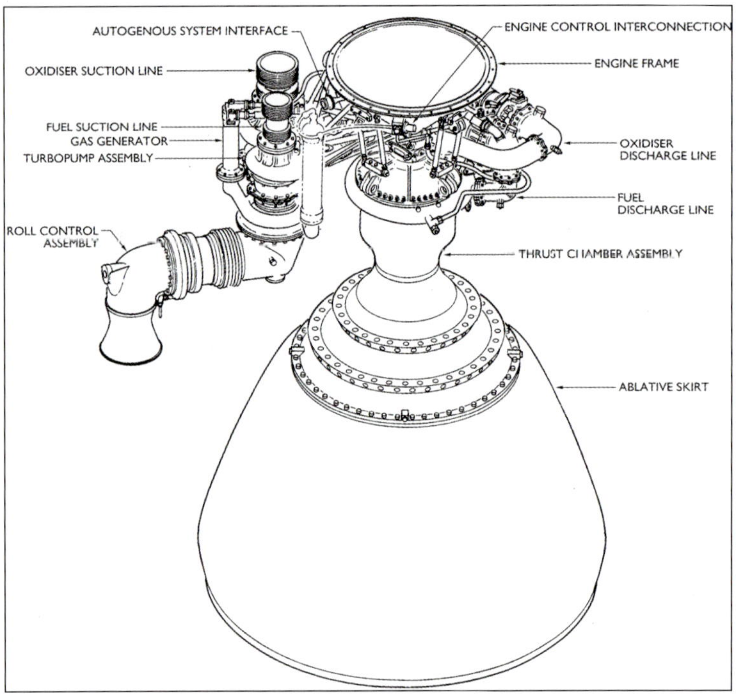

ABOVE Diagram of the LR-91 engine as used in the second stage of the Gemini-Titan launch vehicle. *(USAF/Courtesy of Don Boelling – titan2icbm.org)*

Unusually for American rockets, the LR-87 had two combustion chambers and nozzles which made it appear that the vehicle had two first stage engines. From a systems standpoint, this was mostly true. Only the means to produce gas to pressurize the tanks was common to what were considered two subassemblies of a single engine. All other subsystems like turbine gas generators and turbopumps were separate.

The average thrust from the LR-87-7 engine was 2MN. At launch, the thrust was 1.9MN owing to the capping effect of Earth's atmospheric pressure. As the air thinned to a near vacuum as the vehicle gained height, the thrust rose to over 2.1MN.

RIGHT Gemini-Titan 3 builds up to full thrust after producing an orange cloud of unburned propellant from the gas generator that powered the engine's turbopumps. *(NASA)*

Second stage

The second stage of the Titan II vehicle was much shorter than the first at 8.5m (27.8ft) but it maintained the same 3m diameter. Its tanks held 22,000 liters of propellant with the oxidizer tank at the top. Both tanks mostly consisted of the domed end pieces, giving them a very ellipsoid appearance. There was very little cylindrical section of wall in the middle of a tank.

Stage two burned the same propellants as the first but used an Aerojet LR-91 engine that had a single combustion chamber with a single large nozzle optimized for vacuum. It was thus a more efficient engine than the LR-87, delivering a thrust of 440kN.

The ignition of the Titan II's second stage was called fire in the hole because the first stage was still attached when the LR-91 started up. The structure between the two stages included apertures just above the first stage to allow the exhaust gases to escape. The upper dome of the first stage oxidizer tank was coated with a protective material.

Flight

The final seconds of the Titan's countdown differed from the later and more familiar Saturn V and Shuttle launches. Those later launchers ignited their engines while the count still had a few seconds to go, finally lifting off when the count reached zero. The Titan II, on the other hand, counted down to the moment of ignition. Once the engine had successfully reached its required thrust, the vehicle was released by the detonation of explosive nuts at each end of the studs that held it to the launch pad.

First stage flight typically lasted 2min 37sec and took the vehicle to a height of 63km and a speed of 11,000km/hr by the time it was 97.5km downrange. Once the first stage tanks

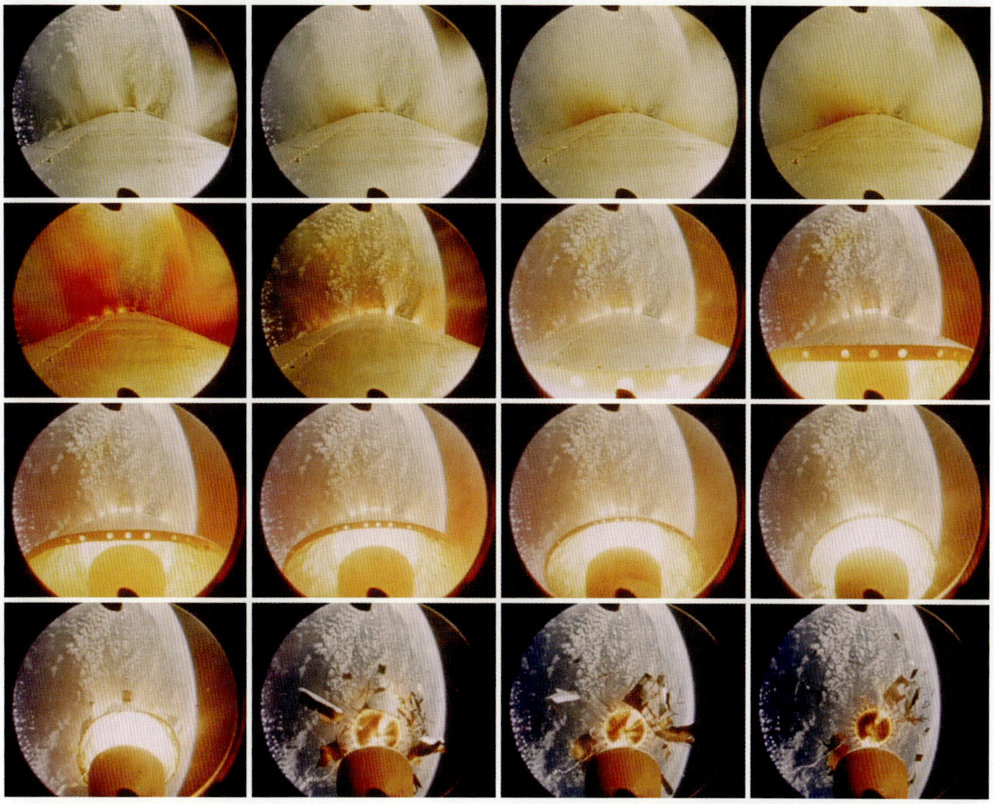

LEFT A sequence of still frames from a movie camera mounted on a Titan II to record the moment of staging and ignition of the second stage engine. At first oxidizer streams out of the holes on the interstage followed by fuel which then ignites. With the second stage at full thrust, the two stages separate as the heat and pressure from the supersonic exhaust causes the break-up of the interstage structure. *(USAF/David Woods/ Courtesy of Mark Gray – spacecraftfilms.com)*

were empty, the second stage engine was ignited, its exhaust venting through the ports in the interstage. A set of studs and explosive nuts similar to those which had attached the first stage to the pad were then detonated to cast the first stage adrift and allow it to splash into the Atlantic Ocean. As the two stages separated, the sheer power of the LR-91's exhaust blast was enough to entirely blow the panels out of the interstage.

Engineers got an opportunity to see the effects of staging when the upper part of the oxidizer tank of the first stage for Gemini 5 was recovered by the USS *Dupont* more than 700km downrange. It was their first chance to closely inspect how the upper dome had reacted to the blast from the LR-91 engine.

The flight of the second stage typically lasted 3 minutes. It took Gemini 1,000km downrange and 161km in altitude. At the same time, it reached a speed of 7.8km/sec parallel to Earth's surface. This directly inserted the spacecraft into its initial orbit, as a basis for orbital maneuvers. The drag from the tenuous air would cause the second stage to spiral down and eventually burn up.

LEFT The oxidizer tank from the first stage of GT-5 is recovered from the Atlantic Ocean by the USS *Dupont*. *(NASA)*

LEFT Fifty years after its recovery, Gemini 5's oxidizer tank, the only surviving section of any of the Gemini launch vehicles, lies in a storage yard in Huntsville. *(Courtesy of Mike Jetzer – heroicrelics.org)*

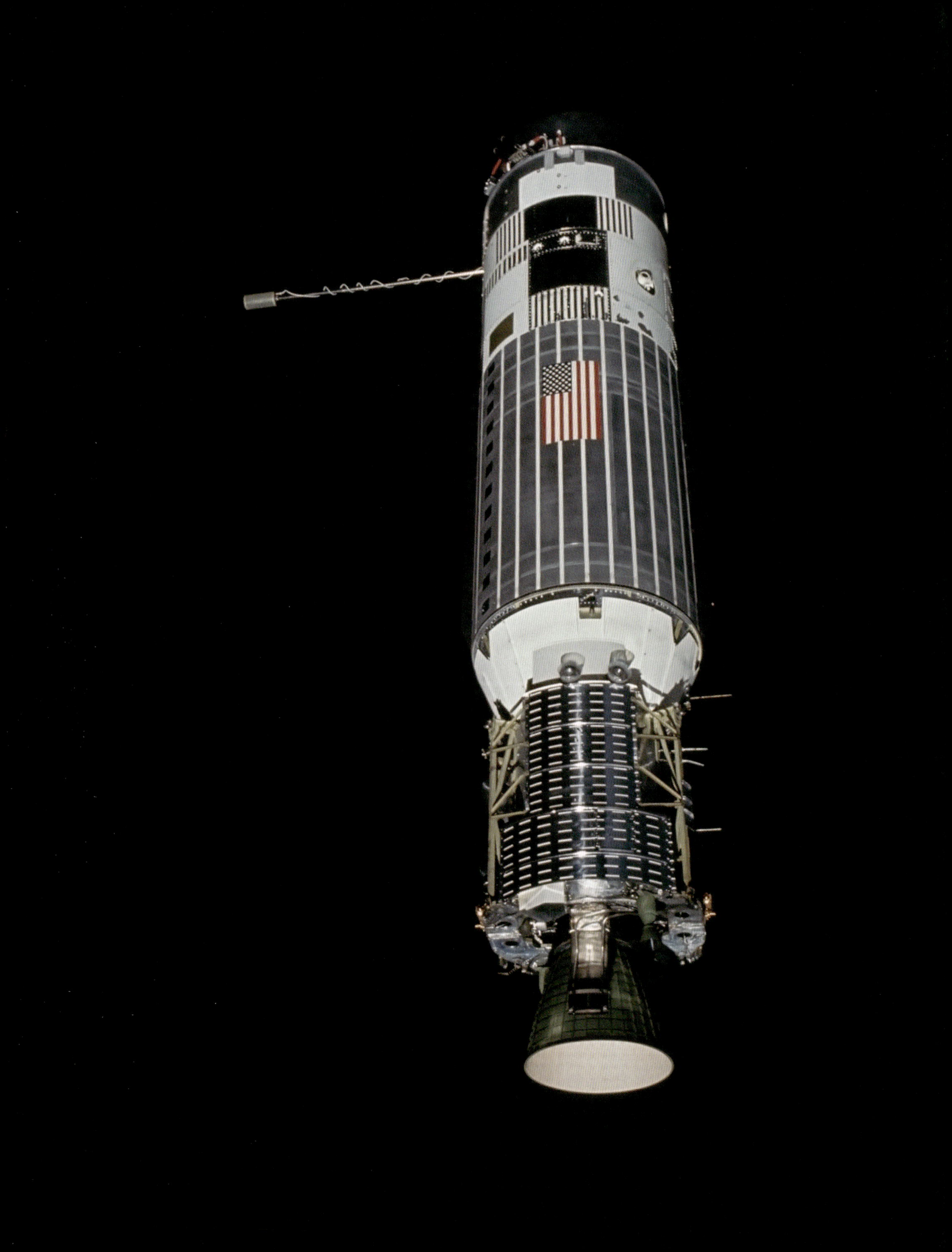

Chapter Three

Gemini-Agena target vehicle

Away from the limelight of space spectaculars, one aspect of space flight that greatly interested governments was reconnaissance. When the Soviet Union took the honors for the first artificial satellite, it set a precedent for one country to be able to fly over another country's territory, a fact that was not lost on the American intelligence community. If high quality photographic systems could be placed in an appropriate orbit, they would eventually pass over an enemy's landscape to take pictures revealing the whereabouts of military assets, particularly ICBM sites.

OPPOSITE The Gemini 12 Agena in orbit as Jim Lovell and Buzz Aldrin station-keep alongside. *(NASA)*

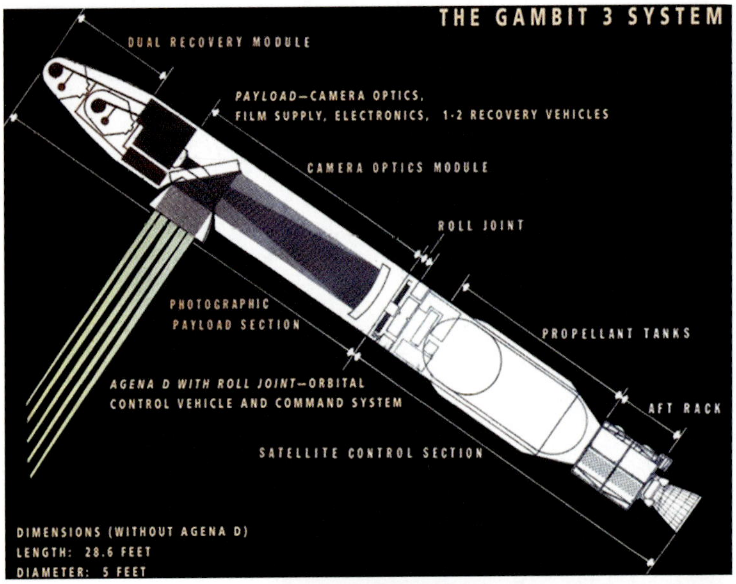

LEFT Diagram of an early US reconnaissance satellite, Gambit 3, with an Agena D propulsion system at the aft end. This variant of the Agena was the starting point for the Gemini Agena vehicles. *(National Museum of the U.S. Air Force/NRO)*

RIGHT A MIDAS II satellite with its Agena A propulsion unit being hoisted to the top of an Atlas booster in May 1960. MIDAS was a program to use satellites to detect the launch of ballistic missiles from space. *(National Museum of the U.S. Air Force)*

Even before the launch of Sputnik signalled the start of the public space race, the US military had quietly initiated a program for a generic satellite platform that could be turned to a range of possible uses, with photographic reconnaissance chief among them. The propulsion section that developed from this program became *Agena*. This not only served as the upper stage of the vehicle that delivered a payload to orbit, it then became a carrier for that payload.

The most common payload for the early Agena was a series of photoreconnaissance satellites that came under the general codename of *Keyhole*, particularly those belonging to the *Corona*, *Gambit* and *Hexagon* programs. In order to shield its true purpose, Keyhole was initially publicized as a civilian space development project called *Discoverer*.

These satellites used specialized cameras to take photographs of Earth's surface on huge reels of film. Once this film had been through the camera, it ended up in a re-entry capsule that returned to Earth upon command. As the film capsule slowly descended by parachute, it was captured in mid-air by specially equipped aircraft.

Corona and Gambit launches used the Thor booster with an Agena serving as an upper stage to achieve orbit. The Agena had an additional trick up its sleeve – it could be restarted in space on command from the ground, an ability of great use to the intelligence agencies. Once in space, a restartable Agena could provide the necessary propulsion to substantially change the orbit of a Corona

LEFT Close-up of the Agena D engine as used for the Gambit 3 reconnaissance satellite. The two spheres at the top of the engine were to hold high pressure nitrogen gas for attitude control via the white jets at the upper left of the picture. *(National Museum of the U.S. Air Force)*

satellite so that in the event of a crisis, it could pass directly over any desired area and photograph it.

Agena's ability to be restarted was of use not only to the military. The civilian agency, NASA, found a role for the vehicle on many of its missions of exploration, and it was common for the early probes bound for the Moon and planets to ride Atlas boosters topped by Agena stages that propelled them out of Earth orbit and on a path to their destinations. These included the Ranger and Lunar Orbiter probes that headed for the Moon and the early Mariner probes that were sent to Venus and Mars.

LEFT The Ranger spacecraft was an early probe that was sent to the Moon by an Agena upper stage. Little more than a platform for slow-scan TV cameras, only the last three missions out of a series of nine were completely successful. *(NASA)*

LEFT Lunar Orbiter was an advanced, film-based reconnaissance spacecraft sent to the Moon by an Agena upper stage in the mid-1960s in support of the Apollo program. All five missions in the series were successful. *(NASA)*

Agena for Gemini

Agena's most public role came when it directly supported Gemini in its primary role; to prove and practice the techniques of rendezvous and docking in preparation for Apollo's attempt to land humans on the Moon.

Early versions of the Agena vehicle had the disadvantage that they could be restarted only once; two burns in total. The D variant, however, had the ability to be restarted multiple times and so, with a few added extras and an eye to the kinds of maneuvers NASA might wish to perform on a flight, it became the *Gemini-Agena target vehicle* (GATV).

As well as the basic restartable rocket stage, GATV included equipment to allow a Gemini spacecraft to dock with it and control its functions. A transponder and various antennae were added as part of the Gemini radar system to permit the range and direction of the Agena to be determined from the Gemini spacecraft, and a set of strobe lights were installed to make the vehicle more visible at a distance.

Attached to the front of the vehicle was a cone-shaped docking collar to shepherd the nose of a Gemini spacecraft towards a docking mechanism with which a rigid connection could be made. Once docked, an astronaut could not only control the Agena, but thanks to an instrument panel installed where it could be seen by the crew through their windows, they gained some visibility into its systems.

Not only did the Gemini-Agena target vehicle give NASA's astronaut corps and the mission control teams the vital experience

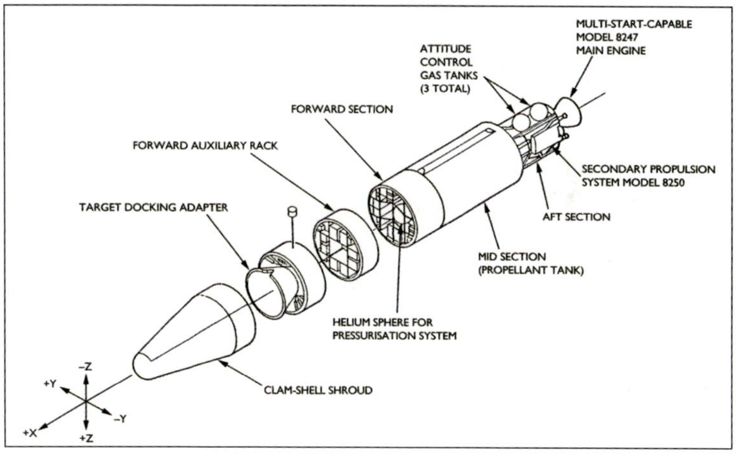

ABOVE The primary elements of the Gemini-Agena target vehicle. *(NASA)*

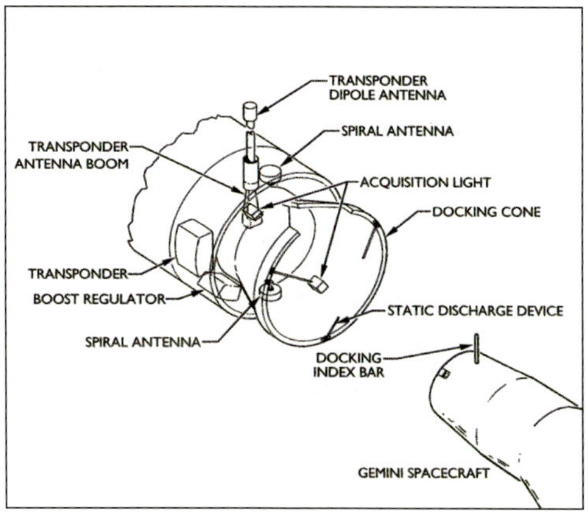

LEFT Major docking elements of the GATV vehicle. *(NASA)*

required to become a truly spacefaring group, its propulsion system lifted Gemini spacecraft to record altitudes, lofty heights which offered a glimpse of the planet as a spectacular, life-giving sphere, a view that would not be surpassed until the Apollo crews left for the Moon.

RIGHT The layout of the GATV status display panel. *(NASA)*

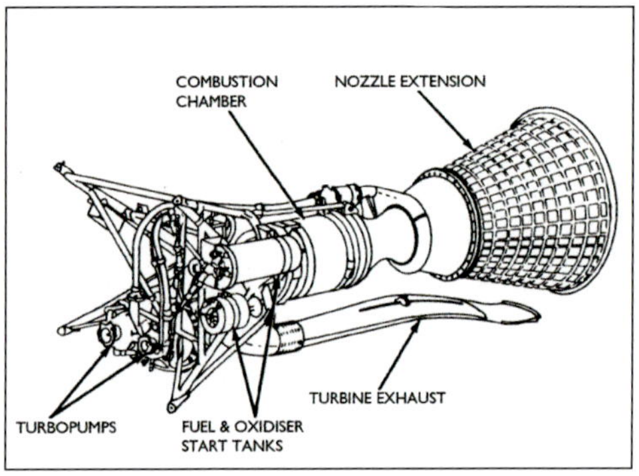

RIGHT Diagram of the Model 8247 rocket engine used in the GATV's primary propulsion system. *(NASA/Courtesy of Mike Jetzer – heroicrelics.org)*

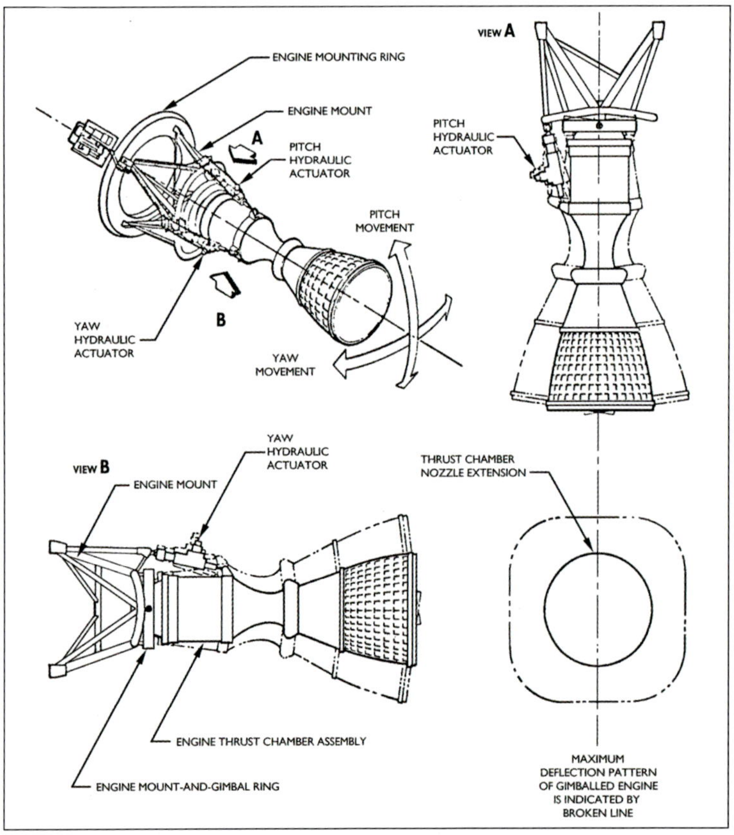

BELOW Diagram to illustrate the ability of the GATV engine to be gimballed for steering. *(NASA)*

GATV

The Gemini-Agena Target Vehicle was 7.93m (26ft) long and 1.52m (5ft) in diameter. When fully fueled, it had a mass of 3,260kg. The main section was built by Lockheed and consisted of a dual propellant tank that fed a Model 8247 rocket engine supplied by Bell Aerosystems. This engine could provide a fixed thrust of 71kN for a total of 4 minutes across multiple restarts.

The aluminium alloy thrust chamber was where the propellants met and burned. It consisted of a cylinder with an injector at one end which sprayed the propellants into the chamber in a manner similar to a shower head. The opposite end of the chamber narrowed then flared out into a skirt that formed the upper part of the nozzle. Prior to being consumed in the engine, liquid oxidizer was fed through passages in the chamber's walls, thereby keeping the metal from being melted. This is called regenerative cooling and is a common method of protecting the chambers of large liquid-fueled engines.

The main part of the nozzle was a separate piece that was attached to the thrust chamber to form a large bell. As exhaust gases leave an engine, they tend to expand in all directions. The function of a nozzle is to limit that expansion to one direction, rearwards, but only insofar as it becomes unwieldy or too heavy to give further benefit. The expansion ratio of Agena's nozzle (the change in area from the throat to its wide end) was 45:1. Fabricated from titanium, it was cooled merely by allowing the heat from the exhaust to radiate away from its outer surface.

This large engine comprised the *primary propulsion system* (PPS). It was mounted on gimbals that allowed it to swivel up to 5° away from the vehicle's centerline. This gave control of pitch and yaw while the main engine was firing. Control of the roll axis was provided by the cold gas system, an array of small thrusters that also allowed full attitude control at other times.

The propellants used by the Agena's main engine were UDMH (a version of hydrazine) as fuel and *inhibited red fuming nitric acid* (IRFNA) as oxidizer. This is a hypergolic combination.

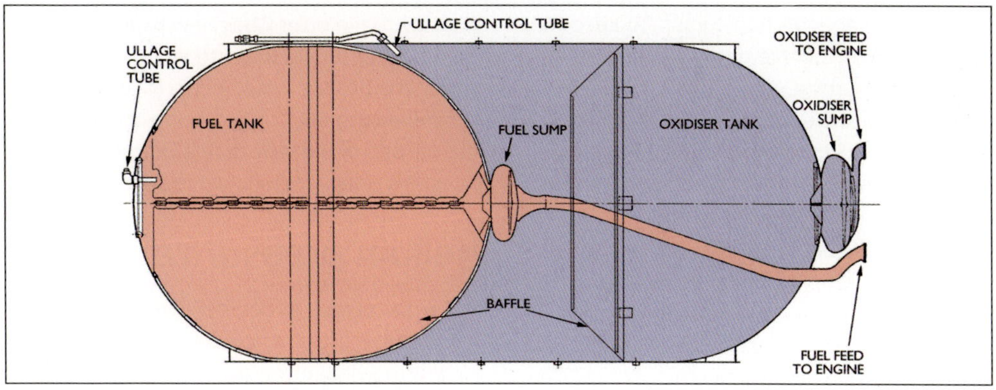

LEFT **Tankage arrangement for the propellants of the GATV.** *(NASA/David Woods)*

BELOW **Schematic of the primary propulsion system of the GATV.** *(NASA/Courtesy of Mike Jetzer – heroicrelics.org/David Woods)*

It is not as powerful as liquid hydrogen and oxygen (as used in the more powerful Centaur upper stage) but it has the advantage that its propellants are storable and can sit in their tanks for extended periods whereas the more powerful propellants must be kept extremely cold and will boil off with time.

Instead of having two separate tank structures to hold each propellant, the designers of the Agena incorporated two tanks into a single pressure vessel using a common domed bulkhead between the two volumes. Separate tanks are intrinsically heavier because of the weight of two bulkheads and the support structure between them. The common bulkhead saved substantial weight. There was a screened sump at the outlet of each tank to hold a small quantity of propellant in readiness for the next firing. This ensured that only liquid and not gas reached the engine at start-up.

Fuel was stored in the volume furthest from the engine and was fed through a standpipe that ran down the middle of the oxidizer tank. Both propellants were forced into the combustion chamber at high pressure using a dual turbopump. This consisted of separate fuel and oxidizer pumps that were both driven off a single turbine. Each pump used a helical screw to drive the propellant to the combustion chamber.

To power the turbine, a little of the fuel and oxidizer were fed to a stainless steel chamber. In this *gas generator*, the combustion of the propellants produced an exhaust gas which passed through the turbine before being dumped overboard via a pipe which ran alongside the main nozzle. The exhaust pipe itself contributed

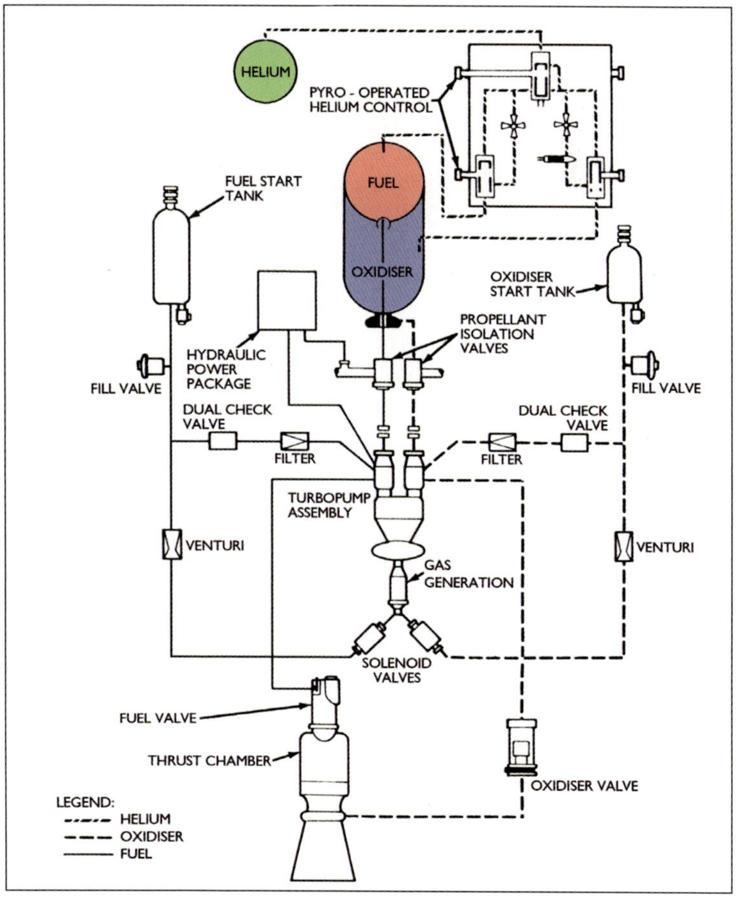

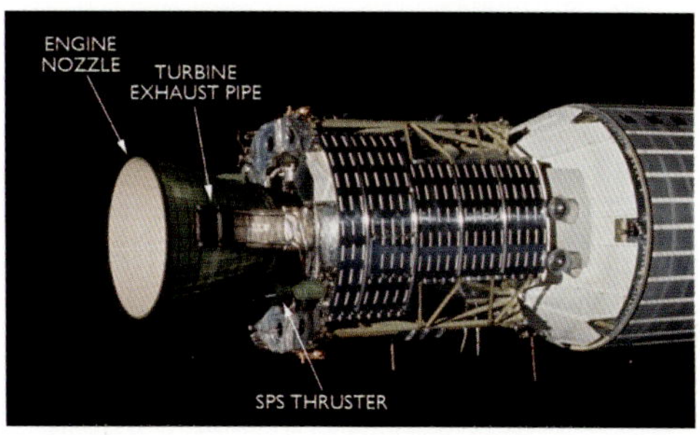

LEFT **Close-up of the 12-Agena to illustrate the SPS thruster, PPS engine nozzle and turbine exhaust pipe.** *(NASA)*

0.9kN to the Agena's total thrust. To keep the temperatures in the gas generator, and hence in the turbine, at moderate levels, the mixture ratio of the propellants in the gas generator was kept deliberately fuel-rich to produce a cooler gas and preclude the need to actively cool these components.

Engine starting

In the original design the start sequence began with a cartridge of solid propellant being ignited in the gas generator. The resulting exhaust would begin to spin the turbine, turn the pumps, and initiate the flow of propellants. Since there were only two such cartridges the engine could be started only twice. NASA wanted their Agena to be capable of starting at least five times, but there couldn't be a cartridge for every start.

For GATV, turbine rotation was initiated for each engine firing by the use of start tanks, each pressurized with nitrogen. A start tank was really a tank within a tank. The outer volume held the nitrogen gas under pressure and the inner tank contained the liquid propellant, fuel or oxidizer. A set of bellows made from steel separated the two.

When the command came to start the engine, valves would open to allow propellants to move from the start tanks to the gas generator. To force them on their way, the pressure in the nitrogen-filled section of each start tank acted on the bellows to squeeze the liquid out. As soon as they met in the gas generator, the propellants would ignite and begin to produce the gas required to spin the turbine until it had reached sufficient speed to sustain its own operation.

Soon, thanks to the rising turbine speed, the pressure in the main propellant lines would increase to the point where it was greater than the pressure of the nitrogen in the start tanks. The bellows would begin to expand, recompressing the nitrogen and allowing the internal part of the tank to refill with liquid propellant, ready for the next restart cycle.

BELOW Cutaway diagram of the fuel-filled start tank in the GATV PPS. Fuel is contained in a volume whose walls form a bellows. When required, nitrogen gas acts on the bellows to force fuel into the gas generator and begin spinning up the turbine. *(NASA)*

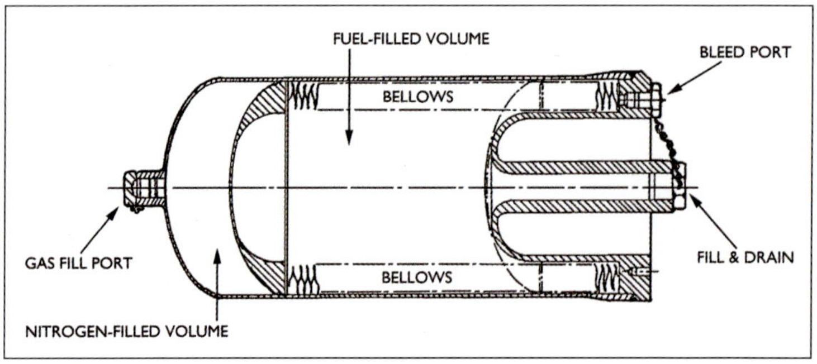

Helium pressurization

For the pumps to operate correctly, the two propellants had to be delivered to their inlets with sufficient pressure. A little of that pressure was brought about during engine operation by the *g*-forces of acceleration which created a head of pressure. The majority of the pressure came from the fact that the tanks were intentionally pressurized by being fed with helium gas. Helium was chosen because, being extremely inert, it wouldn't react with the propellants. It was stored in a separate 50cm tank at the very high pressure of 2,500psi or about 170bar.

Attitude control

When the main engine was not operating, Agena controlled its attitude using a cold-gas system that squirted a mixture of nitrogen and tetrafluoromethane through a set of six valves. Three spherical tanks contained a total of 63.5kg of the gas at a pressure of about 3,600psi. It passed through regulators which took it down to yield two supplies with a pressure of 100psi or 5psi. Either of these feeds was then sent to the thrust valves where their release in controlled squirts delivered a thrust of 45N or 2.2N as appropriate.

Secondary propulsion system

In addition to the main engine, the Agena had a pair of Model 8250 *secondary propulsion system* (SPS) modules, one on each side of the main engine. Each module had a large thruster delivering 0.9kN and a smaller one of only 70N; a total of four, all of which faced aft. The large thrusters were used together for orbital maneuvers that were considered too small for the main engine to accurately complete.

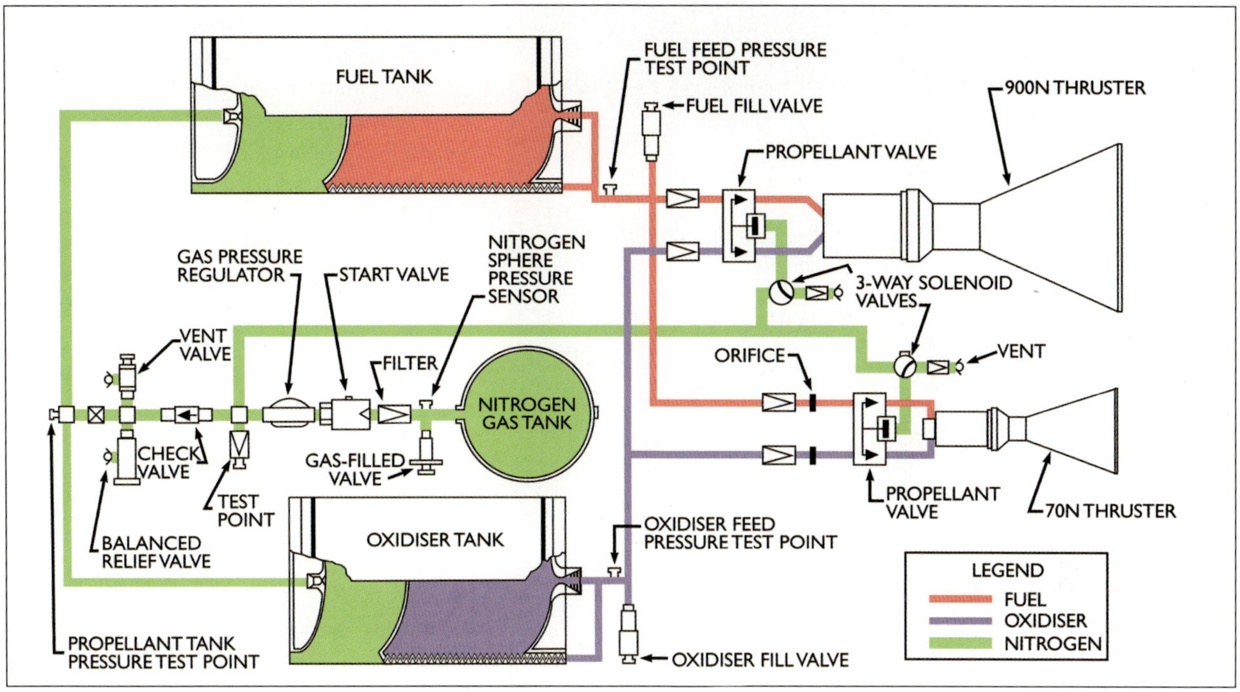

ABOVE Schematic of the secondary propulsion system of the GATV. *(NASA/ David Woods)*

The small thrusters were used for *ullage*, a term that comes from brewing which refers to the top part of a barrel not occupied by liquor. Ullage has a similar meaning in rocketry. In conditions of zero-*g*, the gaseous content of a tank can be anywhere within its volume and the liquid is free to float around in great globs. However, prior to ignition of a liquid-fueled engine, steps have to be taken to ensure that none of the gas enters the pipework leading to the engine. A common way to achieve this is to use small supplementary rocket engines to apply just sufficient acceleration to the vehicle to settle the liquids in its propellant tanks rearwards, forcing the gas to the front, this being the ullage space.

The SPS burned the hypergolic combination of UDMH (a version of hydrazine) along with so-called *mixed oxides of nitrogen* (MON); the latter having a lower freezing point than the more conventional nitrogen tetroxide oxidizer. Each module had its own pair of tanks which operated in a similar manner to the main engine's start tanks, whereby the propellant was stored within a set of steel bellows inside the tank and nitrogen gas was used to apply the pressure required to force the liquid out.

Target docking adapter

At the front end of the GATV was a docking adapter supplied by McDonnell. The most obvious component of this unit was a large, incomplete cone nearly 1.5m across. This cone was used to shepherd the nose of a Gemini spacecraft towards three latches that engaged with receptacles on the spacecraft. A missing

LEFT Close-up of the docking cone of the 12-Agena. On the upper left is the docking index bar that protruded from the nose of the Gemini spacecraft. On Gemini 12, it included a cap. *(NASA)*

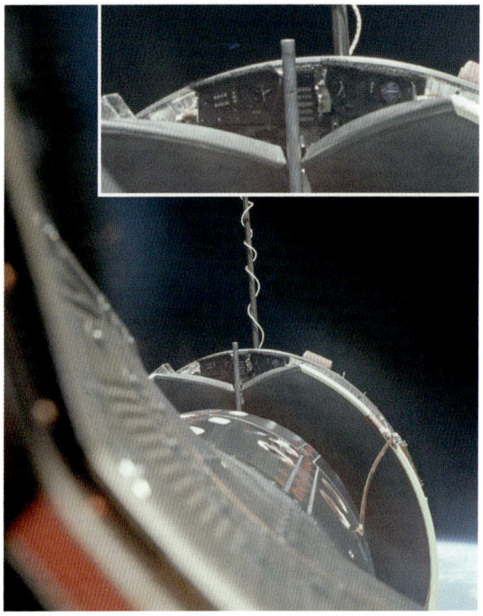

RIGHT Mike Collins took this photograph of the 10-Agena after John Young had docked their Gemini 10 spacecraft with it. The index bar is seated at the apex of the V-shaped notch in the docking cone to ensure proper alignment of the two vehicles. Also visible on the right is one of the static discharge rods that was attached to some GATVs. Inset is a close-up of the Agena's status display panel. *(NASA)*

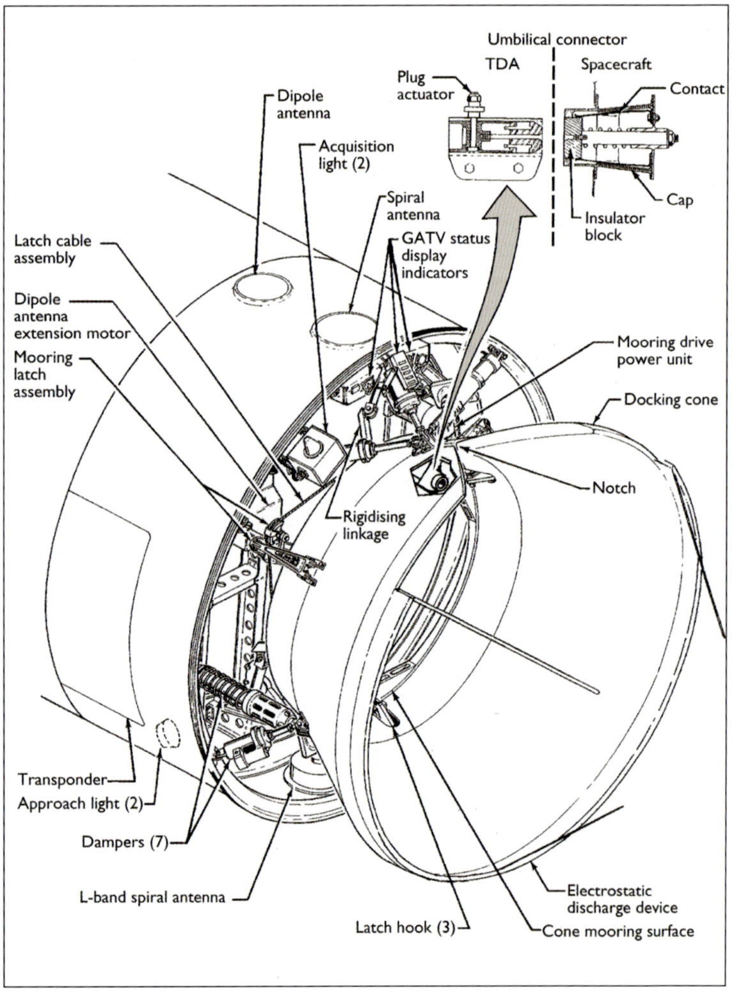

LEFT Diagram of a typical docking adapter on the GATV. *(NASA)*

section on one side of the cone formed a V-shaped notch that accepted an index bar protruding from the side of Gemini's nose to ensure the proper alignment of the two vehicles around their long axes.

A set of dampers connected the cone to the rest of the Agena. These absorbed the energy of the relative movement to ensure that the two vehicles were stabilized prior to being pulled together for a rigid connection. In the process of rigidization, an electric motor pulled the docking cone, and hence the spacecraft in towards the Agena, compressing the shock absorbers until the cone settled against three hardpoints. Undocking reversed the process by extending the docking cone and releasing the latches.

Additional docking equipment included three copper prongs that discharged any static electricity between the two vehicles just prior to docking. Four lights were mounted on the adapter to aid docking: two flashing lights that could be seen at a distance and two that illuminated the docking cone. The process of docking linked up umbilicals that gave the astronauts direct control of the Agena's functions.

Rather than install a dedicated instrument panel inside the Gemini spacecraft for the Agena, each GATV included an instrument panel that was visible to both astronauts through their windows. It indicated the status of the propulsion systems (including how long they had been operating), the docking system (particularly whether or not it was rigidized) and the status of the attitude control system. A sunshade was included but astronauts reported that the panel was often difficult to see in the glare of an unfiltered Sun.

Control of the Agena was carried out by the pilot in the right seat who had access to an *encoder controller* which allowed him to send three-digit codes to the Agena. It consisted of two concentric dials on which the first two digits could be set. Below that was a lever with which the final digit, always a zero or a one, could be entered by moving it to the left or right. The action of moving the lever also transmitted the code to the Agena.

Augmented target docking adapter

Agena was not the only craft that Gemini was designed to dock with. After the loss of the Agena for the Gemini 6 mission, NASA arranged for McDonnell to build the *augmented target docking adapter* (ATDA) as a standby that could be sent up at short notice in the event that the Agena for a subsequent mission was lost. This would enable the program to maintain its hectic schedule.

What set the ATDA apart from the GATV was that it had no large propulsion unit and so could not change its orbit. Nevertheless, the ATDA would permit crews to practice the program's most important task; rendezvous and docking.

Only 3.6m long, 1.5m in diameter and weighing less than 800kg, the ATDA could be launched directly into orbit by an Atlas booster. It had all the systems to fulfil its role; radar transponder, stabilization system, attitude control, lights, power, and of course the docking adapter. Indeed, most of its systems used components meant for Gemini. For example, the only ADTA that was ever launched, which was in support of the Gemini 9 mission, controlled its attitude using an RCS unit that had been taken from the Gemini 6 spacecraft and refurbished.

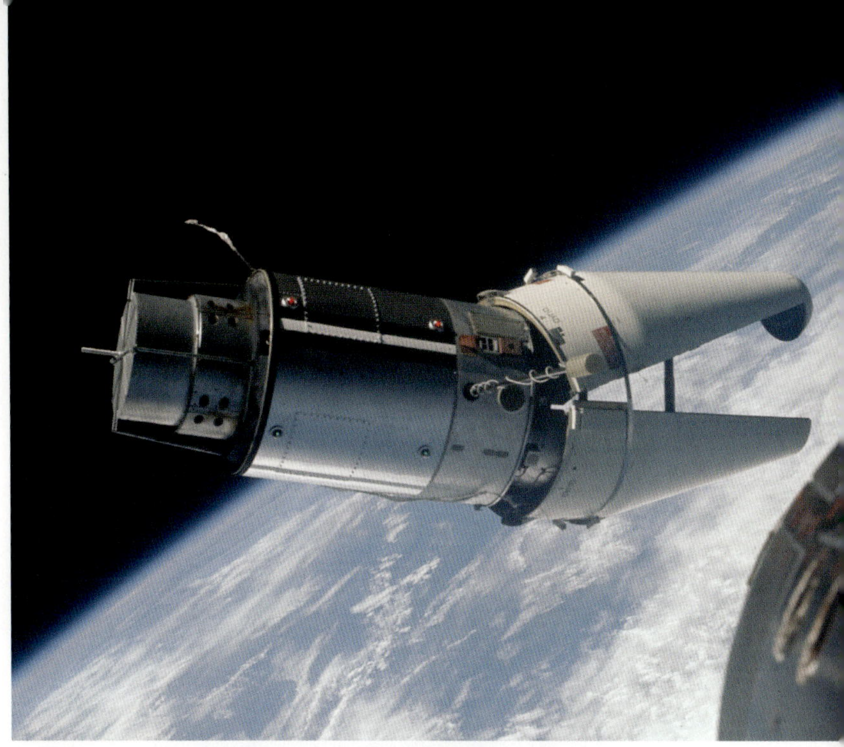

ABOVE The augmented target docking adapter flown for the Gemini 9 mission. The aerodynamic shroud had failed to jettison, rendering the vehicle useless for anything other than rendezvous practice. Visible on the left end of the vehicle is the re-entry control system package that was salvaged from the Gemini 6 spacecraft and refurbished for this mission to provide attitude control. *(NASA)*

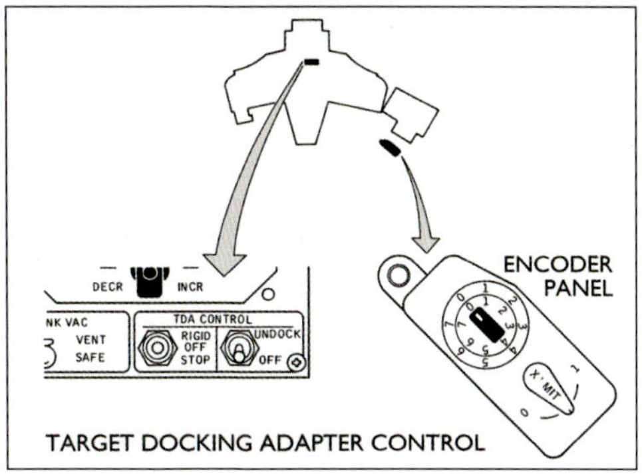

MIDDLE Diagram of the encoder controller panel that was used to send commands to the Agena from the Gemini spacecraft. *(NASA)*

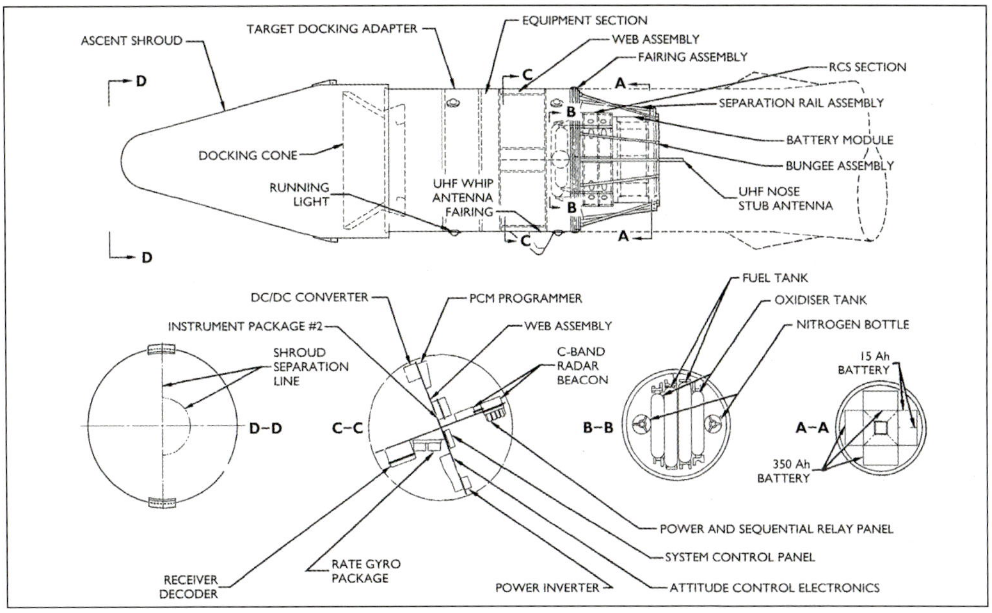

LEFT Diagram of the ATDA and its systems. *(NASA)*

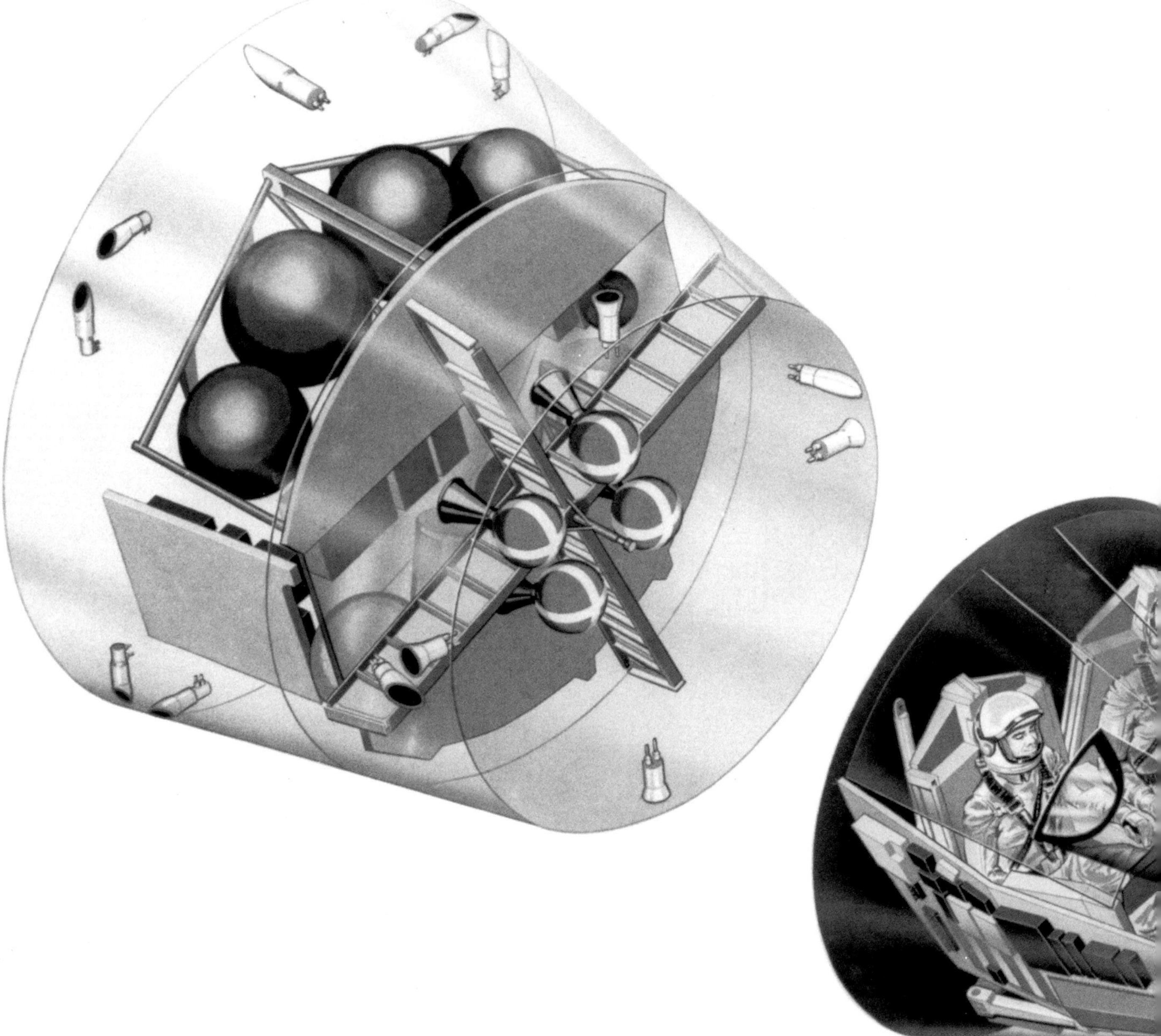

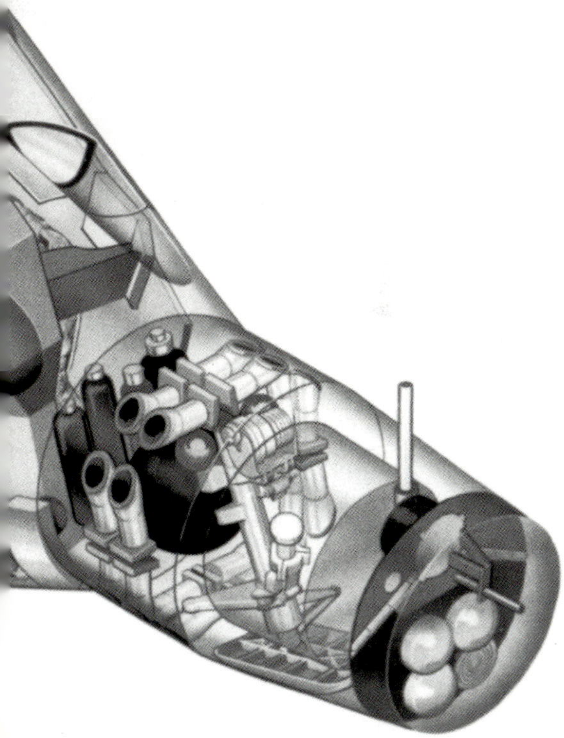

Chapter Four

Spacecraft structure

Overview

Gemini was a modular spacecraft built by the McDonnell Aircraft Corporation in St Louis, Missouri; now absorbed into Boeing. It consisted of a re-entry module and an adapter module and had a total mass of about 3,800kg, depending on its mission. Both modules were further divided into sections, each with their own specialized function.

OPPOSITE **Artist's cutaway drawing of the complete Gemini spacecraft.** *(NASA)*

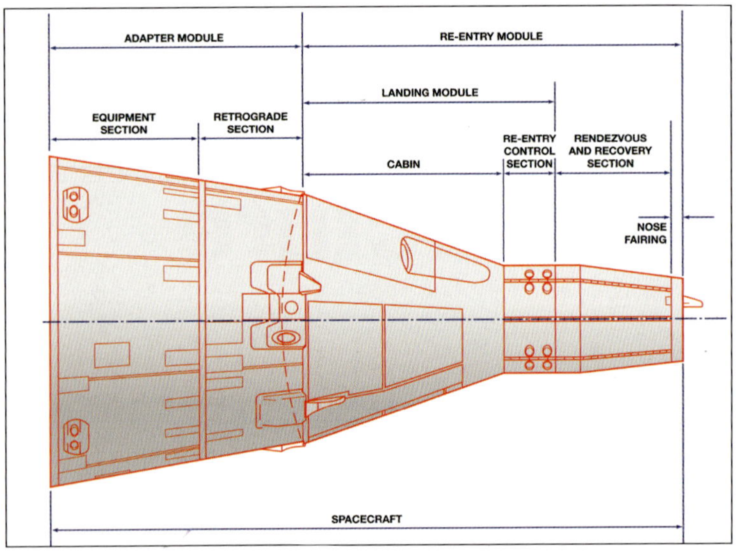

The largest part of the re-entry module was the re-entry section which was conical in shape with a heatshield across its large end, similar to the Mercury spacecraft. Use of a truncated cone for a re-entry vehicle is a design that has proved durable even into the 21st century, having been used for Apollo and, more recently, NASA's *Orion* and SpaceX's *Dragon* spacecraft.

Mounted at the narrow end of the cone was a cylindrical Re-entry Control System section that contained 16 thrusters for use at the end of the mission. Atop of that, forming the nose, was the Rendezvous & Recovery section.

Although built as a single unit, the adapter module was comprised of two functionally separate sections. Next to the spacecraft's heatshield was the retrograde section which

ABOVE The commonly accepted nomenclature of the Gemini spacecraft. *(David Woods)*

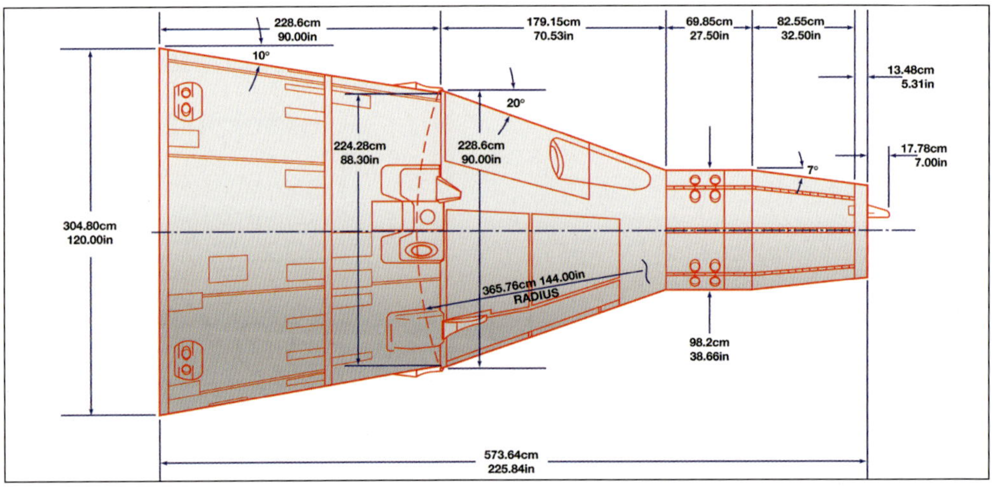

RIGHT Dimensions of the Gemini spacecraft. *(David Woods)*

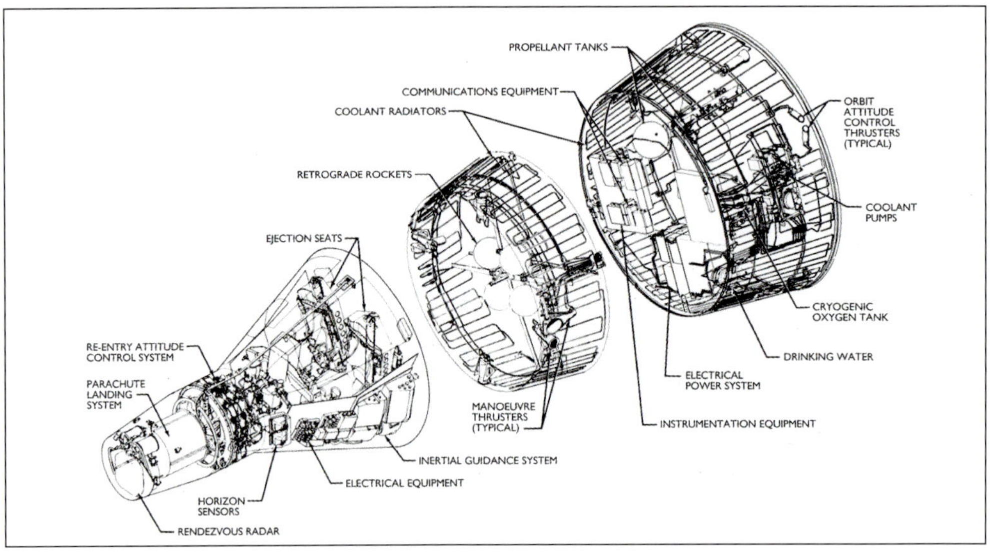

RIGHT Arrangement of equipment on a battery-powered Gemini spacecraft. *(NASA)*

RIGHT **Wide-angle view of the Gemini 9 re-entry module on top of its launch vehicle.** *(NASA)*

carried a set of four powerful solid-fueled rockets to terminate the spacecraft's orbit. Behind that was the equipment section that held systems for propulsion, attitude control, and the supply of electrical power. On some missions, special apparatus intended for spacewalkers would be carried at the very rear of this section.

Re-entry module

The demands that moulded the design of the re-entry module were many and conflicting. It had to be light so that the Titan II could lift it. But it also had to be immensely strong to withstand the aerodynamic and acceleration loads that would act upon it during launch and re-entry. In its final moments, it needed to endure the shock of impact with water without springing a leak, then act as a boat until the crew were recovered. All of these requirements led engineers to assemble the structure largely from titanium and magnesium, metals that exhibit strength while being light in weight.

In space, the spacecraft's pressure hull, which was the astronauts' home for the duration of the mission, had to withstand the outward force of the cabin's atmosphere in the vacuum of space which, at 5psi, was about one-third of Earth's sea-level pressure. The two astronauts were seated with their backs to the heatshield. This arrangement helped them withstand the punishingly high acceleration forces they experienced when ascending to orbit and returning to Earth – both of which typically peaked between 6 and 7*g*.

Above each crewman was an outward-opening hinged hatch. This was large enough to allow an ejection seat and its astronaut passenger to rapidly escape from a failing rocket. In normal use, this hatch could easily be opened either from inside or out. This design feature, had it also been applied to the early Apollo spacecraft, might have saved the lives of three astronauts killed when their Apollo 1 spacecraft caught fire during a ground test. That spacecraft's inward-opening door effectively

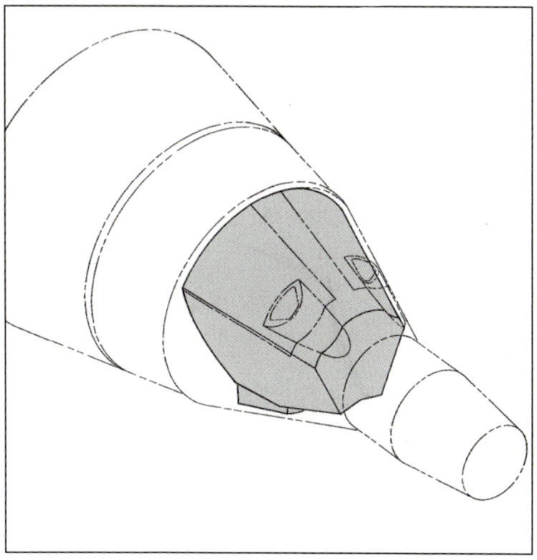

LEFT Diagram to show the location of the pressure hull within the Gemini spacecraft. *(NASA)*

BELOW An exploded view of the major structural elements of the Gemini re-entry module. Note that the spacecraft included landing skid doors though, ultimately, landing skids were never incorporated. *(NASA)*

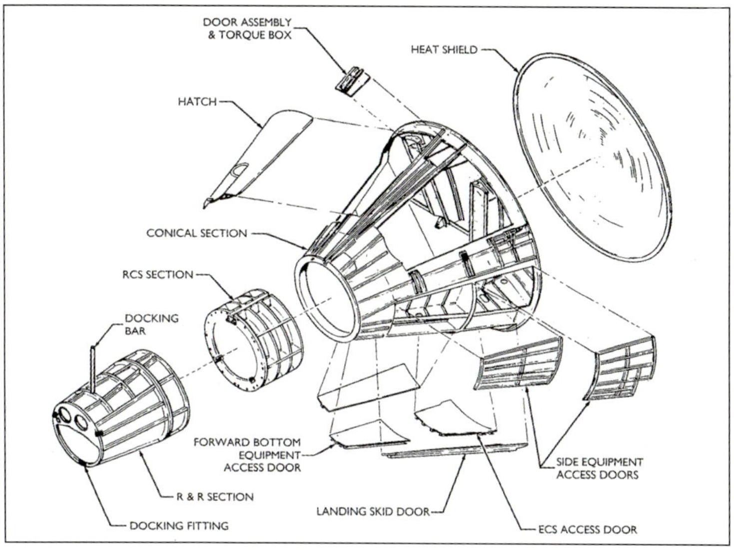

trapped the crew. Given their experience with Gemini, McDonnell engineers assisted the Apollo manufacturer, North American Rockwell, with the redesign of the hatch in the fire's wake.

With their backs facing aft, the crewmen faced forwards, towards the pointy end of the ship. In front of each man, and built as part of the hatch, was a triple-paned, half-moon-shaped window 8in wide and 6in deep. This was primarily so that the commander would be able to watch and guide the final stages of rendezvous and docking. However, special attention was given to the clarity of the pilot's window since he was usually assigned a program of photography.

On the early Gemini flights it was discovered that the windows were being fogged during the ascent to orbit so an outer protective pane was

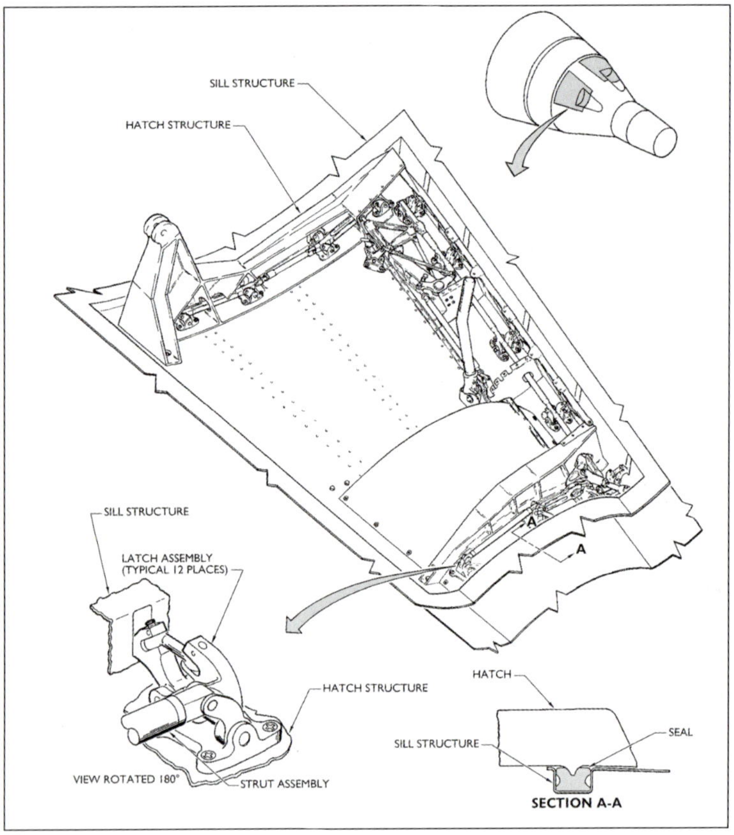

ABOVE Diagram of the catch mechanism and seal on a Gemini hatch. *(NASA)*

BELOW The open hatches of Gemini 3 reveal Gus Grissom and John Young during countdown practice a few days prior to launch. *(NASA)*

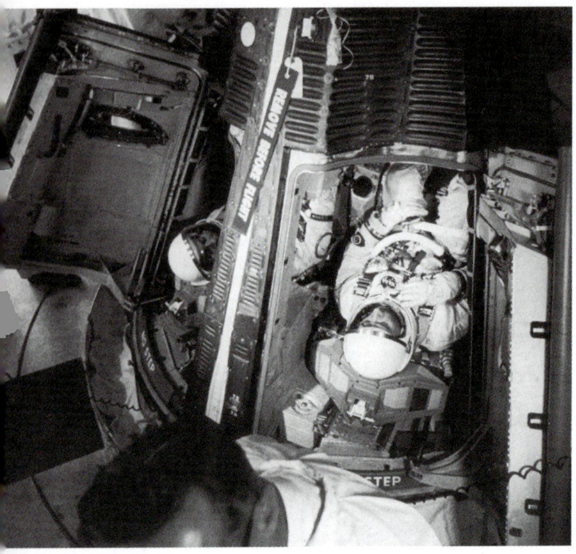

BELOW Exploded view and cross section of Gemini's outer window assembly. *(NASA/David Woods)*

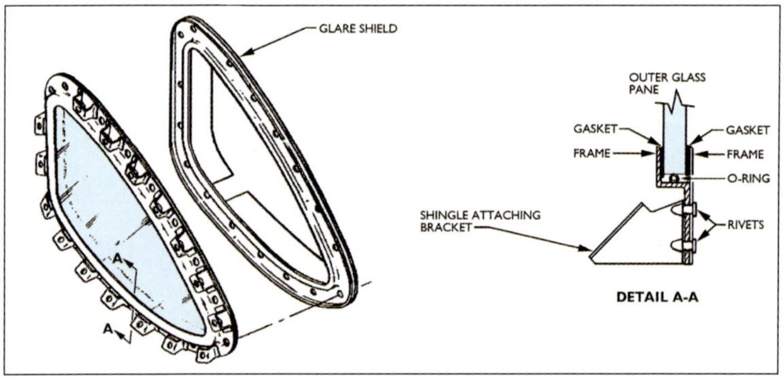

BOTTOM Cross section of Gemini's triple-paned windows. *(NASA/David Woods)*

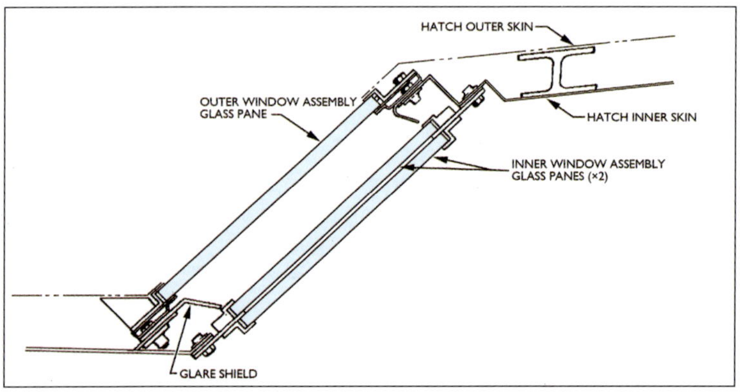

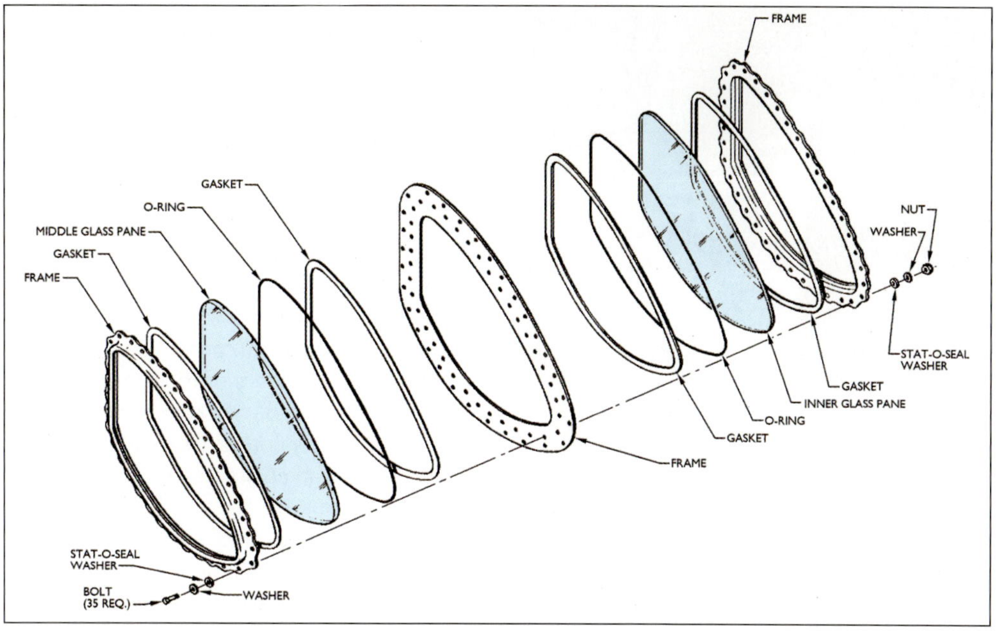

LEFT Exploded view of Gemini's inner window assembly. *(NASA/David Woods)*

added to the pilot's window. These panes were cannibalized from earlier flown spacecraft, and once in space the pilot could jettison this glass to reveal a pristine window pane beneath.

Much of the spacecraft's equipment was placed outside the pressure hull but within the exterior surface of the ship. This not only made it more accessible when repairs were required, it kept the interior free for all the ancillary gear the astronauts would require for their long duration flights. The pressure vessel was constructed out of titanium panels mounted on a titanium frame. Each panel consisted of two layers, each 0.25mm (0.01in) thick with one layer being beaded; that is, stamped with grooves to increase its stiffness. Most of the panels had their beaded layer on the inside but the aft bulkhead had them on the outside.

The shape of the pressure vessel was such that it allowed for three equipment bays

BELOW Major components of the spacecraft's pressure hull. *(NASA)*

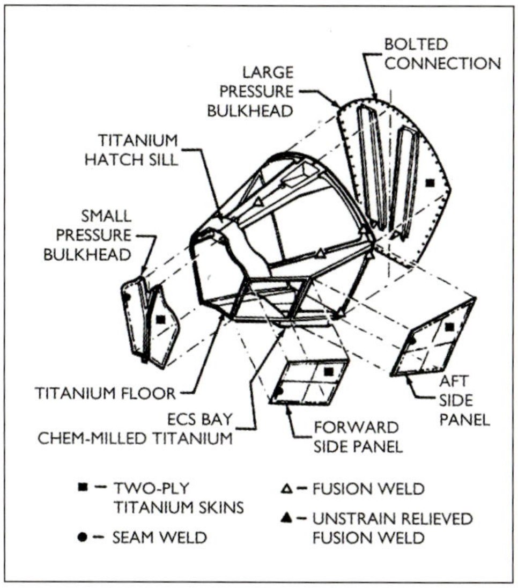

BELOW Jim Lovell, commander of Gemini 12, by the bluish Earthlight coming through his small hatch window. *(NASA)*

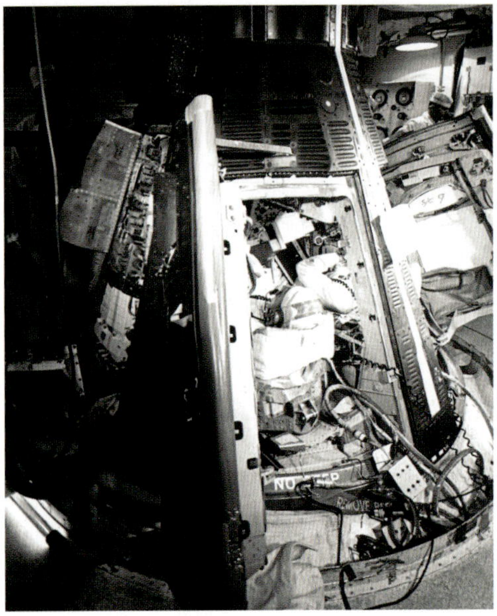

RIGHT Gemini 9 during preparations for flight. On the left, some of the spacecraft's external doors are open to expose the equipment bays within. *(NASA)*

between its walls and the outer skin of the spacecraft. These bays were unpressurized and could be accessed by the removal of skin panels. There was one on each side of the spacecraft and a third beneath the floor. They held most of the electronic systems, so the equipment had either to be capable of operating in a vacuum or be housed in its own pressurized container.

Offset center of mass

An important feature of the re-entry section was that its center of mass was positioned about 45mm (1.75in) away from its geometrical center. In other words it was designed to be slightly heavier on one side, unlike the Mercury spacecraft in which any offset was unintended. This small change meant that as a Gemini spacecraft passed through the atmosphere on re-entry, it could be guided to a desired landing site.

When a Mercury spacecraft re-entered, it had no means to control its flight path. It followed a purely ballistic trajectory, like an artillery shell. If its center of mass was unintentionally offset, causing it to exhibit a slight tendency to fly to one side, then that was treated as a problem. The astronaut would cancel out such a tendency by making the spacecraft slowly roll around its long axis during its passage through the atmosphere.

Already, for Mercury, there were enough variables that could affect its landing spot; the strength of the retrorockets' thrust, the precise

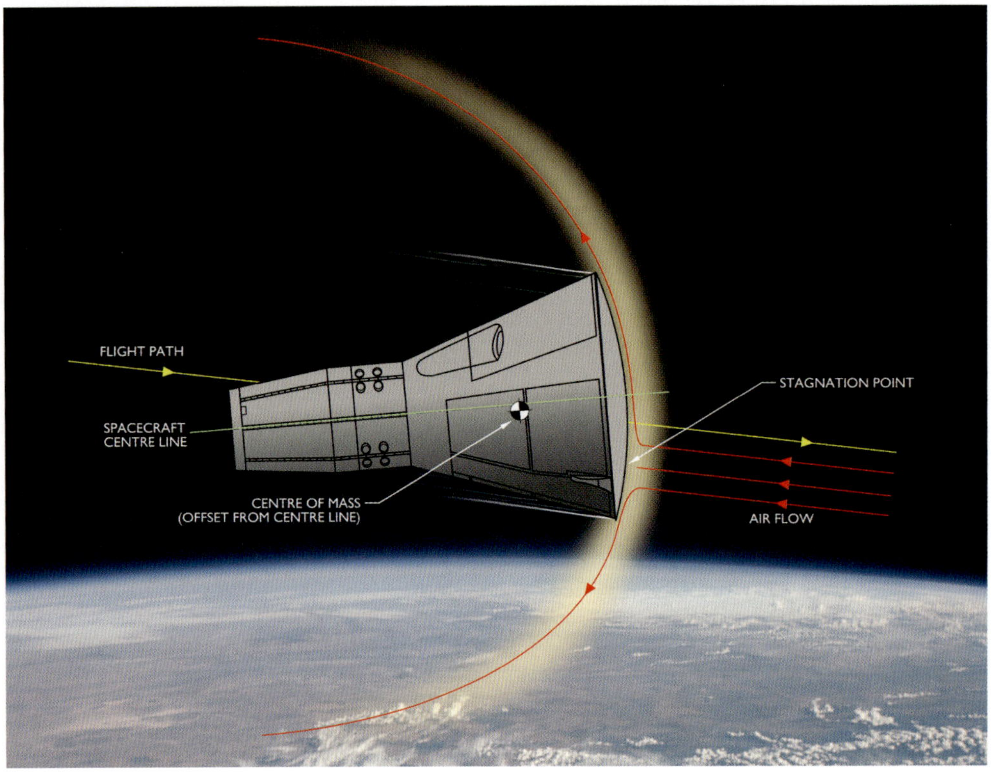

RIGHT Diagram to show how the spacecraft's offset center of mass caused it to re-enter in a lop-sided manner that permitted limited control of its flight path. *(David Woods/ Kevin Woods/NASA)*

timing of their firing, and the density of the atmosphere along the flight path. With a starting speed of nearly 8km/sec, even tiny deviations from the ideal produced great uncertainty in the spacecraft's final splashdown point and that made an accurate landing more a matter of chance. For Gemini, the displacement of its center of mass to one side was deliberate and it provided the ship with a small degree of control of its re-entry; enough for it to steer to a given landing spot. Gemini was the first manned spacecraft to take advantage of this technique.

The heavy side of the spacecraft was set away from the hatches and towards the astronauts' feet. This ensured that, upon re-entry, the spacecraft would tilt slightly to one side with respect to the oncoming hypersonic airflow. As a result, it took a slightly different flight path when compared to a purely ballistic re-entry and this was always in the direction that their feet were pointing. It had essentially gained a tiny amount of aerodynamic lift and could, in a very crude sense, fly. To use the terminology of the aerodynamicist, it had been endowed with a lift to drag ratio that was greater than zero.

Lift to drag ratio is a number that is of great interest to aerodynamicists because it indicates how well an aircraft's wings work. For example, for a sailplane or glider, the upward force generated by its wings passing through air is about 50 times larger than the force of drag that is slowing the aircraft down. For a jet liner, the ratio is in the region of 17:1 while a Space Shuttle coming in to land had an L/D ratio of only 4.5. For Gemini, the offset center of mass gave it an L/D ratio of about 0.2, a very small number for an aircraft but an important amount of lift for a spacecraft streaking through the atmosphere at hypersonic speeds.

This property gave the astronauts a means to steer the re-entry flight path merely by rolling the craft around its long axis. To veer left, they rolled around so their feet would point left. To extend their flight path, they pointed their feet out towards space, thereby flying a slightly higher flight path that kept the spacecraft out of the thicker layers of the atmosphere for longer, reducing the drag on the craft and thereby allowing it to fly further. To shorten their flight path, they pointed their feet Earthward to dig deeper into the thicker atmosphere, which slowed them down more than would otherwise be the case. Apollo took this technique further by having an L/D ratio of 0.37 for an even greater degree of control of its flight path during re-entry.

ABOVE The nose of Gemini 12 photographed from an open hatch. Oversized washers around the fixing screws of the beaded panels cover the large holes in the panels that allow for thermal expansion. *(NASA)*

Spacecraft skin

During a flight, any part of the spacecraft's surface not exposed to the Sun could cool down to well below zero Celsius. At the same time, surfaces on the sunward side could heat to well over 100°C. But the passage of the spacecraft through the atmosphere upon re-entry was much more of a trial. Brutal compression of the air ahead of the heatshield created superhot plasma which cocooned Gemini in a fireball of its own making. As well as eroding the heatshield, which was designed to take the punishment directly, it heated the rest of the outer surface to over 500°C, severely testing the exterior skin of the re-entry module. Even passage through the atmosphere during launch and ascent generated enough aerodynamic heating for some areas to reach over 300°C.

To withstand these temperatures, most of the conical section's outer skin was made from René 41, an alloy produced chiefly from nickel, chromium, cobalt, and molybdenum. This alloy is popular in aerospace applications that require high strength at extreme temperatures. For the spacecraft it was shaped into overlapping

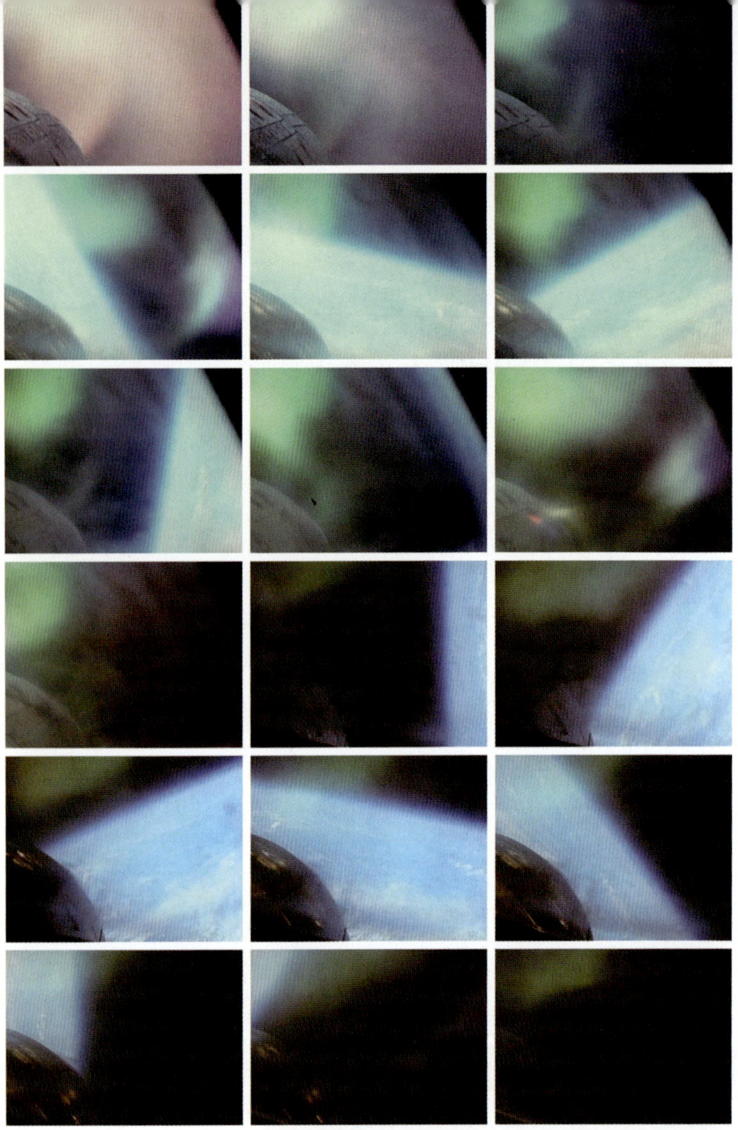

LEFT It was customary for crews to film the view out of their window during re-entry. This montage from Gemini 9's re-entry shows the varying colors of the plasma produced by the spacecraft's shockwave. In the ninth image, an RCS thruster can be seen firing, glowing red and creating a disturbance in the plasma. *(NASA/David Woods/ Courtesy of Mark Gray – spacecraftfilms.com)*

tiles called shingles that were beaded. These shingles were fastened to the spacecraft's structure with screws. The screw holes were made deliberately large to accommodate the expansion and contraction that the shingles would undergo in the wide range of temperatures to which they would be exposed, and oversized washers covered up the gap.

The upper two sections of the re-entry module also had shingles but these were unbeaded and made from beryllium, an extremely light metal which is also strong and able to withstand high temperatures. It is also notably toxic, and great care is required during its manufacture. All the re-entry module surfaces were coated with a black ceramic-based paint which aided the loss of heat from the shingles by thermal radiation.

Heatshield

The aft end of the cabin section comprised a large heatshield that spent most of the mission covered by the adapter module. Exposed just prior to re-entry, it bore the brunt of the heating caused by the spacecraft's hypervelocity plunge into the atmosphere.

Although the air at the edge of space is tenuous, the speed of the spacecraft caused a shockwave to form in front of the heatshield. The extreme compression of the air generated temperatures in the range 4,000–5,000°C. This would vaporize any solid material that came into contact with the shockwave. Presenting a blunt shape to the hypersonic airflow obliged the shockwave to form a short distance away from the structure. This limited the temperature of the heatshield to 1,600°C, which could be handled by the process of ablation.

Ablation works by accepting that the heat of

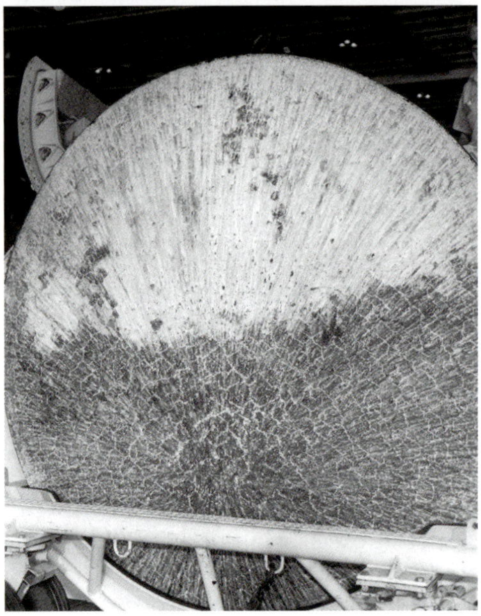

RIGHT Gemini 10's heatshield photographed on the recovery ship. Its passage through the atmosphere has produced a distinctive radial pattern that has its center well off to one side, showing how the offset center of mass has caused it to re-enter lopsided. *(NASA)*

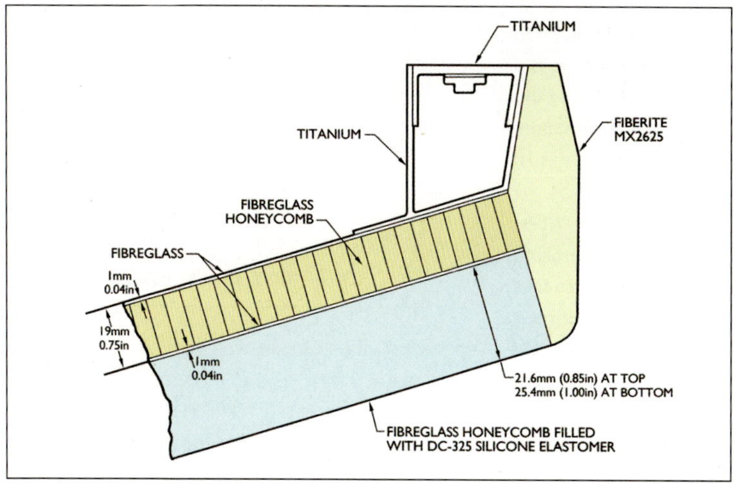

RIGHT Cross section of the edge of the Gemini heatshield. *(NASA)*

re-entry will damage and erode the heatshield. But if the right material is chosen, its surface will char and form an insulating layer as it erodes. So long as the total erosion is less than the thickness of the heatshield, it will suffice to protect the rest of the spacecraft until the speed has reduced sufficiently for ablation to cease.

Engineers covered the entire aft end of the re-entry module with a dish-shaped structure built in two layers. The inner layer was a sandwich, 19mm (0.75in) thick, of fiberglass honeycomb that was faced with fiberglass sheeting. The outer layer was also of fiberglass honeycomb, but with each cell filled with a silicone rubber compound, Dow Corning DC-325. To take account of the spacecraft's offset center of mass and the fact that one side of the shield would endure greater heating, the outer layer's thickness was varied from 21.6mm (0.85in) where the heat load was at its least, to 25.4mm (1.00in) at the edge which turned into the airflow. The rim of the heatshield was finished off with a ring of solid glass fiber and resin material that both served as an ablator for re-entry and as a solid structure to take the weight of the spacecraft as it sat atop its launch vehicle.

Adapter module

In contrast to the black re-entry module, the rear of the spacecraft was the white-painted adapter module, so called because at its simplest, it adapted the spacecraft's 228.6cm (90in) diameter at the heatshield to the 304.8cm (120in) diameter of the Titan II rocket. But rather than leaving this conical ring as an empty shell, engineers used the adapter essentially as a service module to give Gemini far more capability than the Mercury spacecraft.

Functionally, the 228.6cm (90in) long adapter module was itself split in two. The first 85.1cm (33.5in) of its length next to the re-entry module was called the *retrograde section* because it carried four retrorockets that would fire against the spacecraft's motion to slow it down at the end of its mission. It also accommodated some of the spacecraft's maneuvering thrusters.

The rest of the adapter module's length (143.5cm or 56.5in) comprised the *equipment section*. This was home to the spacecraft's electrical power source, be it batteries or fuel cells, and the majority of its propulsion system including propellant tanks. It held a tank of oxygen for the astronauts' breathing supply. If fuel cells were used, there were additional tanks to supply the necessary reactant gases for power generation.

Since it was never intended to survive re-entry, the adapter module's skin could be designed for other uses and it became a large radiator to dissipate excess heat from the

BELOW Diagram of the primary elements of the adapter module. *(NASA)*

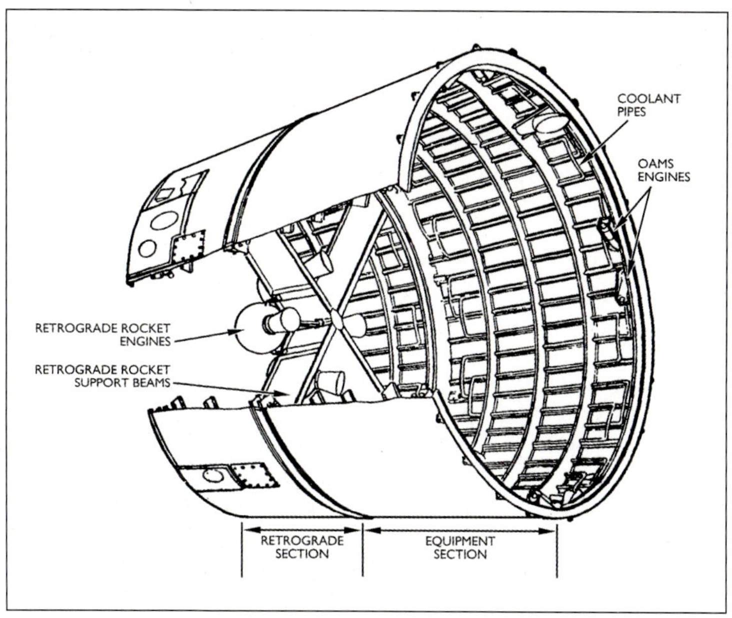

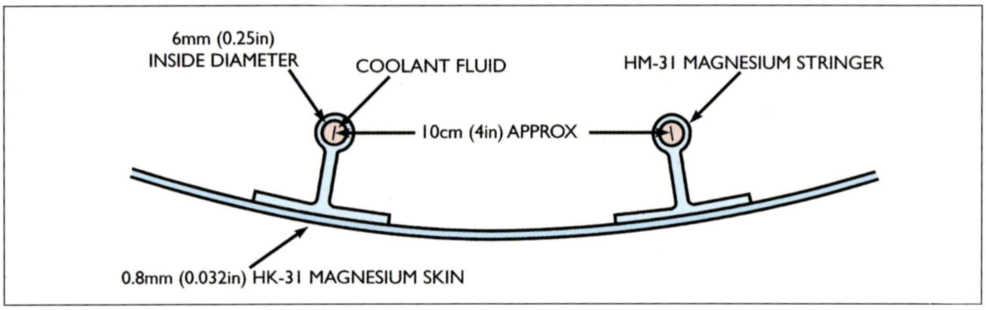

RIGHT Cross section to illustrate the construction of the adapter module's skin. *(David Woods)*

BELOW When Ed White became America's first spacewalker, he carried a 35mm camera and took this shot of Gemini 4's adapter module near where it had separated from its launch vehicle. Damage to the paintwork is apparent. *(NASA)*

spacecraft. Its structure was built around a set of aluminium rings that dictated its conical shape. The module's outer skin was formed by attaching a series of narrow panels lengthways to these rings. These panels were made from a magnesium-thorium alloy for lightness and included integral stringers to provide additional stiffness.

Pipes were fabricated into the stringers along their length and connected at their ends to form a circuit in which coolant could flow. Since the stringers were structurally part of the skin panels, heat from the spacecraft's environmental control system passed from the liquid coolant to the panels' exterior surfaces and was then radiated to space. White ceramic paint was added to the outside to improve the efficiency of the radiation due to its high emissivity (a measure of how well it could emit infrared radiation). Metallic surfaces have a poor emissivity, so the interior surface of the adapter's skin was lined with aluminium foil to limit the transmission of heat to the internal components.

As the end of a mission approached, the equipment section of the module was jettisoned by the detonation of an explosive charge that ran around the circumference of the module. It physically cut the outer skin at the junction with the retrograde section. Separation of the retrograde section from the re-entry module was handled in a different fashion because the heatshield sat between the two. Its rim was not metallic and was not structurally fixed to the adapter module; it and the re-entry module merely sat on top of the adapter module.

To hold it in place, three titanium straps were bolted to the re-entry module. The opposite ends of these straps had a screw fitting which engaged with receptacles on the adapter module and which could be tightened to put the straps in tension. After the retrograde burn was complete, explosive charges across the straps were detonated to sever them and jettison the retrograde section.

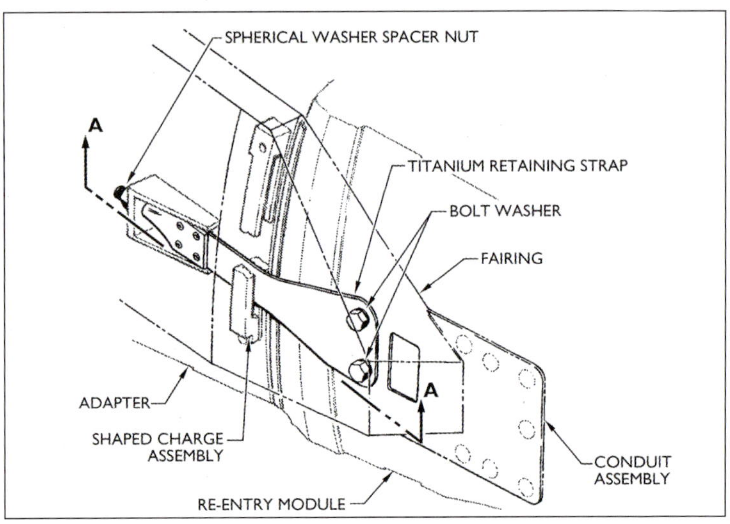

LEFT Diagram of the titanium straps that held the re-entry and adapter modules together. *(NASA)*

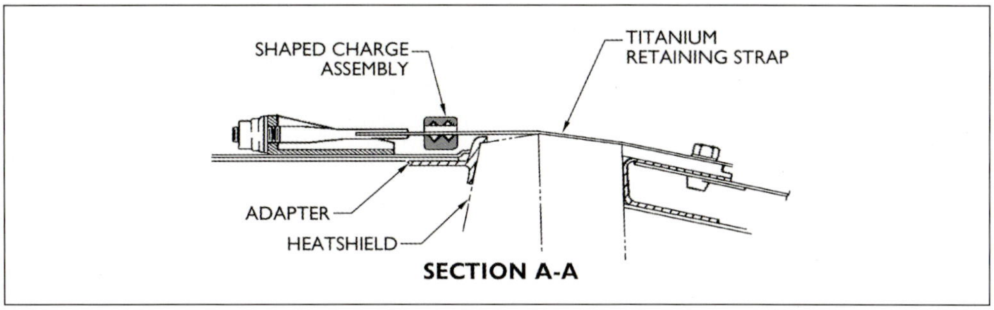

LEFT Cross section to illustrate where an explosive charge cut the retaining straps. *(NASA)*

The open end of the adapter section was covered with a glass fiber cloth that had been coated with an extremely thin layer of gold by the process of vapor deposition. This cloth served to protect the equipment within from the extremes of space by both reflecting the Sun's heat and inhibiting excessive cooling by infrared radiation into space.

BELOW A view of Gemini 7 with the thermal cloth that covered the large end of the adapter module. The white adapter modules of the early spacecraft had strips of silvered tape attached. The streamers at the aft-end of the spacecraft are left over from the explosive separation from its launch vehicle. *(NASA)*

Chapter Five

Propulsion

In order to get to where it has to go, a spacecraft needs a form of propulsion. For the Mercury spacecraft, maneuverability was severely limited. Although it could be rotated to point in any direction, it had no propulsion to change its orbit. Once the launch vehicle had released it, the spacecraft would continue on its way until its retrorockets caused it to fall back to Earth. That was it.

OPPOSITE Engineers test-mount retrorockets on the crossed I-beams of a retrograde section. *(NASA/Courtesy of Rob Getz - stellar-views.com)*

To make rendezvous work, Gemini needed the ability to change its flight path, to alter the size and shape of its orbit, to gently pull up beside another spacecraft and stop. The spacecraft was festooned with three dozen rocket motors, large and small. One set of eight gave its astronauts control of their attitude, so that the vehicle could be pointed in any desired direction. Another eight changed its speed; slowing down or speeding up, and moving sideways or up and down.

At the end of the mission, a cluster of four powerful solid rocket motors dropped the spacecraft out of orbit.

Finally, near the nose of the spacecraft was a unit which carried two independent sets of eight thrusters to provide redundant attitude control during re-entry.

To enhance the capability of the Gemini system, some missions docked with an Agena vehicle that had a large rocket engine. With the aid of an Agena, one crew was able to reach an altitude of 1,373.3km (741.5nmi) and set a

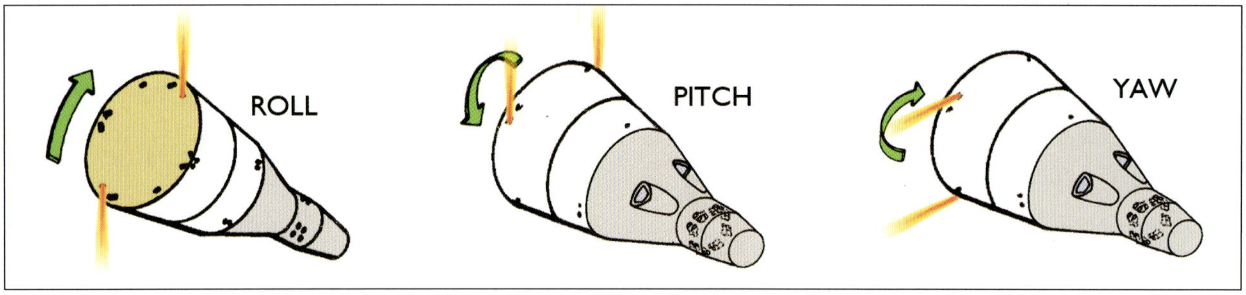

ABOVE Action of the attitude control thrusters. *(NASA)*

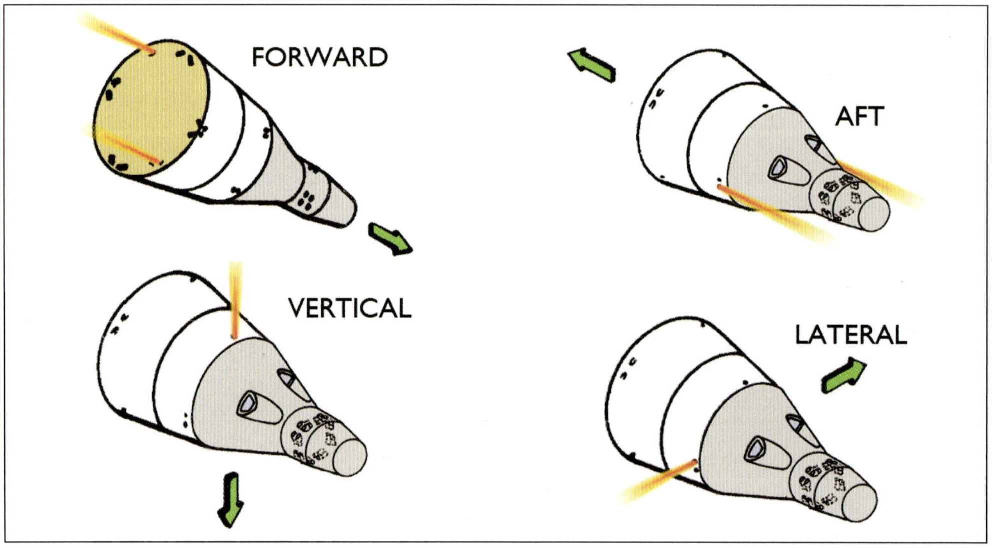

RIGHT Action of the translation thrusters. *(NASA)*

BELOW Action of the thrusters for the re-entry control system. *(NASA)*

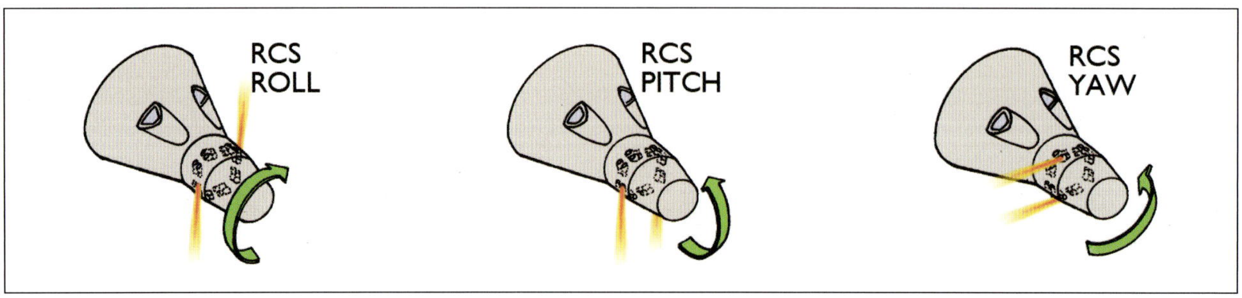

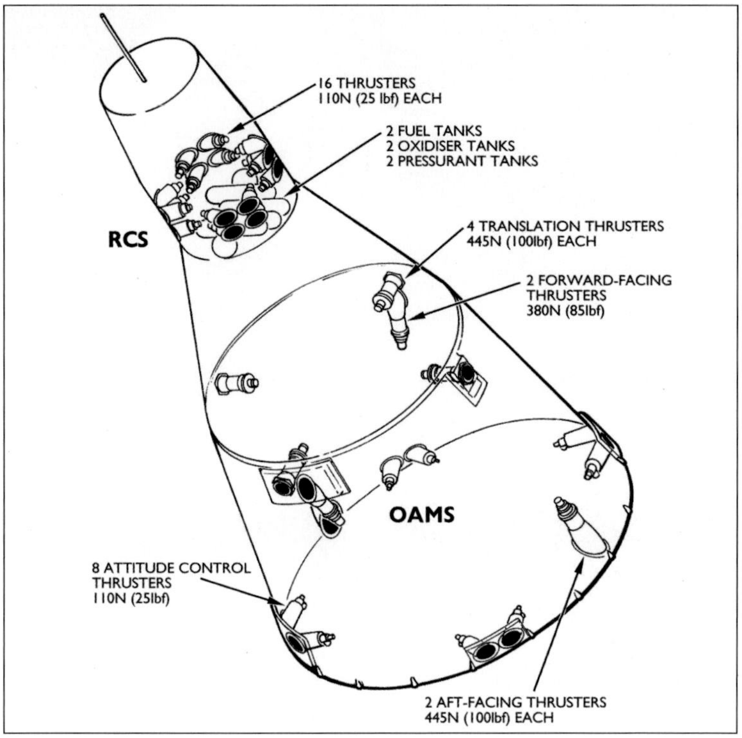

LEFT Diagram of the thrusters on the Gemini spacecraft. *(NASA)*

BELOW Mounting of the four rocket motors in the retrograde section. *(NASA)*

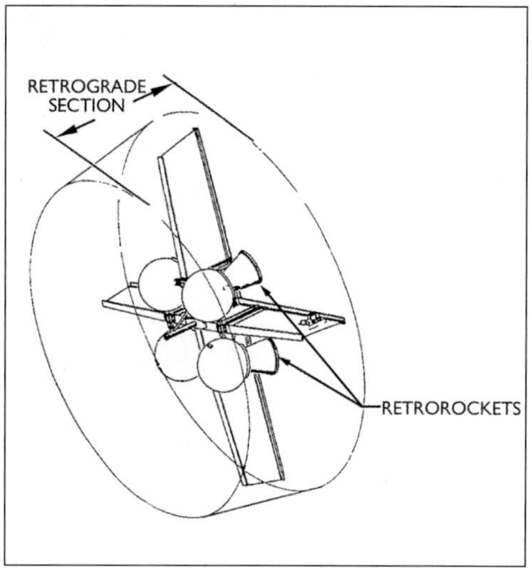

record that stood for over two years until the flight of Apollo 8 to the Moon.

Orbit attitude and maneuver system (OAMS)

In NASA's parlance, the Titan II rocket was deemed to be the primary propulsion system in the Gemini-Titan system. Once it had done its work to get Gemini into orbit, it was discarded. Any further propulsion came from the OAMS, which also provided the spacecraft's attitude control. It consisted of 16 little rocket engines of varying power mounted at strategic positions on the adapter module, along with the necessary propellant tanks, valves, plumbing, and a pressurizing system to force propellant to the engines.

Eight engines were arranged around the base of the adapter section and each applied a force of 110N (25lbf). They were fired in pairs as appropriate for control of the spacecraft's attitude. The other eight engines were used for

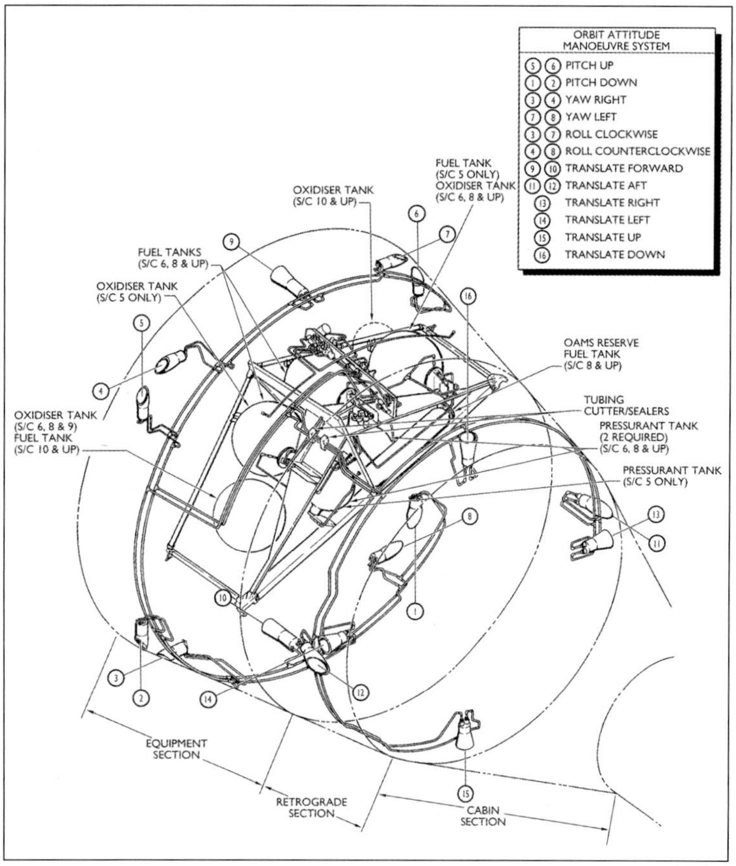

RIGHT Diagram of the OAMS, its thrusters, tankage, piping and associated systems. *(NASA)*

RIGHT Interior of an equipment section with the OAMS tanks mounted at the top. *(NASA/Courtesy of Mike Jetzer – heroicrelics.org)*

propulsion or *translation*, two words that mean the same thing; to make the ship move in one direction without intentionally rotating it. Six of these fired with a force of 445N (100lbf) and the other two were 380N (85lbf) motors.

Unlike Mercury, which used a single propellant for its thrusters, OAMS burned two substances that have become ubiquitous in space flight for two reasons: they can be stored for long periods and they are hypergolic and thus spontaneously ignite upon contact with each other. Hypergolic engines are extremely reliable and controllable and therefore highly suited to the fine control of spacecraft.

The propellants were *monomethylhydrazine* (MMH) as fuel and nitrogen tetroxide as oxidizer. A generation of spacecraft, manned and unmanned, from television broadcast satellites to our most distant probes, have used this type of propellant combination for propulsion and attitude control. Probably the most famous is Apollo 11's *Eagle* that delivered Neil Armstrong and Edwin "Buzz" Aldrin to the lunar surface. On Gemini, the propellants were stored in an array of spherical tanks within the adapter module, up to six depending on the mission.

Each engine had a fuel and an oxidizer valve, both of which were normally held shut by spring action. To operate the engine, the two valves were opened simultaneously, often very briefly, to allow the propellants into a combustion chamber. A valve could be opened by passing an electric current through a *solenoid* to overcome the force of the spring.

A solenoid is an electromagnetically operated actuator. By applying a current to a wire coil, it becomes an electromagnet. Its temporary magnetic field then moves a metal actuator that sits within the turns of the coil. In the engine, the actuator opened the valve against

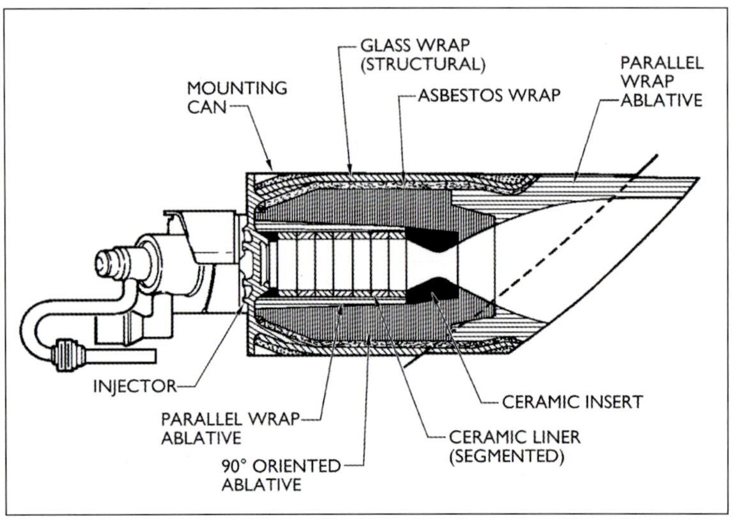

BELOW Cutaway diagram of a 110N (25lbf) thruster. *(NASA)*

the spring. All the control signals to open these valves were handled by the *attitude control and maneuver electronics* (ACME).

OAMS pressurization

When combustion occurs, the heat generated produces a high pressure within the combustion chamber in order to expel the exhaust gases out of the nozzle at great speed. It follows that the propellant must be forced into the chamber at an even greater pressure, as otherwise the liquid would be pushed back towards the tanks. Rather than use pumps with moving parts that could fail, the OAMS used a high pressure gas system to keep the tanks at a higher pressure than the chamber. This ensured that propellants would continue to flow while the valves were open.

Helium was used as the pressurizing gas in the OAMS. By introducing the gas into the tank at high pressure, the tank's contents would be fed out at the same pressure. But a means had to be found to avoid helium reaching the engines. Under gravity, a half-empty tank of liquid naturally ends up with the gas at the top so that if the outlet is at the bottom, only liquid will come out. But if the same tank is being used in a weightless environment, the liquid will tend to float around in great globs and there would be a good chance that gas, not liquid, would emerge from the outlet.

On a large rocket system like the Agena, small rocket motors were used to gently settle fluids at the bottom of their tanks prior to major burns. This cannot work for very small control thrusters because there cannot be such a preparatory burn.

The solution used on Gemini, and on many subsequent spacecraft, was to keep the gas and liquid separate by storing the liquid within a flexible bladder inside the tank. Pressurizing gas was then fed between the

BELOW Schematic of the OAMS propellant supply and pressurization systems. *(NASA/David Woods)*

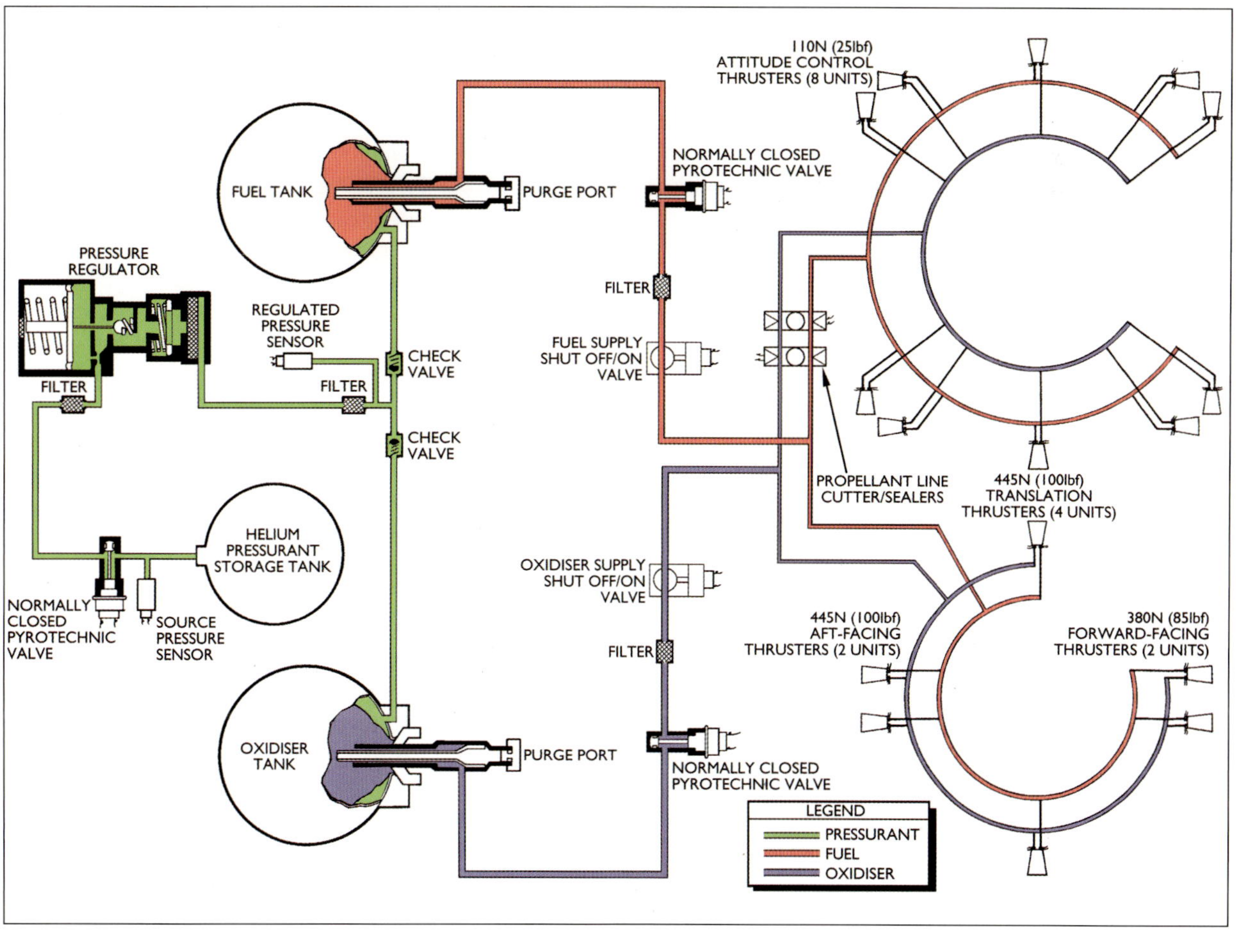

tank's walls and the bladder, thereby ensuring that only liquid propellant would leave the tank's outlet. The corrosive nature of the propellants dictated that the bladder be made from *polytetrafluoroethylene* (PTFE, also known as Teflon), a substance noted for its inability to react with almost anything.

Up to two spherical tanks stored the helium gas at the very high pressure of 3,000psi. It was then fed to the propellant tanks via explosively operated valves; one to open the feed at the start of the mission and another to close it if a leak in the system required it.

The helium was then fed through a pressure regulator to ensure that it would reach the propellant tanks at the much lower pressure of 295psi, about twice the pressure a thruster would generate in its combustion chamber, to guarantee that propellant would be delivered with every use.

The pressure regulator was essentially a spring-loaded valve. The pressure downstream of the valve operated against the spring so that if the pressure was too low, the spring would open the valve and allow more helium to flow from its storage tank until the downstream pressure was high enough to force the spring back and allow the valve to close again.

Other components in the system included sensors to measure the pressure on either side of the regulator, one-way valves to ensure flow in a single direction, and manually operated shut-off valves, plus filters to keep contamination from the engines. Gemini 4 and 7 included diaphragms that would burst before anything else in the system, safely venting excess pressure overboard. It was especially necessary for Gemini 7's long duration mission as the pressure in the helium tank rose due to heat leaking into it over time.

Such a failure of the OAMS or any other malfunction that disabled the system was serious. For example, a thruster on Gemini 8 began to fire intermittently, causing the spacecraft to spin at an accelerating rate. The unwanted rotation had become almost intolerable when Neil Armstrong decided to shut down the OAMS and use his re-entry thrusters to regain control. The flight was aborted and he and Dave Scott returned to Earth at the first opportunity.

De-orbit solid rockets

As the end of a mission approached, there was only one remaining propulsive maneuver to carry out, and it was a big one. It was far beyond the capability of the OAMS which, by this time, had probably just about emptied its tanks. Moreover, since this was the maneuver that would return the crew to Earth, very high reliability was called for. Failure of this burn was likely to be lethal by marooning the two astronauts in orbit.

As was often the case, when a critical action was called for in a spacecraft, the engineers turned to pyrotechnics to ensure operation. Although liquid-fueled rockets are very controllable, they are relatively complicated with valves, plumbing and pressurizing systems. The most dependable rocket technology was (and is) the simple solid-fueled rocket motor. A single electrical signal is all that is required for assured operation.

The *retrograde rocket system* (RRS) employed four solid rocket motors to perform the de-orbit maneuver on Gemini. These were manufactured by Thiokol, a company which, in a later form, would build huge solid rocket boosters for the Space Shuttle. The motors were fired in sequence against the direction of travel to decelerate the vehicle out of orbit.

Before the burn, the crew got rid of the equipment section of the adapter module by firing an explosive charge which cut the module's skin right around its circumference to set it free. This exposed the four retrograde rocket motors attached to a pair of crossed aluminium beams in the retrograde section.

Once the de-orbit rocket burn had been completed, the retrograde section was discarded to fully expose the heatshield which covered the aft end of the remaining spacecraft. The three titanium straps that held the retrograde section to the re-entry module were cut by redundant explosive charges.

Each retro consisted of a titanium alloy sphere, 30.5cm (12in) in diameter, filled with a solid propellant of polysulfide with ammonium perchlorate. A star-shaped cavity on the inside of the propellant increased the surface area available for combustion in the initial moments of firing. This helped to make the thrust more

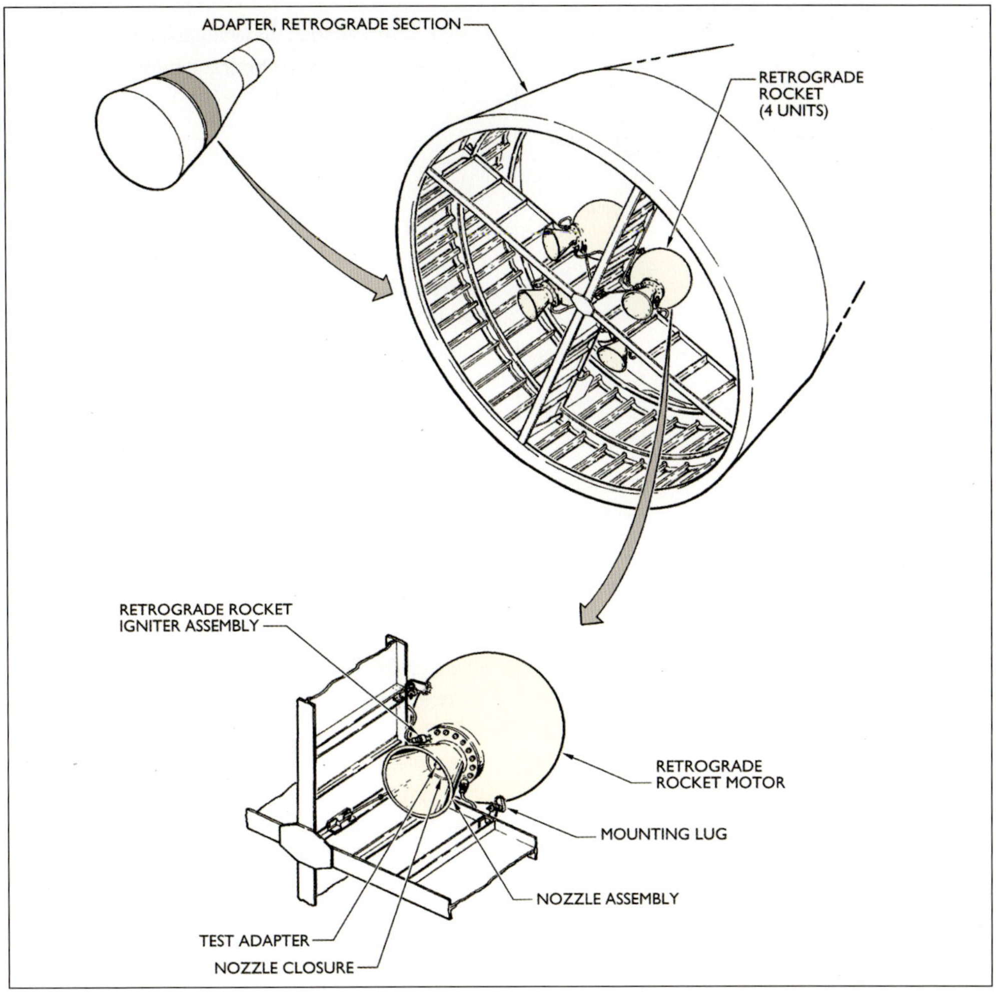

LEFT Diagram to illustrate the positioning and mounting of retrograde rocket motors. *(NASA)*

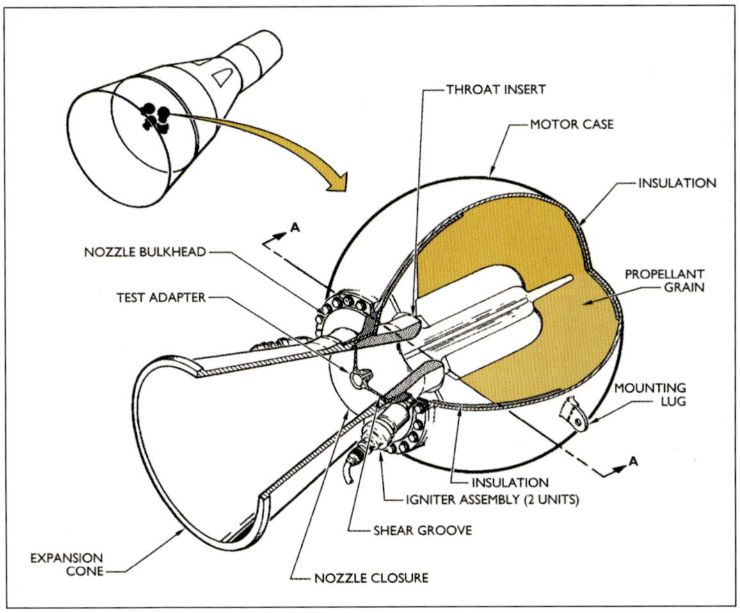

BELOW LEFT Cutaway diagram of solid-fueled retrograde rocket motor. *(NASA)*

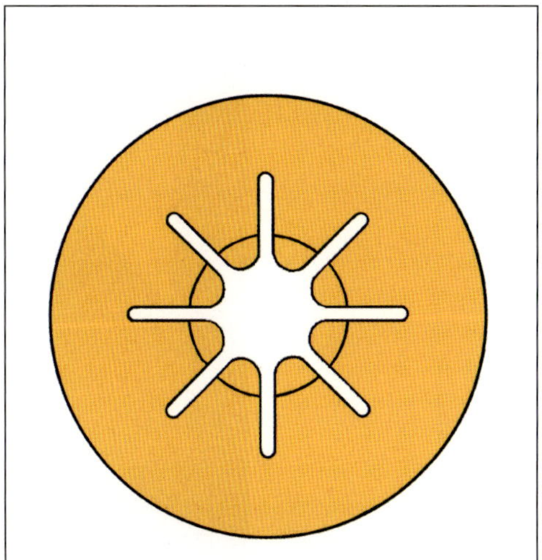

BELOW Cross section of a retrograde rocket to show the grain pattern designed to smooth the motor's thrust profile. *(NASA)*

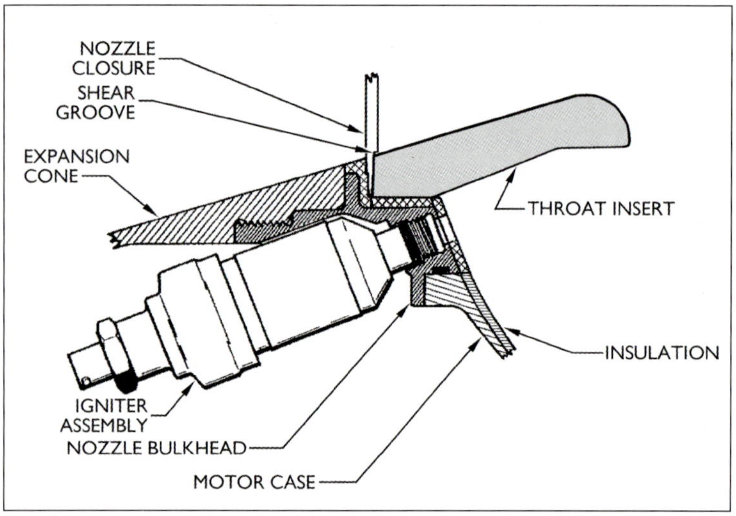

LEFT Cross section showing position of a Pyrogen igniter in a retrograde motor. *(NASA)*

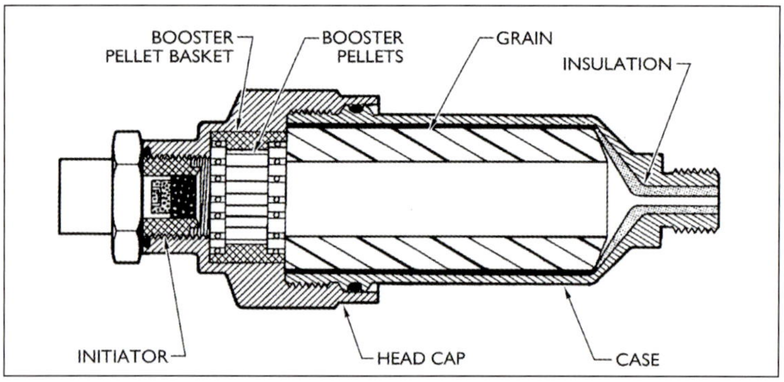

ABOVE Cross section of a Pyrogen igniter. *(NASA)*

RIGHT A Gemini retrograde motor. *(Courtesy of Scott Schneeweis collection – spaceaholic.com)*

even as the engine burned, otherwise it would be small at first and increase as the size of the burning cavity became enlarged.

Ignition was achieved by a redundant pair of Pyrogen igniters, essentially tiny rockets that produced a flame when electricity was passed through them. That flame was directed over the solid propellant's internal surface to initiate combustion. The resulting hot gases then exited the motor through a nozzle to produce a force of 11kN (2,490lbf).

Engineers provided many ways to fire the igniters and start these motors. The normal technique was to use an onboard electrical timer. If that failed, a manual command from either astronaut could send power from any of the seven batteries through redundant circuits to the independent igniters. Each motor burned for about 5.5 seconds. On a normal mission, they were fired sequentially so that as one motor faded the next was ignited, thereby creating an almost constant thrust that lasted 22 seconds. However, on one occasion, at the end of Gemini 5's mission, the fourth motor was significantly late.

The retrorockets had an additional life-saving function. If, during the latter part of its flight, the Titan II rocket were to show signs of imminent failure, then the astronauts would use the retro package to separate and move clear before making a controlled landing in the ocean.

Re-entry control system (RCS)

After the OAMS had been jettisoned, there was still a requirement for the spacecraft to maintain control of its attitude. To begin with, it had to be held in a retrograde attitude, heatshield first, for the retrorockets to do their work properly. This attitude was also known as BEF for *blunt-end-forward*. Once the retrorockets had been jettisoned, the heatshield-first attitude was maintained until the aerodynamic forces on the ship imposed their own stability.

During its high-speed passage through the atmosphere, the spacecraft had to be able to

ABOVE **RCS unit during assembly.** *(NASA/ Courtesy of Mike Jetzer – heroicrelics.org)*

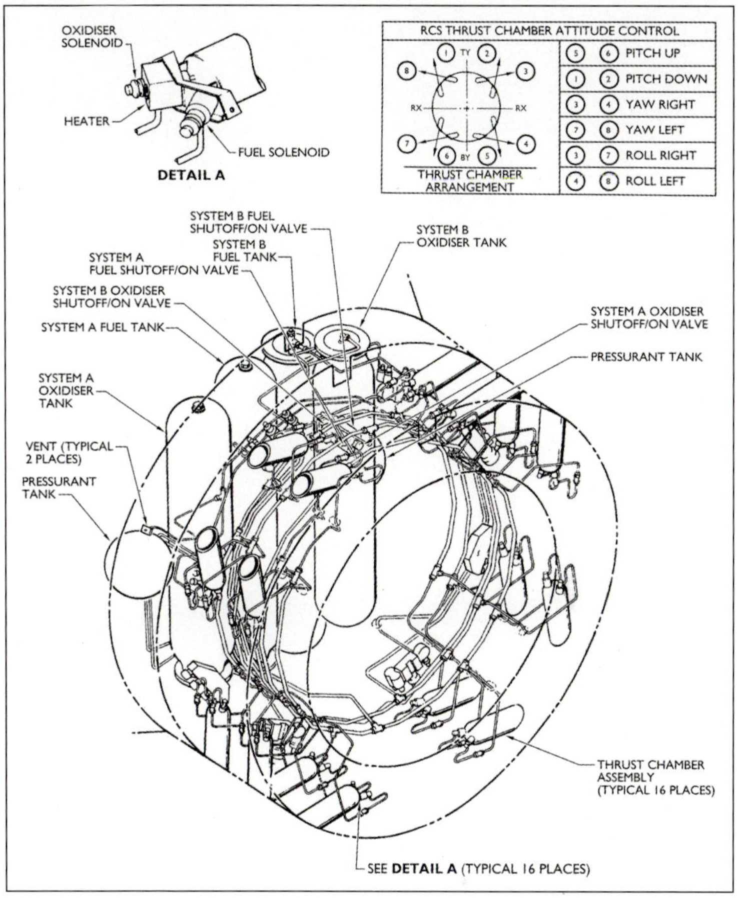

RIGHT **Diagram of the RCS, its thrusters, tankage, piping and associated systems.** *(NASA)*

rotate around its long axis in order to steer to its designated landing site, one where a naval ship was standing by to recover the astronauts. This steering was made possible by the offset center of mass of the re-entry module.

Controlling the attitude during re-entry was the responsibility of the re-entry control system, a cylindrical package of thrusters and tanks mounted at the apex of the spacecraft. It consisted of two rings of eight thrusters, with each ring being a completely independent system with its own propellant tanks to provide redundancy. A fuel tank for one system held 8.95 liters and the oxidizer tank held 7.2 liters. The pressurizing system for each was also independent with a tank of nitrogen gas for each ring. The use of nitrogen instead of helium reflected the system's intended limited lifetime and smaller size.

The thrusters were the same as those used for attitude control on the OAMS, and used the same propellants. They provided 110N of force (25lbf) each and they fired in pairs to achieve rotation in yaw, pitch and roll.

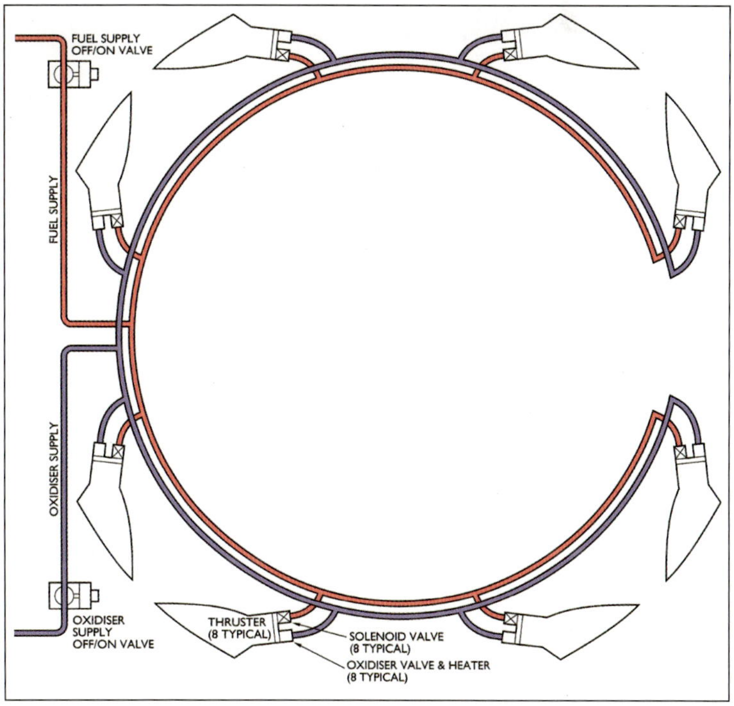

RIGHT **Schematic of the propellant supply for an RCS ring.** *(David Woods)*

UNITED
STATES

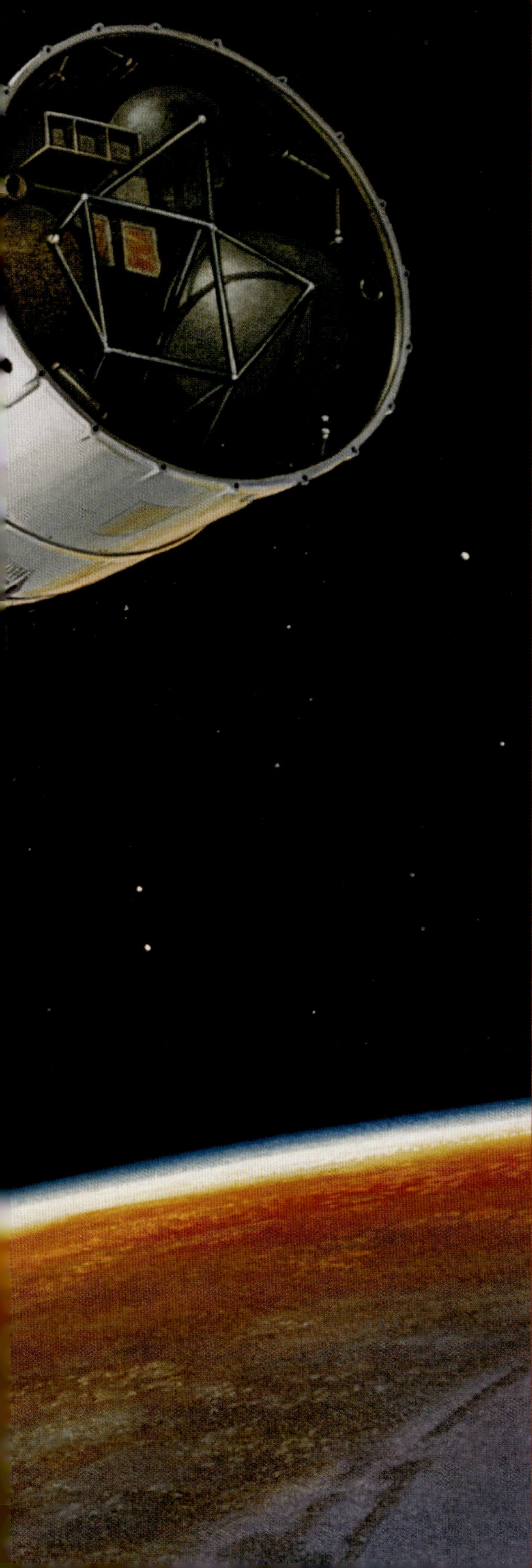

Chapter Six

Guidance and control

In its pursuit of the Moon, NASA had to learn the fundamentals of flying in space because it had been determined, after a protracted debate, that a flight to our nearest celestial neighbor would require two spacecraft to achieve rendezvous, an exercise which at that time was perceived as being dangerous, difficult, and extremely demanding of crews and equipment. Gemini would be NASA's classroom and top of the curriculum was to prove and practice the techniques required for safe and successful rendezvous.

OPPOSITE Artist's impression of the Gemini 6 and Gemini 7 spacecraft station-keeping next to each other after the first controlled rendezvous in human space flight. Rendezvous is only possible with advanced guidance and control systems. *(NASA)*

ABOVE The Gemini 6 spacecraft photographed from Gemini 7 after it had achieved rendezvous. The white box on the spacecraft's nose is a radar unit. Beneath the three domes are rotating spiral antennae that were used to determine not only the target's distance and speed of approach, but also its direction. *(NASA)*

Central to achieving rendezvous was the need to know where the spacecraft was in relationship to a target vehicle. Then, using the available information, the astronauts, with help from mission control, had to calculate the necessary maneuvers for a successful rendezvous, and then carry them out. Throughout, the spacecraft had to be able to point itself and therefore its engines in a precise direction, preferably autonomously. This was the responsibility of *guidance and control* (G&C).

The major subsystems in the Gemini spacecraft involved with the guidance role were the radar and the inertial guidance system along with a host of other subsidiary units like the master clock and various interface systems to carry information and commands. Control of the spacecraft's attitude and trajectory was achieved using thrusters arranged around the outside of the adapter module. These were fired according to commands that came directly from the crew, from the guidance systems, or from signals generated by horizon sensors.

Radar

To successfully execute a rendezvous task, the first requirement was to find out where the target was. For Gemini this target was usually an Agena vehicle, though with two exceptions. One was the spectacular simultaneous flights of Geminis 6 and 7. Gemini 7 was a long duration flight that became a manned target at short notice when the Agena intended for Gemini 6 exploded shortly after launch. Another was Gemini 9 when the loss of its Agena led to NASA flying a substitute target.

With good lighting, it was often possible to see the target directly and use simple instruments to determine its direction. Astronaut

Buzz Aldrin achieved this on Gemini 12 by using a sextant. However, visual sighting was less useful when the target was very far away and such manual techniques could not easily measure the target's distance. A much better solution was to use radar to make these measurements accurately and under varying conditions. Once the Gemini radar system had locked onto the target, it could determine not only in which direction it lay, but also how far away it was (its range), and how fast it was approaching (its range-rate).

The word *radar* began as an acronym for RAdio Detection And Ranging. It was developed during the Second World War as a means to detect ships and aircraft at much greater distances than feasible by eyes alone. At its simplest, radar works by transmitting a radio signal and detecting what comes back in the form of an echo. This is *passive* or *primary* radar, and it relies on the fact that metal structures are very good at reflecting radio waves. The range can be determined by precise measurement of the time between the transmitted pulse and the returned signal. If the antenna has a narrow beam, it will also be able to determine the object's direction. The object plays no part in its detection other than to reflect a signal.

For the Gemini role, primary radar had disadvantages. A radar system for Gemini had to work when the spacecraft and Agena were close together as well as when they were very far apart. A passive system struggles with close proximity because the speed of light (and radio waves), at 300,000km/sec, is so fast that the transmitter could still be sending its outgoing pulse when the reflection arrives and is swamped by the power of the transmitter. Also, it is important that the radar identifies only the desired object, the Agena, and is not misled by other objects that may also reflect its pulses, either on the ground on in orbit nearby.

Gemini/Agena therefore used an active radar system, one in which both vehicles took an active part in making it work. The Gemini spacecraft carried the transmitter/receiver, also known as an *interrogator*, and the Agena carried a *transponder* which, rather than just reflecting the incoming pulse, used it as a trigger to send its own reply pulse. On the Gemini side, the interrogator was a sealed unit weighing nearly 33kg built into the nose of the spacecraft. It had four antennae; one to transmit pulses and three to receive the returned pulses. The transponder was a 14kg unit built into the side of the Agena near the docking equipment. Its two antennae were located on either side of the cylindrical spacecraft.

In such an active system, the interrogator sent out a short pulse of radio energy at a particular frequency. When the Agena's transponder received the pulse, it returned another pulse with two characteristics. First, the reply pulse was at a different frequency. (Imagine a parent calls to a child and hears a reply in a recognizable voice that distinguishes it from others.) Second, the transponder waited for a predetermined time before transmitting its reply. This was to allow the system to operate when at very close range, for example during

ABOVE The Gemini 7 spacecraft photographed from Gemini 6. Instead of a radar unit, this spacecraft carried a transponder in its nose. The brass-colored spiral antenna of the transponder is visible on the spacecraft's nose. *(NASA)*

RIGHT **Range and range-rate instrument as installed in front of the Gemini commander.** *(NASA)*

the final stages of a rendezvous. The radar merely had to subtract the time delay from its measurement to determine the target's range.

Measurement of range was carried out in two separate circuits; one using digital processing and the other an analog technique. The digital version, essentially a binary number, was fed to the spacecraft's computer to be used as part of its calculation of the maneuvers to be made to reach the target. This number was generated by counting accurate clock pulses between the moments of transmission and reception.

BELOW **An engineer inspects the rotatable spiral antenna on a Gemini radar unit.** *(NASA)*

The analog version of the range measurement was produced to drive a gauge on the crew's instrument panel that indicated the range to the target and the range-rate. To generate this signal, engineers arranged that at the moment of radar pulse transmission, a voltage would begin to rise smoothly and linearly. The rise was stopped at the moment of reception. The upper level of this voltage was therefore proportional to the target's range. With a bit of processing, the unit could produce a signal to drive the range instrument. By measuring how this range signal changed, a range-rate signal could be derived which told the crew how fast the target was approaching or receding.

The four antennae for the radar unit were constructed as metal spirals mounted on glass fiber discs 114.3mm (4.5in) in diameter. By arranging the three receiving antennae in a pattern that formed a right-angled triangle, the direction to the target could be determined. Therefore, with the spacecraft in its heads-up attitude, two antennae were on a line perpendicular to the ground. This pair measured the angle to the target in the vertical axis. Likewise, the pair that were on a line parallel to the ground did the same in the horizontal axis. By combining the measurements, an angle to the target was calculated and sent to the computer.

The receiving antenna common to both pairs was fixed and the other two could be rotated. By rotating the spiral of one antenna in comparison to the fixed antenna, the phase of the incoming signals could be made to match. The angle to the target was in turn related to the angle to which the antenna had been rotated.

Engineers added an additional capability to the radar system which made use of the fact that the pulses could carry information. Each pulse from the interrogator included commands from the Gemini spacecraft to the Agena, allowing the crew to control it remotely once the transponder had been acquired. The transponder then acknowledged that it had received and accepted the command. After docking, commands to the Agena were routed via an umbilical link.

Inertial Guidance

The guidance and control of any reasonably sophisticated spacecraft requires knowing "which way is up." In other words, the spacecraft needs to know how it is orientated with respect to the universe around it. Without this knowledge it cannot aim cameras, instruments, or any antenna that has a highly directional radiation pattern. Worse, if it does not know which way it is pointed, it cannot aim its engines properly to undertake the required maneuvers. What is needed is some kind of fixed reference against which a spacecraft's orientation, usually referred to as its *attitude*, can be measured.

Around the time of the Gemini program, engineers had been developing missile systems that would deliver nuclear warheads across continents. Their missiles needed to be accurate over long ranges, necessitating careful measurement of attitude and motion. The solution they developed, *inertial guidance*, used the properties of the traditional gyroscope to stabilize the orientation of a small platform.

A traditional gyroscope is simply a mass that is made to spin at high speed. This spin has an important effect; as the mass spins, its axis becomes very reluctant to rotate and tries to remain pointed in the same direction. Get a toy gyroscope spinning and it can be placed on the end of a pen without falling over. Bicycles of all sorts rely on this property to stay upright. A cyclist does not balance on a bike; once its wheels are turning the resultant gyroscopic effect works to keep them upright.

If it is well engineered, this gyroscopic effect can be employed to maintain the orientation of a physical platform, and in the early years of the technology it was usual to mount this platform within a set of nested gimbals which isolated the rotation of the vehicle from the platform and provided a means to measure the relative angles between the two. The platform formed the core of what is usually called an *inertial measurement unit* (IMU). This contained three gyroscopes, each fitted with an electric motor to keep it spinning. The axis of each gyroscope was orientated perpendicular to the other two, making them *orthogonally mounted*.

The axis of each gyroscope would resist the tendency of the platform to rotate and therefore would apply a force to its mountings. This force was measured and used to control motors in the gimbals that would return the platform to its initial orientation. Thus the platform would appear to remain unmoved relative to the *inertial frame of reference* defined by the stars, enabling it to measure the precise attitude of the spacecraft as that rotated around the *stable platform*.

A second ingredient in this inertial system was the *accelerometer*. As the name implies, this is a device which measures acceleration. As these usually work along one axis only, a conventional guidance platform had three of them and, like the gyroscopes, they were mounted orthogonally. At first it may appear a little counter-intuitive but three accelerometers are all that is needed to continuously follow a vehicle's position in three dimensions. If you measure acceleration then you know how fast your speed is changing. As long as you knew what your starting speed was, your acceleration will allow you to calculate your current speed. To take this further, speed is a measure of how fast your position is changing. Therefore, as before, if you know the position that you started from, then knowledge of your speed will allow you to calculate your current position, all completely derived from a measurement of acceleration.

This is the basis of inertial guidance. In the second half of the 20th century, before GPS satellites had been widely implemented, it was an important means of long distance guidance. It guided jumbo jets across continents, submarines beneath the ocean surface, and rocket-driven missiles towards their targets. In space, inertial guidance underpinned the exploration of the planets and our trips to the Moon.

BELOW **The spinning rotor on this toy gyroscope allows it to sit on the tip of a pen without falling over.** *(David Woods)*

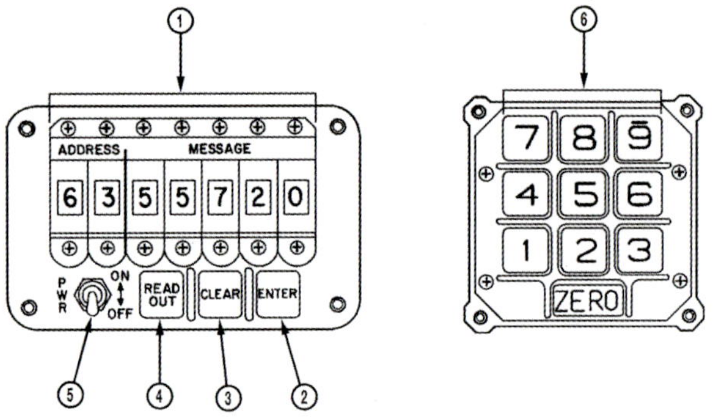

ITEM	NOMENCLATURE	PURPOSE
1	ADDRESS AND MESSAGE DISPLAY DEVICES	DISPLAY ADDRESS AND MESSAGE SENT TO COMPUTER DURING ENTER OPERATION; DISPLAY ADDRESS SENT TO, AND MESSAGE RECEIVED FROM, COMPUTER DURING READOUT OPERATION
2	ENTER PUSH-BUTTON SWITCH	PROVIDES MEANS FOR CAUSING MESSAGE SENT TO COMPUTER DURING ENTER OPERATION TO BE STORED IN MEMORY.
3	CLEAR PUSH-BUTTON SWITCH	PROVIDES MEANS FOR CAUSING ADDRESS AND MESSAGE SET UP BY MDK TO BE CLEARED OR CANCELLED.
4	READ OUT PUSH-BUTTON SWITCH	PROVIDES MEANS FOR CAUSING MESSAGE TO BE READ OUT OF COMPUTER AND DISPLAYED BY MESSAGE DISPLAY DEVICES.
5	POWER TOGGLE SWITCH	PROVIDES MEANS FOR CONTROLLING APPLICATION OF POWER TO MDK AND MDR.
6	DATA INSERT PUSH-BUTTON SWITCH	PROVIDES MEANS FOR CAUSING ADDRESS AND MESSAGE TO BE SENT TO COMPUTER AND TO BE DISPLAYED BY ADDRESS AND MESSAGE DISPLAY DEVICES.

LEFT Control panels for the Gemini computer, both mounted in front of the pilot. *(NASA)*

Inertial guidance system

A number of subsystems came together to form the inertial guidance system, principally the inertial measurement unit and a computer. Other important components included the *manual data insertion unit* (MDIU) that essentially acted like a modern keyboard and screen in that it allowed the pilot in the right seat to interact with the computer.

Another was the *incremental velocity indicator* (IVI) sited in front of the commander, a kind of digital speedometer. For a spacecraft, the concept of speed is conventionally replaced with velocity. This is because the direction of movement has to be considered and not just how fast something is moving. Thus velocity is often expressed as three components that are specified relative to some frame of reference. Therefore the IVI allowed the commander to monitor the spacecraft's velocity as three numbers, calibrated in increments of 1ft/sec.

Inertial measurement unit

At the very center of the guidance system was the IMU. This was a stabilized platform that used three orthogonally mounted gyroscopes to maintain its orientation. It produced a measure of the spacecraft's attitude and its velocity. To isolate it from any rotation which the spacecraft

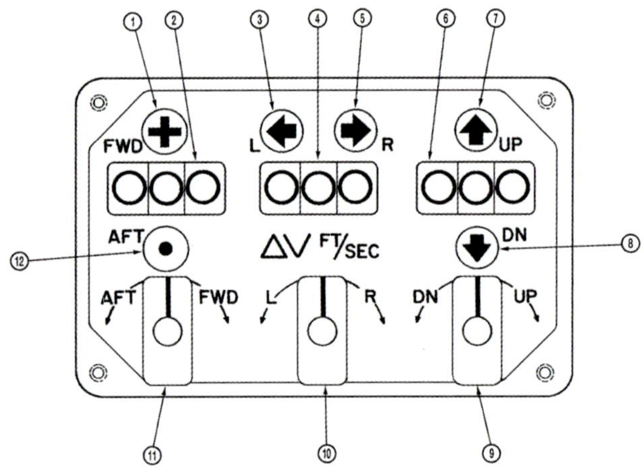

ITEM	NOMENCLATURE	PURPOSE
1	FORWARD DIRECTION INDICATION LAMP	INDICATES THAT PLUS-X AXIS VELOCITY IS INSUFFICIENT
2	FORWARD-AFT DISPLAY DEVICE	INDICATES AMOUNT OF INSUFFICIENT VELOCITY FOR PLUS OR MINUS-X AXIS
3	L (LEFT) DIRECTION INDICATION LAMP	INDICATES THAT MINUS-Y AXIS VELOCITY IS INSUFFICIENT
4	LEFT-RIGHT DISPLAY DEVICE	INDICATES AMOUNT OF INSUFFICIENT VELOCITY FOR PLUS OR MINUS-Y AXIS
5	R (RIGHT) DIRECTION INDICATION LAMP	INDICATES THAT PLUS-Y AXIS VELOCITY IS INSUFFICIENT
6	UP-DOWN DISPLAY DEVICE	INDICATES AMOUNT OF INSUFFICIENT VELOCITY FOR PLUS OR MINUS-Z AXIS
7	UP DIRECTION INDICATION LAMP	INDICATES THAT MINUS-Z AXIS VELOCITY IS INSUFFICIENT
8	DOWN DIRECTION INDICATION LAMP	INDICATES THAT PLUS-Z AXIS VELOCITY IS INSUFFICIENT
9	DOWN-UP ROTARY SWITCH	PROVIDES MEANS FOR MANUALLY SETTING UP Z AXIS VELOCITY ERROR ON UP-DOWN DISPLAY DEVICE
10	LEFT-RIGHT ROTARY SWITCH	PROVIDES MEANS FOR MANUALLY SETTING UP Y AXIS VELOCITY ERROR ON UP-DOWN DISPLAY DEVICE
11	AFT-FORWARD ROTARY SWITCH	PROVIDES MEANS FOR MANUALLY SETTING UP X AXIS VELOCITY ERROR ON UP-DOWN DISPLAY DEVICE
12	AFT DIRECTION INDICATION LAMP	INDICATES THAT MINUS-X AXIS VELOCITY IS INSUFFICIENT

LEFT Layout of the incremental velocity indicator, a crucial instrument to help the commander control the effect of his engine burns. *(NASA)*

BELOW Diagram of the inertial measurement unit and its location within the spacecraft. *(NASA)*

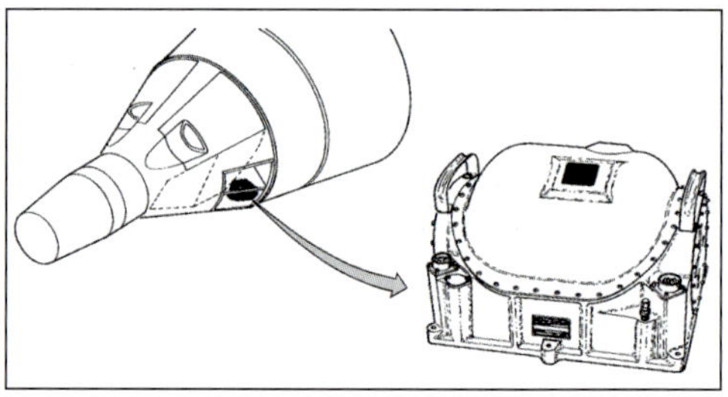

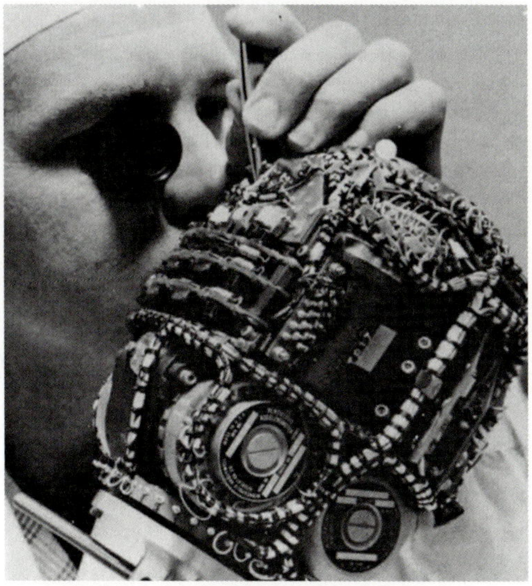

ABOVE **Technician working on a guidance platform that lies at the center of the IMU.** *(NASA)*

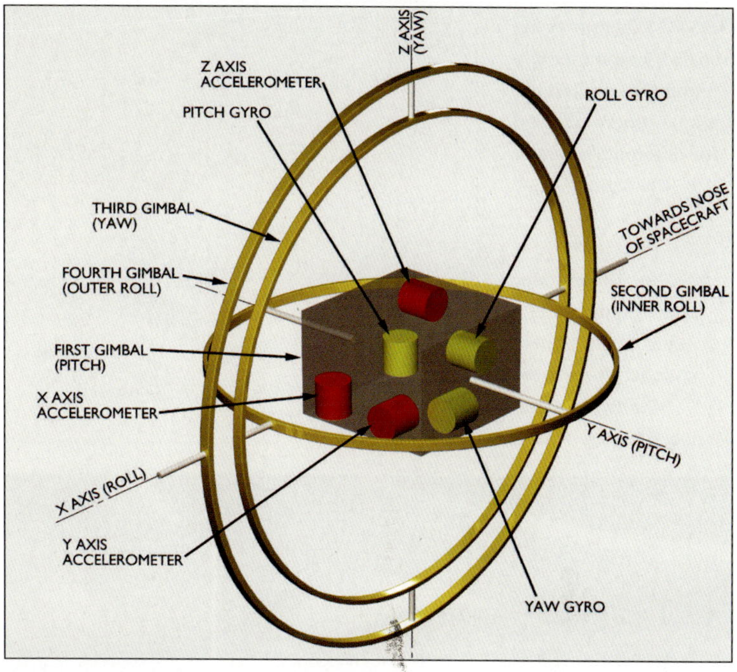

ABOVE **Conceptual diagram of an IMU showing its central stabilized platform with gyroscopes and accelerometers. Surrounding it is the system of gimbals that allow it to maintain its orientation.** *(Kevin Woods)*

might make, it was mounted within a set of four nested gimbals, the axis of each being set 90 degrees from its neighbor, an arrangement designed to ensure that the platform would always retain a fixed orientation irrespective of the spacecraft's orientation.

At the bearing where one gimbal was connected onto the next, there were two types of device. The first device was an electric motor that could rotate the gimbal with respect to its neighbor as commanded by the system endeavoring to stabilize the platform's orientation. The second device, a *resolver*, measured the angle of the gimbal with respect to the next gimbal. Across all the gimbals, the entire mechanism could measure the spacecraft's attitude with respect to the platform. Each bearing had two resolvers, one feeding angle data to the computer and the other one feeding the crew's displays and the attitude control system.

Computer

The Gemini computer was an early example of small-scale computing machines that developed rapidly from the United States' missile and space programs, primarily to support the demands of guidance. Although not as powerful as the machine that would guide the Apollo spacecraft to the Moon, it was an important stage in the evolution of microcomputing. Developed by IBM, it occupied a volume of about 31 liters and had a mass of 25kg.

The computer's memory capacity was a mere 12K words where each word consisted of 13 bits. These binary words could be used to represent a 13-bit address or instruction code. Two words could be treated as a 26-bit data word, including one bit to indicate a positive or negative value. Because of the primitive way in which it worked, the computer's speed is

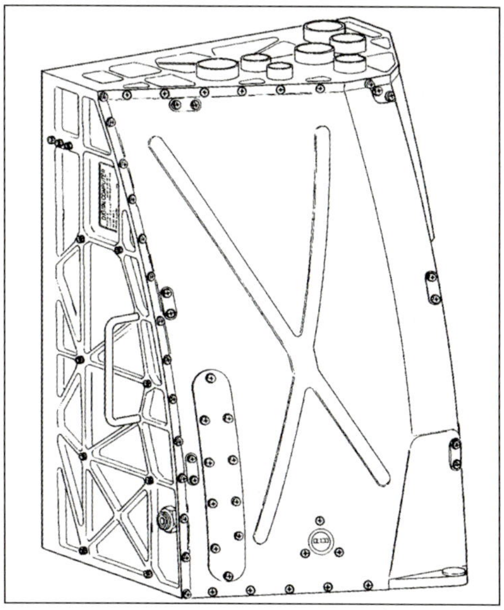

LEFT **Diagram of the Gemini computer, its outer case shaped to allow it to fit in one of the equipment bays of the spacecraft.** *(NASA)*

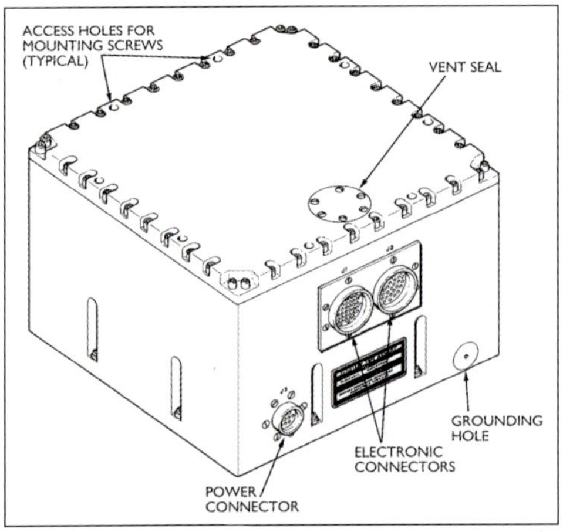

RIGHT Diagram of the auxiliary tape memory unit that carried the various programs used for different modes of the flight. *(NASA)*

BELOW The exterior of the commander's side of the Gemini spacecraft showing the two horizon sensors (inset). *(NASA)*

difficult to compare to modern machines with their GHz clocks, vastly greater storage, and sophisticated data handling. Its clock ran at 8MHz but memory was only accessed with a 0.25MHz clock. According to the specification sheet for simple arithmetic operations, it could achieve 1,200 division sums, 2,400 multiplication sums, or 7,150 addition or subtraction sums per second.

Engineers overcame the computer's limited storage capacity by storing all the programs on magnetic tape within the *auxiliary tape memory unit* (ATMU). With this, they could load one of six modules, each of which had a small selection of programs for various common tasks. For example, by loading module 3 from the ATMU the computer had the *Catch-Up*, *Rendezvous* and *Relative Motion* programs. The *Catch-Up* program aided the astronauts when they needed to fire their aft-facing engines in changing their orbit. *Rendezvous* had the job of interpreting the signals coming from the radar and calculating the maneuvers to bring the spacecraft into close proximity with the target. *Relative Motion* was used to help with maneuvers that were required to move with respect to the target.

Horizon scanner

A gyroscopically stabilized inertial platform, like the IMU on Gemini, was inevitably prone to a small degree of drift and had to be periodically realigned to its desired orientation. On Apollo, this was achieved by an astronaut taking sightings of the stars. For Gemini, stars were not used for reference. All maneuvers were made with respect to the ground below, a concept known as *local vertical*. This is similar to an aircraft flying around Earth. Just about everything it does is with reference to the local vertical.

Likewise, as the Gemini spacecraft flew around Earth, it maintained a constant reference to the ground below so that, with respect to the stars, it slowly rotated at the same rate as it orbited the planet. This is

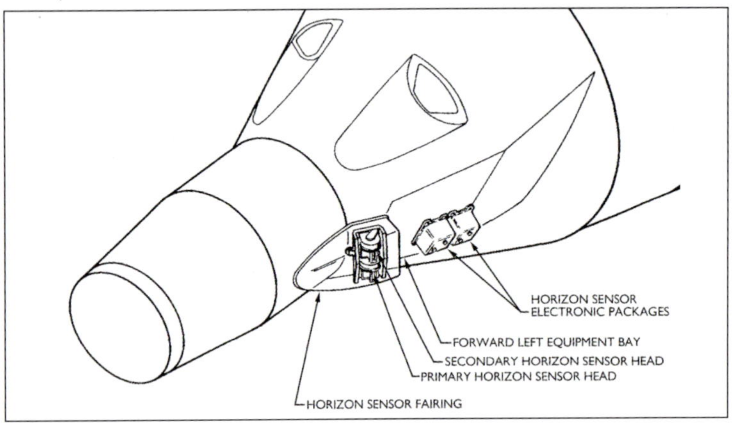

LEFT Mounting and position of horizon sensors and their fairing. *(NASA)*

commonly known as *orbital rate* or *orb-rate* attitude. To the astronauts flying the spacecraft, this made perfect sense. They were used to thinking about flight as being an Earth-centered activity and most of the maneuvers they made had to be achieved with the spacecraft's long axis horizontal, like an aircraft. However, although Earth's gravity is almost as strong at the altitudes flown by Gemini as it is on the ground, its effects were cancelled out by the spacecraft's trajectory. That is, being weightless meant that a concept like "down" could not be determined by conventional means. Instead, the Gemini spacecraft sensed its attitude with respect to the planet by detecting Earth's horizon using infrared sensors.

The horizon sensor was an optical instrument mounted on the outside of the spacecraft near the top of the cabin section. It had two independent sensors for redundancy, and was protected during launch and ascent by a fairing that was jettisoned once the spacecraft was in orbit. The unit itself was jettisoned at the end of the mission.

The sensor used a thermistor (a thermally sensitive resistor) to detect the horizon by scanning between the cold of space and the infrared emission of Earth. The transition between the two indicated the position of the horizon in the scan. This transition was used to generate a signal whose magnitude was proportional to the position of the horizon. Additionally, the entire scan could be moved from side to side so that it sensed the horizon over a range of angles. Once the output of the sensor had been processed it yielded error signals that, within limits, represented how far the spacecraft's pitch and roll deviated from ideal.

The output from the horizon sensor was used in one of two ways. One application was to fire thrusters in direct response to the measured attitude error, thereby maintaining the spacecraft in an attitude similar to an aircraft; heads-up with "wings level," even though there were no actual wings. Alternatively, the output from the horizon sensor could provide the guidance system with an indication of which way was down, to realign the IMU.

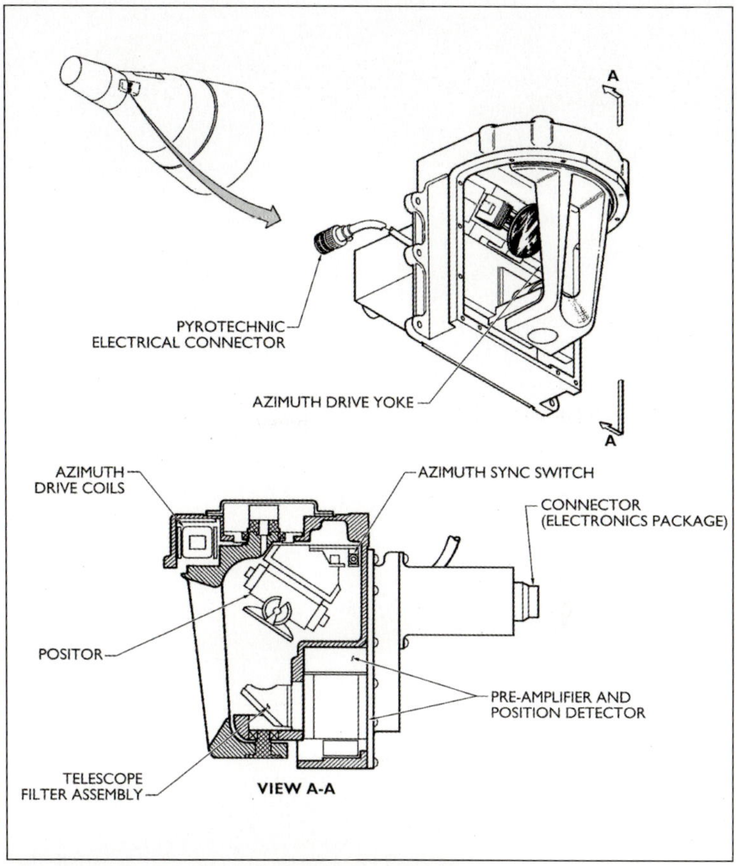

ABOVE Diagram and cross section of a horizon sensor. *(NASA)*

LEFT The Gemini 3 spacecraft undergoing final preparations for launch. Visible at the left is the jettisonable fairing that protects the horizon sensors during launch. *(NASA)*

Chapter Seven

Power and life support

A spacecraft carrying humans must possess the means to keep its occupants alive. Furthermore, if they are to work efficiently, it should keep them as comfortable as possible. On Gemini, this was the task of the *environmental control system* (ECS). It maintained a breathable atmosphere for the astronauts, handled their water and waste requirements, and controlled the temperature of the cabin and equipment.

OPPOSITE Astronaut Buzz Aldrin takes a selfie during an EVA on Gemini 12. He is safely sealed within his suit, sustained by the oxygen and cooling provided by the life support systems in his spacecraft. *(NASA)*

Closely allied to it was the electrical system. So much equipment in the spacecraft required electricity: instruments, computer, guidance systems, pumps, pyrotechnics, radios, radars; a spacecraft without power is essentially dead and, within short order, so is its crew.

The only major loss of power on a manned spacecraft in flight occurred on April 14 1970. As Apollo 13 neared the Moon, a catastrophic fire inside an oxygen tank caused an explosion which robbed the ship of its primary source of electricity. The three astronauts only survived their 3.5-day journey home because they could draw on reserves of electrical power available from batteries in their unused lunar module.

During the Gemini program, the implementation of these systems, particularly the electrical system, changed with mission goals and NASA's continuing learning curve. Initially installed as quite separate systems, they gradually became more integrated. For example, water produced in the generation of electricity became part of the ECS water system. By Gemini 10, the oxygen supply for both systems came from a common tank.

BELOW A mockup of the equipment section of the adapter module with a power unit at the bottom that included tanks of cryogenic hydrogen and oxygen, and two cylindrical fuel cell sections. *(NASA)*

Electrical system

The power requirements of the upcoming Apollo missions to the Moon had set the engineers a tricky challenge. Solar cells were deemed too unwieldy. Given their relative inefficiency at the time, the spacecraft would have required huge panels to supply sufficient power for the needs of a manned spacecraft. Then perversely, the crew would find themselves folding those panels away to protect them from the acceleration of a rocket firing, just as their electricity was needed most. Though batteries could deliver sufficient power for a short flight in space, a mission to the Moon demanded such quantities of electricity that their weight would have been prohibitive.

Yet again, Gemini beat a pioneering path for Apollo by helping to forge new technologies for the supply of electricity on manned spacecraft. Though the initial Gemini flights relied on batteries, the later missions provided a test bed for an immature but promising technology; the *fuel cell*.

Fuel cells

Invented in 1939, the fuel cell had barely moved beyond being an engineer's curiosity by the 1960s. Yet to NASA it seemed to offer a solution to the problem of long-term electricity supply for manned spacecraft. Based on improvements made by General Electric, NASA forced further development of the technology and used Gemini as a test bed for a type of fuel cell known as *proton exchange membrane* (PEM). At the same time, they kept conventional batteries as the spacecraft's primary supply. In the event, PEM fuel cells gave way to cells that used an alkaline solution as an electrolyte instead of a membrane, a technology which proved itself on Apollo as the primary power supply. PEM fuel cells flew on Gemini 5 and all missions from Gemini 7 onwards.

A fuel cell can be likened to a conventional battery cell; a package of chemicals and electrodes that use a chemical reaction to generate electrical energy. The power output of the conventional cell is maintained until the supply of unused chemicals in the cell has run out, at which point the cell must either be disposed of or the reaction be reversed by recharging. The fuel cell is very similar in that it

RIGHT Cutaway diagram of a Gemini fuel cell stack consisting of 32 individual cells. *(NASA)*

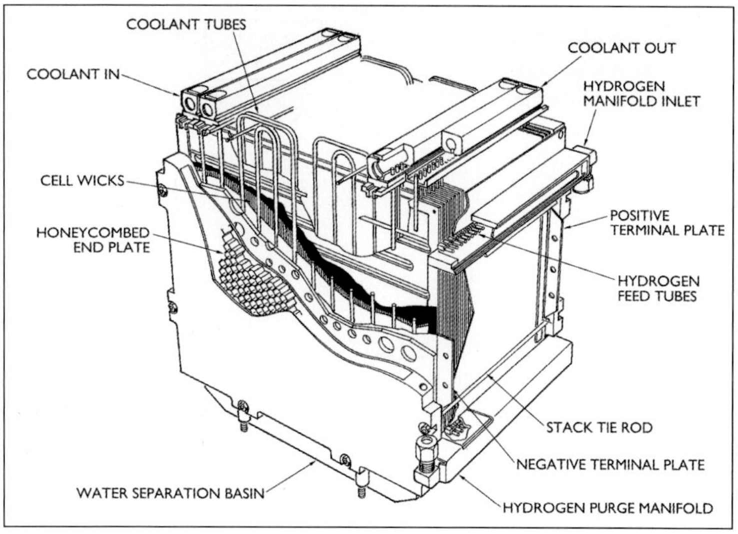

also uses chemistry and electrodes to produce electricity. The difference is that the chemicals upon which its reaction depends can be continually replenished.

This is the reverse of electrolysis of water, a process whereby electricity is passed through water and the water molecules are split to yield oxygen and hydrogen gas. In the fuel cell, these same two gases, the *reactants*, are brought together in the presence of a catalyst. There they chemically combine to produce water, and in so doing, generate copious amounts of electricity along with some heat.

On Gemini, the complete fuel cell system was installed in the adapter module. Two spherical tanks held the reactants. On later missions, the oxygen tank was also the source of breathing air for the astronauts. These tanks were loaded with reactants that were in an extremely cold, liquid form. Once loaded and the tanks sealed, internal heaters raised the temperature and hence the pressure until the contents became supercritical – neither liquid nor gas but an especially dense, homogenous fog which ensured that a partially depleted tank would not contain blobs of liquid floating within a gas. As long as sufficient pressure was maintained, the contents would remain in this single state and the tank would deliver a smooth flow in weightless conditions.

Each fuel cell in Gemini consisted of a thin membrane of plastic that separated the oxygen and hydrogen gases. Porous layers of platinum were bonded to either side of the membrane to form electrodes and to act as catalysts to enable the chemistry to take place. Hydrogen gas was passed across one side of the membrane where the catalyst caused the single electron of each atom to be removed, turning it into an ion. That electron then became part of the flow of electricity from the cell to the spacecraft's systems.

The plastic membrane was permeable, enabling the hydrogen ions, essentially just protons, to transfer to the opposite side and encounter oxygen atoms. With help from the platinum catalyst, and using those electrons that had returned after flowing through the spacecraft's circuits, the hydrogen and oxygen reacted to form water. This water was allowed to soak into cloth wicks which ran across the oxygen side of the cell. Driven by the pressure of the oxygen gas, it found its way into a storage tank. On Apollo with its alkaline fuel cells, the water created by the reaction was good enough to drink. Not so for Gemini, where excessive contamination made it acidic.

BELOW Diagram of the electrical generation system for a long duration flight like Gemini 7. This unit had particularly large tanks to feed reactants to the cells for a longer period. *(NASA)*

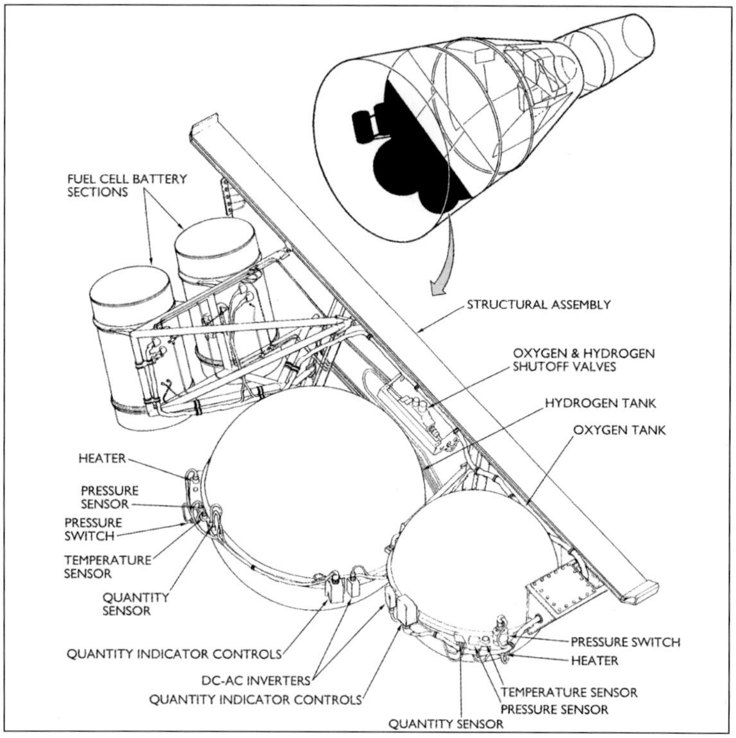

RIGHT Diagram of the operation of a fuel cell of the type installed in Gemini. *(David Woods)*

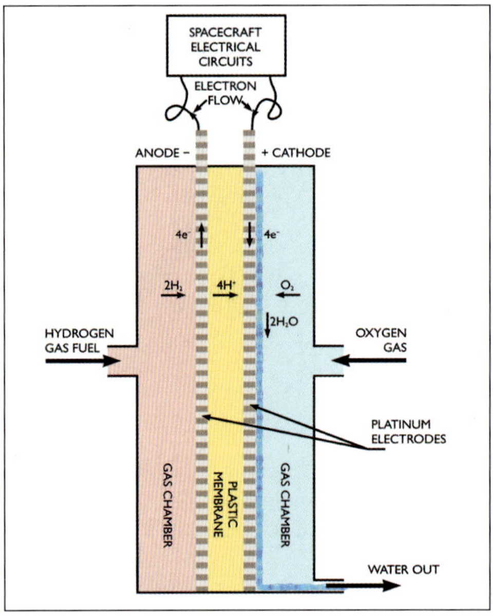

The fuel cells were arranged in *stacks* of 32 cells. Three stacks were then connected in series and built into a casing measuring 0.3 by 0.6m. This was called a *section*, and it could supply 1kW at 23.3 to 26.6V. Each fuel-cell-equipped spacecraft contained two sections along with associated tanks, plumbing and equipment.

As the cells generated power, impurities in the reactants, mostly noble gases like neon and argon, would gradually build up on the surface of the membrane. To flush these contaminants from the cells, the astronauts would purge the cells by passing reactant gas across the membrane at a high rate. A purge was carried out every few hours depending on the current being drawn, and lasted 11 seconds on the hydrogen side and two minutes on the oxygen side.

BELOW Schematic to illustrate the flow of fluids and gases in the Gemini fuel cell system. *(NASA/David Woods)*

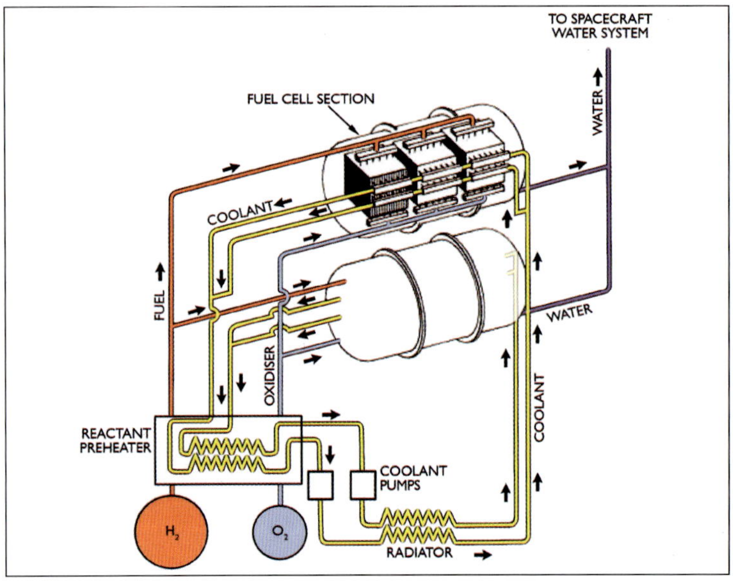

As well as generating electricity, the fuel cells produced heat which was drawn off by piping coolant through the cells. This heat was then used to take the chill off the reactants emerging from their high pressure storage tanks. Any excess heat was removed in the adapter section's radiator panels.

Batteries

The primary power supply came from conventional batteries. Indeed, for Geminis 3, 4 and 6, they were the only source of electricity. Once the equipment section had been jettisoned in the final moments of a mission, taking the fuel cells with it, conventional batteries supplied power through re-entry and on the ocean.

A typical spacecraft had seven batteries in total comprising four 45 amp-hour (Ah) batteries as the primary supply for the start and end of the mission, and three so-called *squib* batteries with a capacity of 15Ah whose sole purpose was to activate various pyrotechnic devices around the spacecraft.

Gemini used silver oxide-zinc batteries, a type which NASA also adopted for Apollo. In fact, the lunar module was exclusively powered with this technology. Silver oxide-zinc combined many properties that made it suitable for space flight: a high energy density, thermal tolerance, and freedom from thermal runaway effects. Although they could be recharged, this ability was not used by Gemini.

Environmental control system (ECS)

The role of the ECS was to ensure the spacecraft would keep two humans alive and functioning in its cabin for up to 14 days in space despite the extremes of heat, cold and vacuum on the outside. This task was far from simple because the needs were many and varied. Their air supply had to be at the correct pressure, with excess water and carbon dioxide removed. A supply of drinking water was required, and waste water and urine had to be handled, including the water generated by the fuel cells, yet the fluids must not be allowed to freeze for fear of rupturing the plumbing. The cabin must be at a comfortable temperature yet the waste heat generated by the astronauts and their equipment must be dissipated. It was the ECS that turned the Gemini spacecraft into a mini, life-sustaining planet.

Breathing

Gemini provided a single gas, oxygen, for astronauts to breathe. This eased the complexity of the air supply system and it reduced spacecraft weight because not only would it require fewer tanks and plumbing, it also reduced the cabin pressure, enabling the pressure hull to be designed for lower stresses and making it lighter.

Oxygen comprizes one-fifth of Earth's atmosphere, but this does not mean that a pure oxygen atmosphere can be supplied at one-fifth of Earth's air pressure. A pure oxygen atmosphere must be supplied at one-third of Earth's air pressure, or about 5psi, to deliver the same concentration of oxygen molecules via the lungs into the bloodstream. This was the in-flight pressure chosen for both Gemini and Apollo cabins.

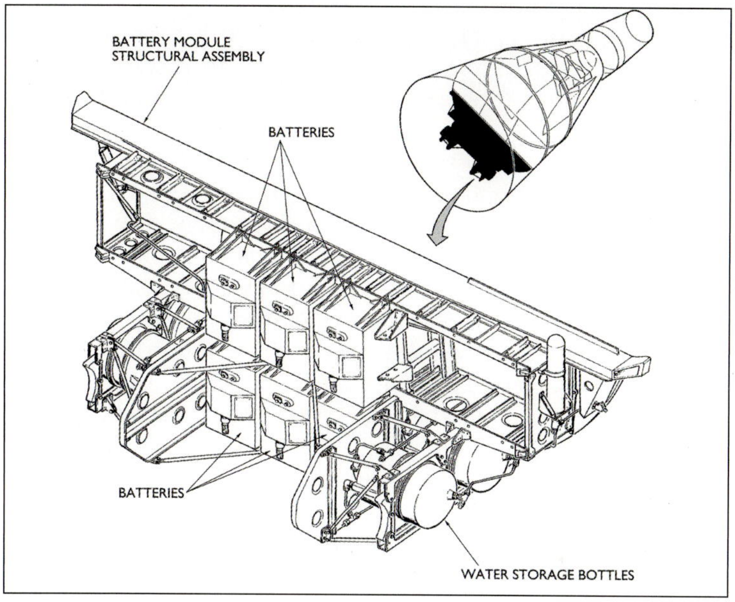

ABOVE Diagram of the battery package used on the early Gemini spacecraft. *(NASA)*

For the early Gemini flights, oxygen for breathing came from a dedicated tank in the equipment section plus two secondary cylinders in the re-entry module for the return to Earth. By the time NASA flew the final three missions, a single large oxygen tank supplied air for the astronauts and reactant for the fuel cells.

Oxygen for the cabin or for the spacesuits was drawn from the tank, warmed, and its pressure

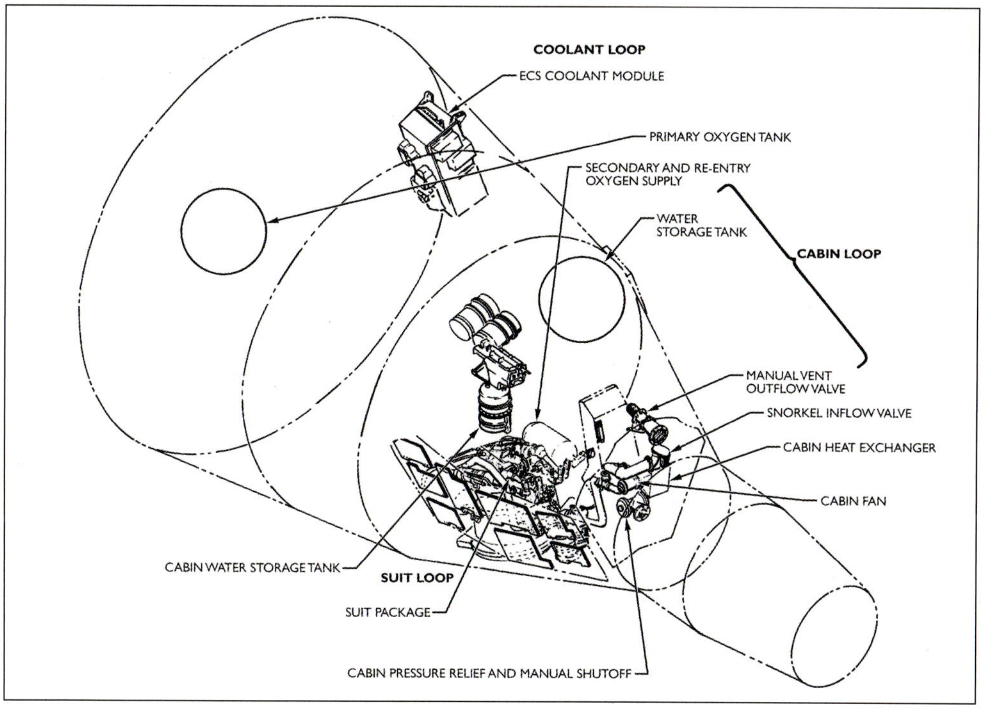

LEFT Diagram of the layout of Gemini's environmental control system. *(NASA)*

reduced via a regulator prior to being fed into one of two supply loops. The most important of these was the suit loop, an independent circuit for supplying air to the astronauts and the only one used during EVA or in the event of the hull being breached. Two compressors worked in parallel to continuously recirculate the air in the loop, passing it through a cartridge of lithium hydroxide to remove carbon dioxide and activated charcoal to remove odors. As oxygen was consumed, more was added from the supply tank to maintain the required pressure in the loop.

The oxygen in the suit loop also served to cool the astronauts, especially during EVA when a spacewalk could generate large amounts of heat through physical activity. Prior to entering the suits, air was passed over a heat exchanger to bring its temperature down. Any moisture which condensed at this stage was removed, either to be dumped or used in an evaporator to provide additional cooling. After leaving the heat exchanger, the air supply was divided to supply each astronaut. A control valve allowed each crewman to adjust the flow through his own suit. As it exited the suit, the air passed through a trap to remove any solid contamination that had been picked up. It then returned to the compressors via a valve that allowed the system to either be shut off or a high flow rate of oxygen to be fed directly to the suits.

The cabin air was fed from a regulator valve that maintained the pressure at 5.1psi. The return circuit was via the suit loop whenever the suits were not sealed. To guard against the cabin being over-pressurized while in space, or being excessively squeezed from outside upon return to the atmosphere, a relief valve in the hull permitted flow in either direction when certain maximum pressures were encountered. Another valve allowed the astronauts to feed oxygen directly from the source tank into the cabin to repressurize it after an EVA.

Water

Drinking water for the astronauts had to be brought from Earth. Initially, it was stored within a bladder which itself was inside a tank. Oxygen was fed into the gap between the tank wall and the bladder to pressurize the tank and force its contents to a drinking nozzle. On later missions, storage of the drinking water was combined with that for the fuel cell. There were two spherical tanks in the adapter module, each containing fuel cell water stored within a bladder. The space outside the bladder held drinking water in one tank and pressurizing oxygen gas in the other. In this manner, the drinking water was pressurized by both the oxygen gas supply and the fuel cell water (itself pressurized by the oxygen gas in the cells).

An additional small tank acted as a reservoir in the cabin and the astronauts accessed their water from a dispenser. An arrangement of 156 wire heaters was installed throughout the water system in the equipment section to prevent freezing.

Waste water, either as urine or as condensate from the cooling of the astronauts' air, went one of two routes. It was either dumped directly into space or it was fed to an evaporator (discussed in the next section). Medics were keen to gather information about the astronauts' metabolism. This included measuring urine volume. In *Carrying the Fire*, Gemini 10 and Apollo 11 pilot Michael Collins took delight in listing the 20 steps required to go to the loo in Gemini. He was discussing the *chemical urine volume measuring system* (CUVMS), a collection of valves, ports and pumps which, along with a collection cuff, allowed the crewman to express his urine into a bag and then, having chemically marked it, take samples prior to dumping the rest.

Thermal control

Gemini had a cooling system reminiscent of that in a car. Coolant flowed in a loop, taking heat from where it was unwanted, adding it to where it was needed, and dissipating the excess in a radiator. The coolant was a silicate ester fluid that remained liquid across a large temperature range (-54°C to 177°C) and had a low viscosity at very cold temperatures. The spacecraft had two coolant loops and, for redundancy, either was sufficient to handle the thermal requirements of the spacecraft.

The largest component of the system was the skin of the adapter section itself which formed two enormous radiators. It was constructed from narrow panels that ran lengthways. On their internal faces were stringers with pipes fabricated along their length. The primary and secondary coolant loops were interwoven through these pipes with U-shaped connecting pieces. Since the adapter module comprised two distinct units, the radiators were split likewise in order to form the skins of the equipment and the retrograde sections.

From the radiators, one flow path for the coolant led through temperature control valves to the evaporator, also known as a boiler. Here a supply of water drawn either from condensate in the cabin or from urine was fed into space by a thermostatically controlled valve. Upon reaching a vacuum, it evaporated, resulting in a steep drop in temperature. If extra cooling were required, coolant could be diverted through the evaporator.

Having been brought down to the required temperature, the coolant entered the cabin and passed through two heat exchangers; one to cool the air in the suit loop and the other to cool the cabin air. It then passed onto a *cold plate* for the spacecraft's tape recorder. Cold plates were flat sheets of aluminium that sandwiched a series of passages through which coolant flowed. Each one was in two layers to accommodate flow from both the primary and secondary cooling circuit. Items of equipment, mostly electronic, were mounted onto these plates as a means of removing their waste heat. On exiting the cabin, the coolant passed through additional cold plates, first in the equipment bays of the re-entry module and then through another set on returning to the adapter module.

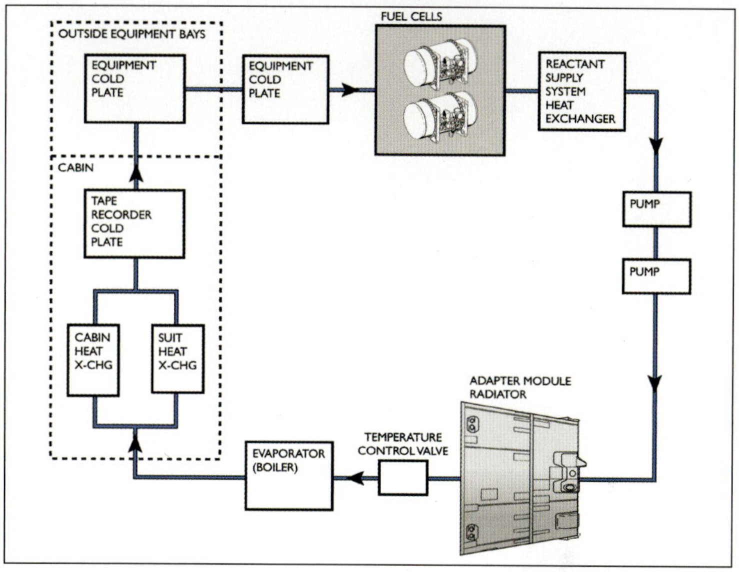

Another branch of the coolant loop went directly to the external cold plates. Having been warmed, the fluid could begin to give up its heat as needed. Its next destination was the fuel cells where it warmed the oxygen and hydrogen reactants before they were fed across the membranes of the cells. It also passed through a heat exchanger to warm the crew's breathing oxygen from the deep cold of cryogenic storage. The final part of its route was a series of redundant pumps that kept the fluid moving around the circuits.

ABOVE Simplified schematic of the spacecraft's thermal control system. The secondary circuit has been ignored. *(David Woods)*

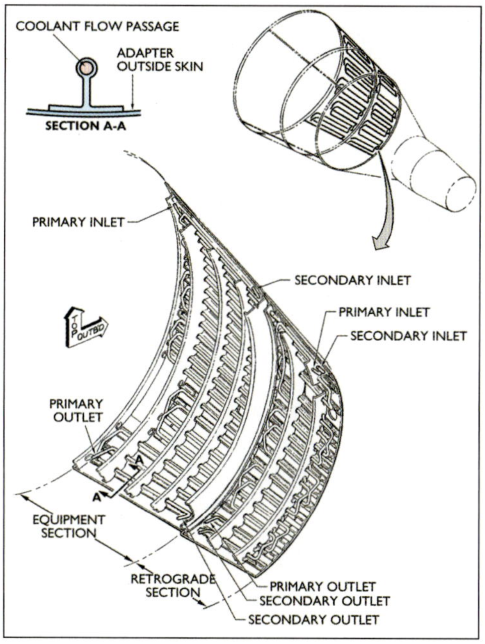

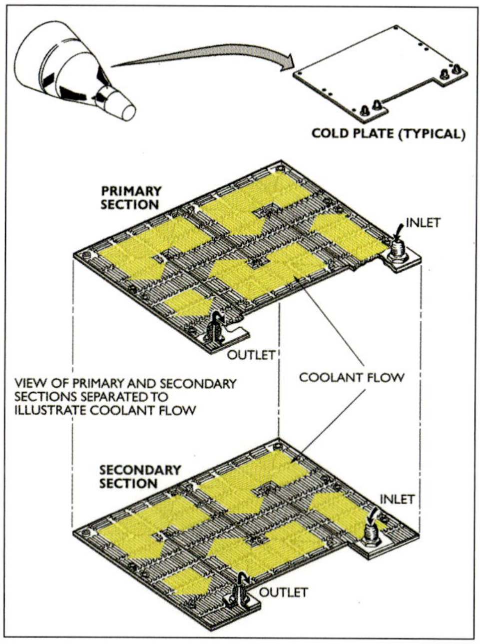

FAR LEFT Details of the coolant loops that were formed within the skin of both sections of the adapter module. *(NASA)*

LEFT Diagram to illustrate the flow of coolant in a cold plate. *(NASA)*

BEAT
ARMY
UNITED
STATES

Chapter Eight

Pyrotechnic systems

In common with other manned spacecraft of the era, Gemini was festooned with dozens of pyrotechnic systems, large and small. Engineers had come to recognize that initiating a charge was often the most reliable way to ensure that something would happen.

OPPOSITE This photograph of the Gemini 6 spacecraft shows two of the red covers that contain the titanium straps that hold the re-entry module to the adapter module. Prior to re-entry, these straps are cut by explosive charges. The crew of Gemini 6, both US Navy aviators, are baiting the commander of Gemini 7, a West Point graduate, about the result of a long standing football fixture played between the US military services. *(NASA)*

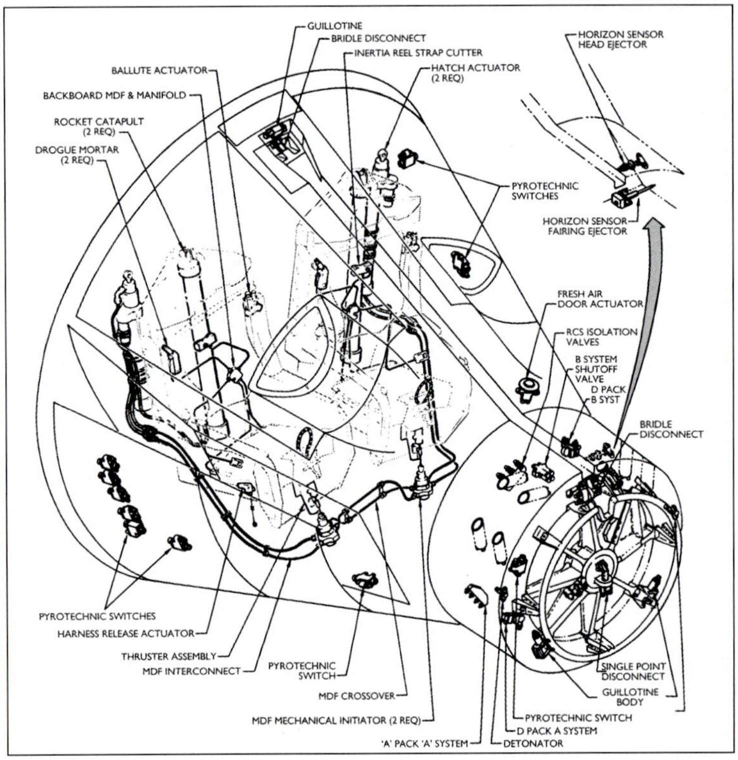

ABOVE Diagram to show the placement of pyrotechnic systems in a Gemini re-entry section. *(NASA)*

BELOW Diagram to show the placement of pyrotechnic systems in a Gemini adapter module. *(NASA)*

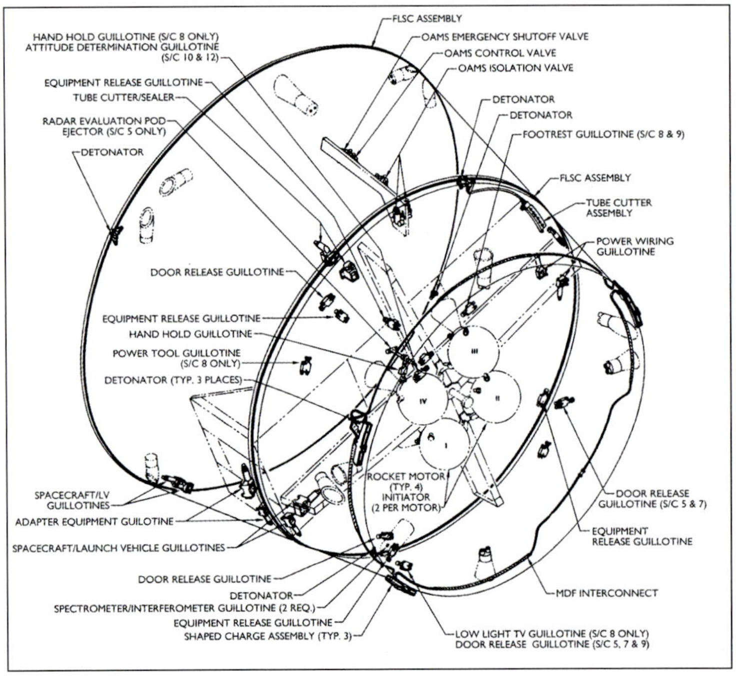

For example, at the small end of the scale, when it came time to pressurize the OAMS propellant tanks in the adapter module, cartridges would be fired to operate valves to allow helium to flow from high pressure storage tanks, through regulators and on to the fuel and oxidizer tanks where its pressure was crucial to the proper operation of the OAMS thrusters.

At the other end of the scale, when it came time to end a mission, the equipment section of the adapter module had to be jettisoned in order to expose the four rocket motors of the retrograde section. The cut was achieved by detonating the linear charge around the circumference of the adapter at the plane where the two sections were to separate. This event also involved driving guillotine blades through plumbing and wire bundles.

Slow burn or fast?

The huge range of pyrotechnic devices employed on a Gemini spacecraft can be narrowed down to a handful of types, depending on the task they had to achieve. These were initiated either by cartridges or detonators. Cartridges were non-explosive. Instead, they burned relatively slowly to produce a gas whose pressure would then operate some device. Detonators were, as their name suggests, explosive devices that were used to initiate larger events. To help engineers sequence events, cartridges and detonators came in types which either fired immediately on

BELOW Cross section of a typical Gemini detonator. *(NASA)*

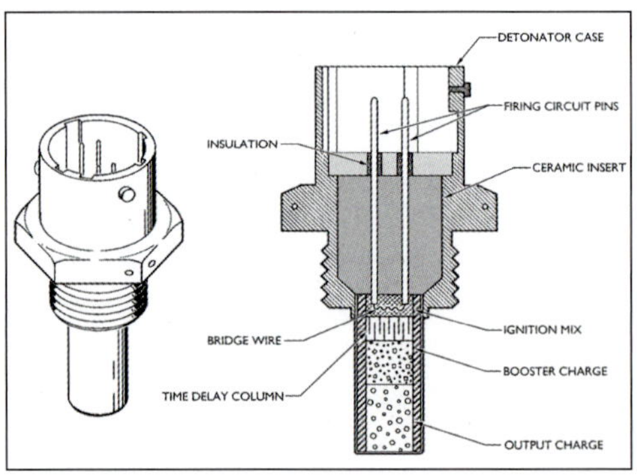

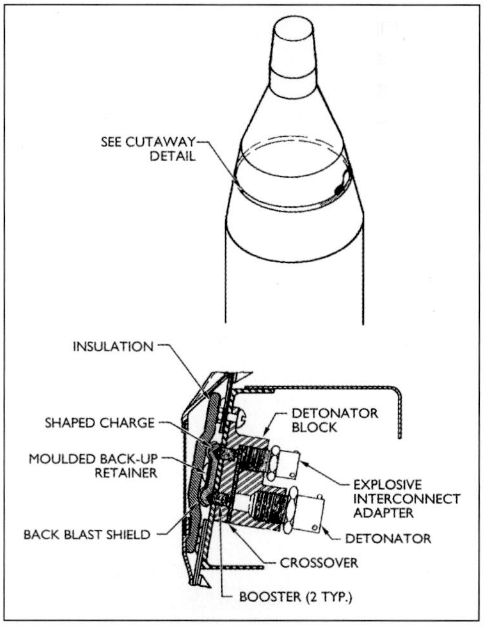

ABOVE Cross section of the explosive interface between the retrograde and equipment sections of the adapter module. *(NASA)*

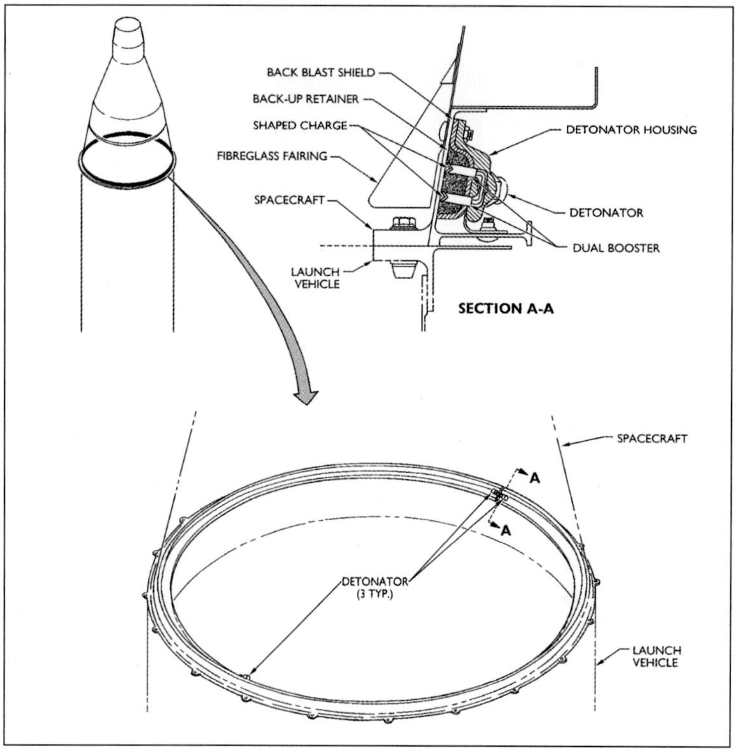

ABOVE Cross section of the explosive interface between the spacecraft and the launch vehicle. *(NASA)*

command or after a specific delay provided by what was essentially a short internal fuse.

Whenever major parts of the spacecraft had to be cut apart, engineers used an arrangement called a *flexible linear shaped charge* (FLSC). Produced in lengths, this could be affixed around curved surfaces. The charge itself was encased in a lead sheath within a V-shaped groove that directed the resulting shock wave towards the spacecraft's skin, vaporizing it and, in essence, performing a cut.

FLSC was used to separate the spacecraft from the Titan II launch vehicle using two redundant strips to ensure operation. Another strip severed the adapter module to expose the retrorockets. Then when it came time to lose the retrograde section, FLSC strips cut the three titanium straps that bound that section to the re-entry module.

Prior to separating parts of the adapter, it was necessary to deal with fluid and electrical services that crossed the boundary. Pyrotechnic cartridges were used to drive a blade through pipes that carried hypergolic propellants. The same action also crimped the ends of the pipes to seal them and prevent leakage of their volatile contents. Before cutting wire bundles, it was necessary to properly disconnect the circuits in order to prevent electrical shorts causing damage. This was ensured with a *pyroswitch* which used the gas from the ignition of a cartridge to drive a piston that opened a set of electrical contacts. Once the electrical circuits had been isolated, cartridge-driven guillotines could be fired to sever entire cable bundles.

A range of devices attached to the spacecraft depended on pyrotechnics for their operation or removal. For example, each

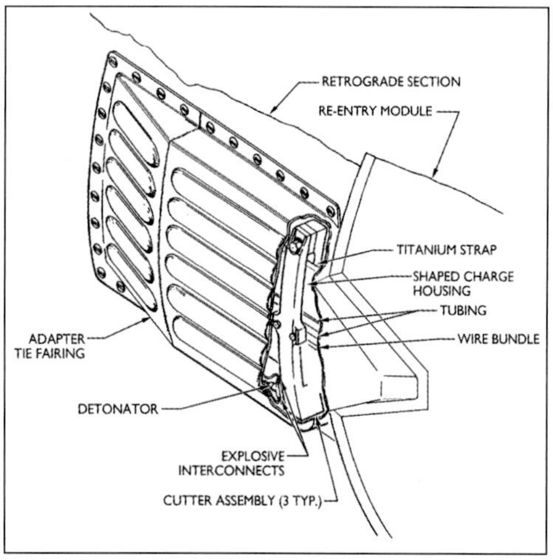

LEFT Cutaway of the explosives designed to sever the straps that held the re-entry module to the adapter module. *(NASA)*

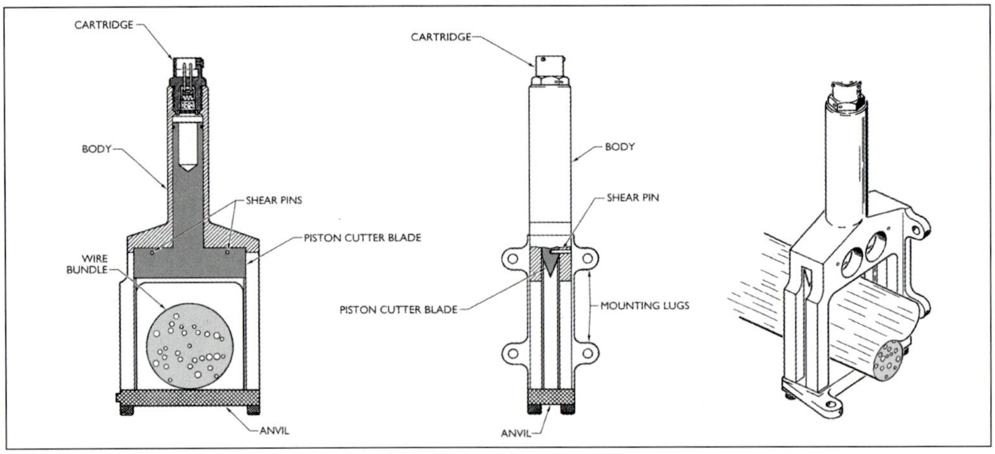

RIGHT Three perspectives of an explosively driven guillotine for cutting wire bundles. *(NASA)*

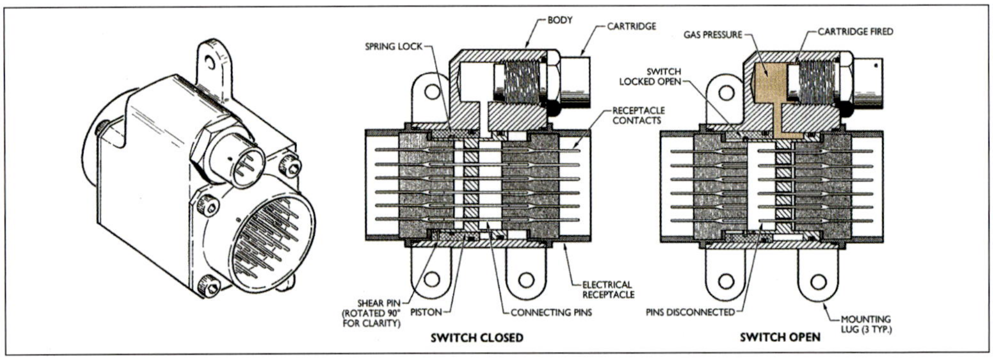

RIGHT Cutaway of the closed and open configurations of a pyrotechnically operated switch. *(NASA)*

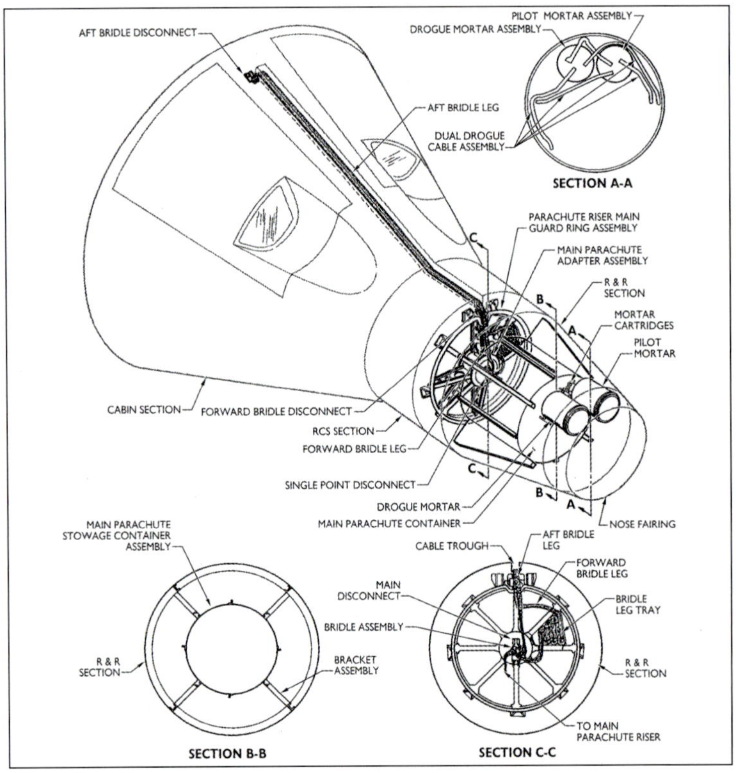

BELOW Diagram and cross sections showing the elements of the spacecraft's Earth landing system. *(NASA)*

spacecraft had a delicate optical horizon scanner mounted on the exterior of the re-entry section. An aerodynamic fairing protected it during launch and ascent. Once in orbit, the gas pressure from two pyrotechnic cartridges jettisoned the fairing to allow the scanner to "see." To restore the re-entry module's aerodynamic lines for the return to Earth, the scanner was jettisoned by another pair of cartridges at the same time as the retrograde section was discarded.

As well as the multiplicity of pyros around the spacecraft, and on the launch vehicle for that matter, two systems concerned with returning the astronauts to Earth's surface alive had the operation of pyrotechnic devices at their heart; the landing system and the ejection seats.

Earth landing/recovery

At the nose of the Gemini spacecraft was the *rendezvous and recovery* (R&R) section which contained the parachutes and other equipment necessary to bring the spacecraft to a safe landing in the ocean and aid its recovery. The systems within were built by Northrop Corporation. Many of its elements were deployed directly upon command from the crew, unlike the Apollo system which automated the entire landing sequence using barometric switches and sequencers.

Just as in an aircraft, the instrument panel included a conventional altimeter, familiar to pilots. It operated using the same principle whereby air pressure varies with altitude in a way that is well understood. The altimeter sensed the static air pressure through a set of four small ports on the surface of the cabin section near the nose where air would not be rammed into them by the vehicle's motion.

The static air pressure from this vent not only operated the altimeter, it also acted on two barometric switches that illuminated two indicators on the instrument panel. The first marked when the spacecraft had descended to 40,000ft (12.2km), by which time the drogue parachute ought to have been deployed. The second operated at 10,600ft (3.2km) which was a cue for the main parachute.

As the re-entry module descended to about 15km altitude a mortar was fired which deployed a nylon drogue chute from a canister in the R&R section. This canopy had a diameter of 3m and was constructed from ribbons of material to form a conical shape. Designed for deployment at high altitude and at high speeds, the drogue was attached to the nose at three points and it both slowed and stabilized the ship until it reached an altitude of about 3.2km.

Initially, the drogue chute was deployed in a *reefed* mode; that is to say, it was restrained from fully inflating by a *reefing line* that kept the parachute's risers gathered together for a period to lessen the jolt that would be experienced by the spacecraft and crew on its initial deployment. After a delay of 16 seconds, pyrotechnics cut the reefing line to permit the canopy to fully inflate.

At 3.2km, the second barometrically operated light illuminated as a cue for the crew to initiate deployment of the main parachute.

ABOVE **The interior of Gemini 7 showing the position of the altimeter (indicated).** *(NASA)*

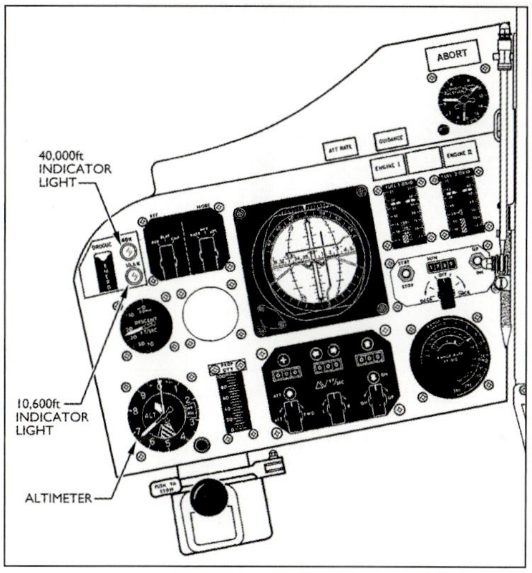

LEFT **Diagram of the commander's instrument panel showing the altimeter and barometric indicators. Note that this panel layout includes a range/range-rate meter, absent on Gemini 7 because that spacecraft had no radar.** *(NASA)*

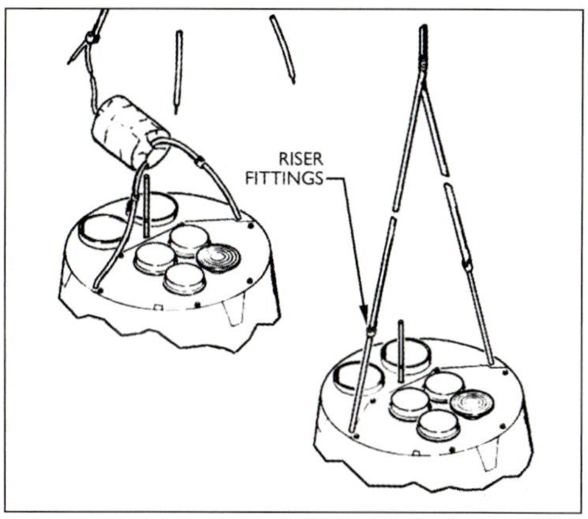

FAR LEFT **Diagram of the deployment and three-point suspension system of the drogue parachute.** *(NASA)*

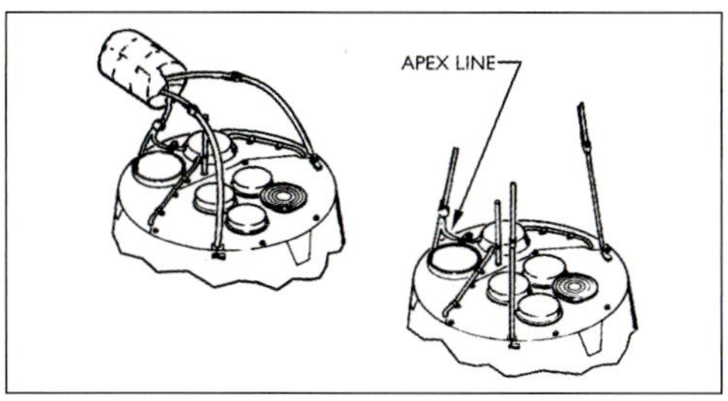

LEFT **Diagram of the deployment and two-point suspension system of the pilot parachute, itself pulled out by the release of the drogue.** *(NASA)*

RIGHT Diagram of main parachute in reefed condition and under single-point suspension. *(NASA)*

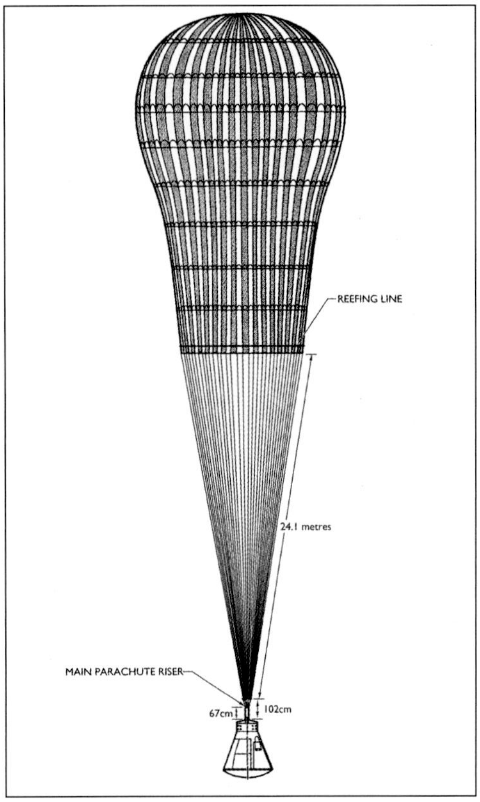

BELOW Diagram of main parachute in fully inflated condition and under two-point suspension. *(NASA)*

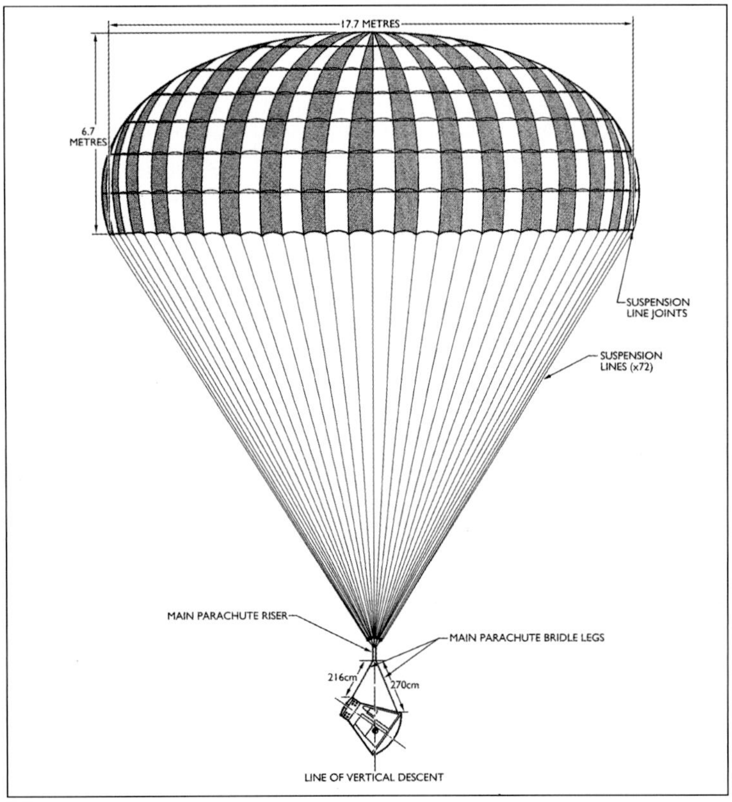

Three cartridge-powered guillotines severed the drogue's attachment cables, and as it departed it pulled a line that extracted the pilot parachute from its canister. For a short time, the spacecraft descended on two parachutes, one above the other.

The pilot parachute was a 5.6m nylon canopy attached to the R&R section at two points. It was also reefed at deployment. After 2.5 seconds, electrical wires to that section were disconnected by a pyroswitch and the wire bundles guillotined just before it was pyrotechnically released. As the section was carried away by the pilot parachute it pulled the main parachute from its container.

Gemini's final descent to the ocean was under a parachute that was deployed at an altitude of 3km. Its reefing line was pyrotechnically cut after 10 seconds, and once the canopy had inflated to form a hemispherical shape with a diameter of 17.7m it reduced the rate of descent to less than 10m/sec.

Meanwhile, six seconds after the pilot chute was deployed, its reefing line was pyrotechnically cut to fully inflate it so that the R&R section could be recovered from the water.

In the moments after main parachute deployment, the re-entry module was suspended by a single bridle on the nose. Having the heatshield facing straight down was an attitude which would have resulted in a very sudden and jarring impact with the water.

However, because the original intention had been to land under a paraglider, the re-entry section was designed to change from single-point suspension to a two-point configuration in which the capsule was tilted by 55°. This mechanism had been retained because it would soften the water impact. Once the crew saw that the main parachute had properly inflated and that the spacecraft was stable, they pressed a button to pyrotechnically release a second bridle that had been stored in a channel running between the hatches. This sudden change in orientation was quite violent, and on one occasion led to an astronaut's visor being cracked.

After splashdown, the parachute was jettisoned by the astronauts, an action that also powered a recovery light. Radio beacons and voice communications equipment were on hand to aid the recovery effort and fluorescent green–

yellow dye that was stored below the water line in water-soluble packaging in the nose was released into the water.

Ejection seats

A major difference between Gemini and the Mercury and Apollo spacecraft was the use of ejection seats as the escape mechanism for the astronauts. The others had used nose-mounted rockets to pull the spacecraft clear of a wayward launch vehicle. Yet Gemini was not the only example of their use in space flight.

The first human in space, Yuri Gagarin, made a single orbit of Earth before he re-entered the atmosphere. Then at 7km altitude, he used an ejection seat to leave his Vostok and descend to Earth under his own parachute. Precisely 20 years later, on the first flight of the Space Shuttle, its crew rode to orbit on ejection seats

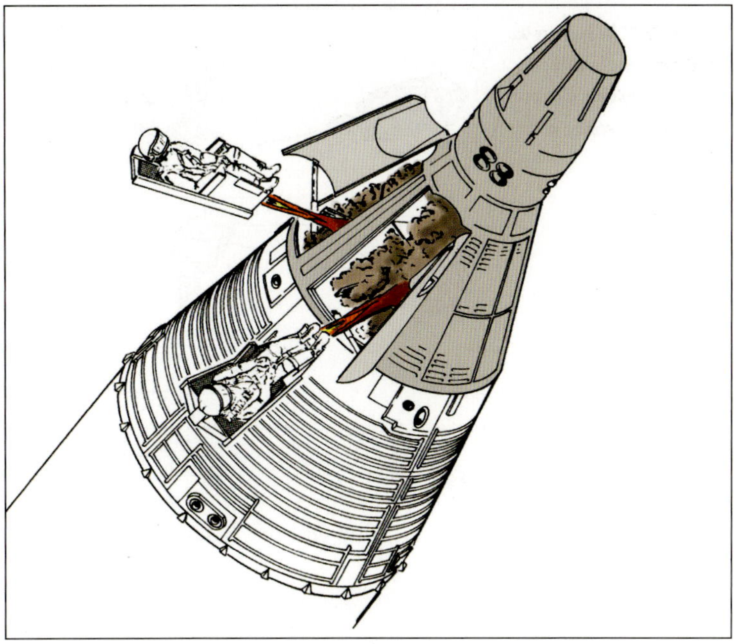

ABOVE Sketch of crew ejecting from a Gemini spacecraft. *(NASA/Courtesy of Mike Jetzer – heroicrelics.org)*

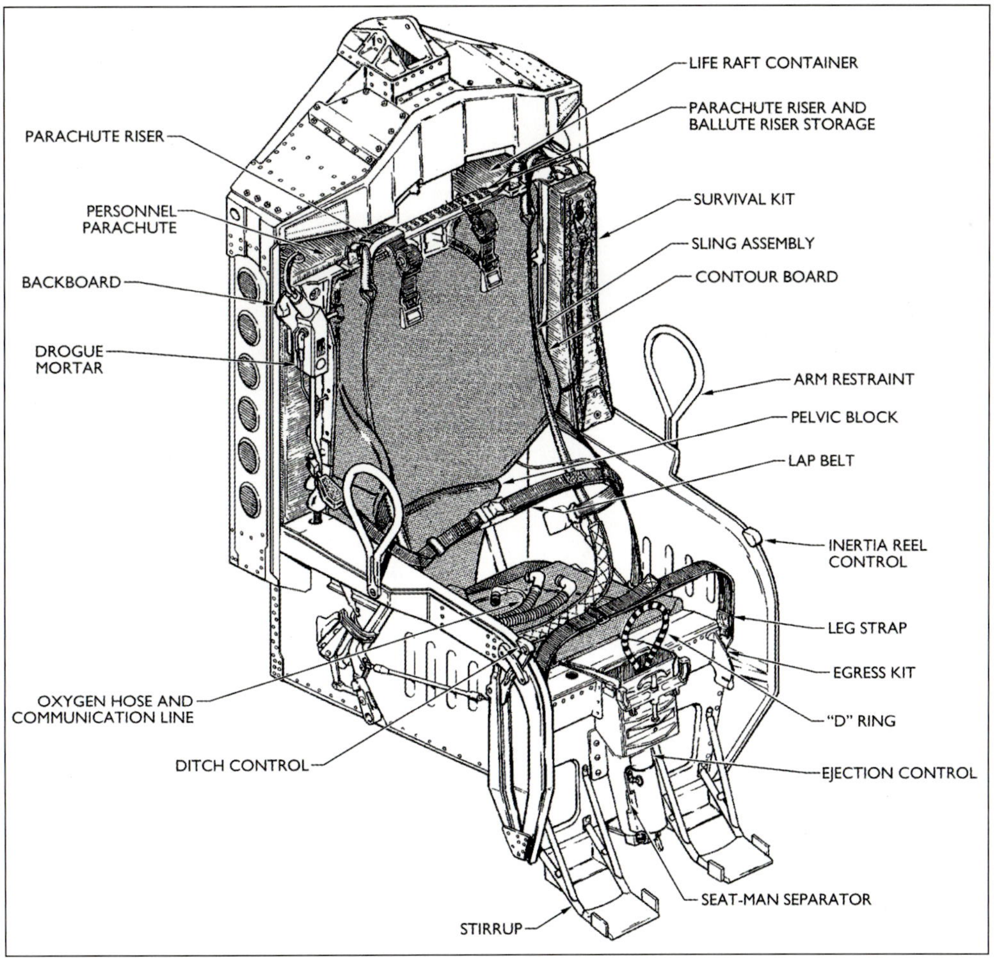

LEFT Diagram showing details of the Gemini ejection seat. *(NASA)*

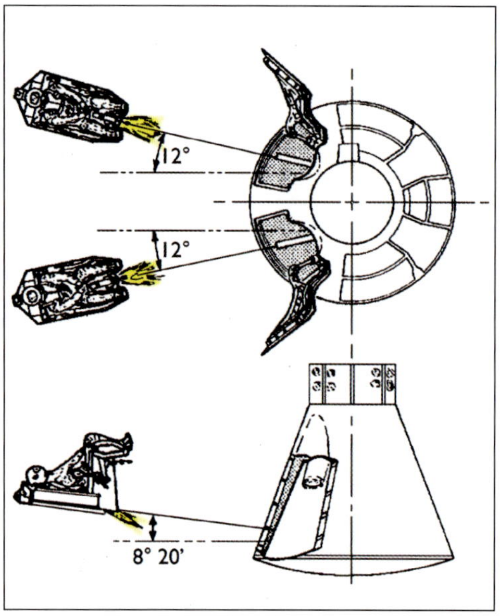

RIGHT Diagram to indicate the geometry of crew ejecting from a Gemini spacecraft. *(NASA)*

in case their new launch system, untested without humans, went awry.

The Gemini escape system was very similar in concept to that used in military aviation. All a crewman had to do was to pull on a D-ring and both men would be simultaneously extracted from the spacecraft and lowered to Earth by parachute under entirely automatic control. It was to be used in an emergency situation either at the start or the end of a mission; the latter in case of a failure of the parachute system. Although designed to be used at altitudes up to 21km, NASA decided to limit it to an operational ceiling of 4.5km. This was primarily because it was felt that with any conceivable failure of the launch vehicle above this height, it was better for the crew to stay in the spacecraft and use the retrorockets in the adapter module to separate and move clear before making a controlled landing in the ocean.

Each seat was mounted in the spacecraft angled 12° out from the center line to ensure that on ejection they would fly away from each other. They were also angled 8.33° towards the nose so that on the launch pad they were aimed slightly upwards. In the case of an escape while on the ground, they would reach a peak altitude of about 80m as the seat's rocketry propelled them over 200m from the Titan.

The seat was in two main parts; the ejection seat proper with its rocket-powered catapult, and a backboard and egress kit that supported the astronaut until deployment of his parachute. When the D-ring was pulled, pyrotechnic cartridges generated a large volume of gas that unlatched both of the spacecraft doors and swung them open, whereupon a locking pin engaged to prevent them from rebounding. The gas pressure also activated the rocket-powered catapults in each seat.

These rockets fired for only 0.25 seconds but accelerated the astronaut with a bone-crushing 24*g* force. It was hardly surprising that crews were loath to eject. If operated too hastily on the launch pad they would not only threaten

BELOW Trajectory of a Gemini ejection from a stationary launch vehicle. *(NASA/David Woods)*

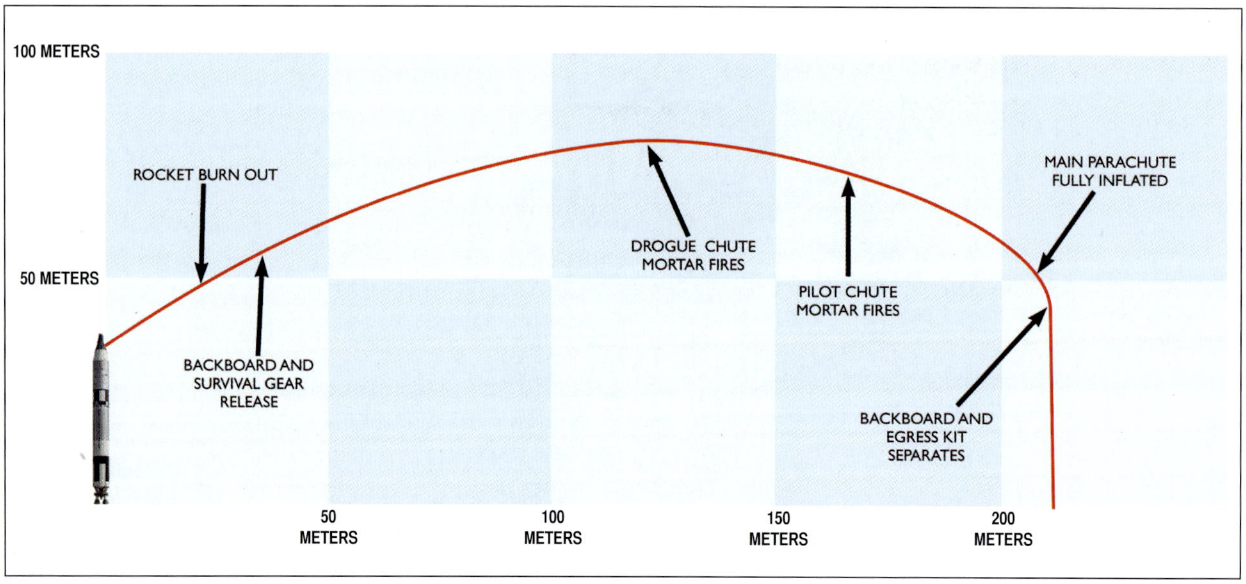

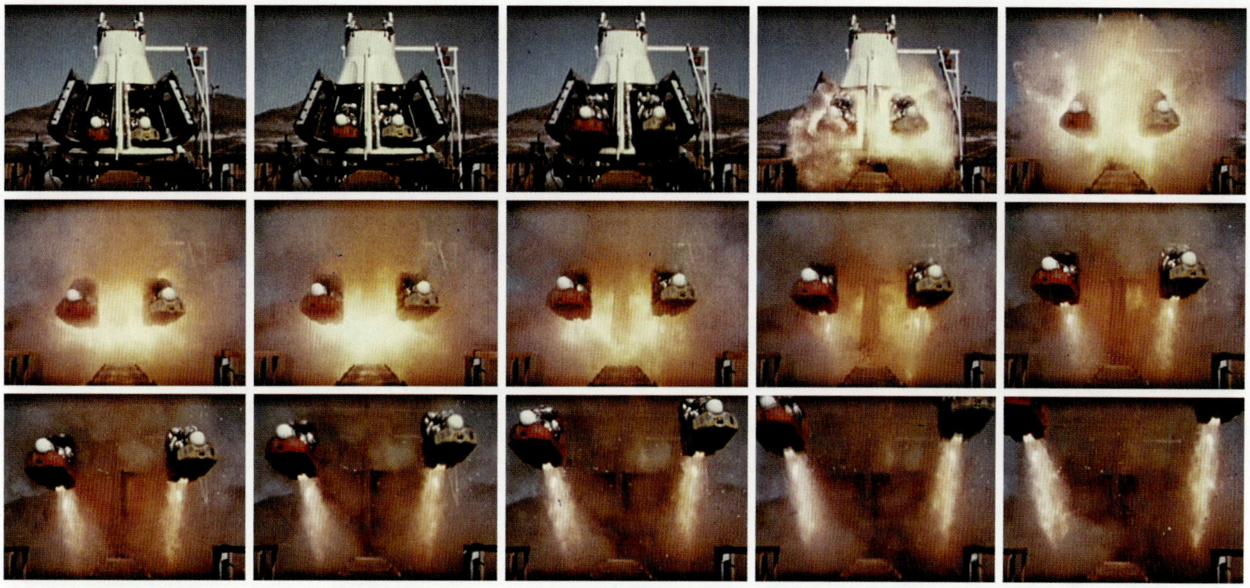

injuries to the crew from the brutal acceleration, the exhaust would also destroy the interior of the spacecraft.

A departing ejection seat pulled on three lanyards that acted to switch the oxygen supply to the astronaut from the spacecraft to a small bailout supply in the egress kit. On later missions, this bailout supply was deleted. A fourth lanyard activated a cartridge with a time delay of 1.08 seconds that separated the astronaut, including backboard and egress kit, from the main body of the seat.

At this point, what occurred depended on barometric switches which fired pyrotechnic charges that deployed or released devices depending on the astronaut's altitude. Above 2.3km, a *ballute* was deployed to control his speed and keep him stabilized until he had descended low enough to use his parachute. Part balloon and part parachute, this device was 1.2m wide when inflated and was automatically released when the astronaut had descended below 2.3km.

Deployment of the parachute was inhibited until the astronaut had descended below 1.7km. If ejection occurred below this altitude, then deployment occurred immediately the astronaut and backboard had separated from the seat. Since it was possible that ejection could occur from the launch pad, it was essential to ensure that the parachute deployed as rapidly as possible in order to inflate before the astronaut hit the ground.

More pyrotechnics then fired a mortar to eject a small drogue that in turn pulled the parachute out. The mortar pressure also triggered further time-delayed pyros that cut the straps to release the astronaut from the backboard and egress kit. As they fell away they released a survival kit that hung beneath him as he descended. The kit included a life raft, food, water, fishing gear, a radio and a machete.

ABOVE Sequence from a movie of a test of Gemini's ejection seats. *(NASA/David Woods/ Courtesy of Mark Gray – spacecraftfilms.com)*

BELOW By blowing air into one of its intakes, a technician inflates an example of the type of ballute used in the Gemini ejection seat for high altitude use. *(NASA)*

Chapter Nine

Crew systems

As a manned spacecraft, Gemini required a range of equipment to allow its crew to operate both within and outside the cabin. Whether or not *extravehicular activity* (EVA) was scheduled, all crews wore spacesuits. They operated and monitored their ship with a large instrument panel that reflected their split responsibilities. A series of communications links allowed them to stay in touch with mission control for at least part of their flight and permitted the ground to track the size and shape of their orbit.

OPPOSITE Astronauts John Young (right) and Mike Collins are fully suited and seated in their Gemini 10 spacecraft as they prepare to conduct a test in an altitude chamber. *(NASA)*

RIGHT Astronaut Ed White floats outside the Gemini 4 spacecraft in his G4C suit. In this, one of the most iconic photographs of the early space age, he is holding a hand-held maneuvering unit in his left hand with a 35mm Maurer camera. The Gemini spacecraft can be seen reflected in the gold layer of his outer visor. *(NASA)*

Spacesuits

Half a century on from the start of the space age, no one leaves the atmosphere without some form of personal protection against being exposed to the vacuum of space. Even in a spacecraft's cabin, the possibility of an unintended decompression requires that some kind of pressure suit is worn or is at least available. Thus the spacesuit has become iconic in the public's imagination as the image of the spaceman, particularly the suits worn by the Gemini astronauts.

Gemini suits were supplied by the David Clark Company of Worcester, Massachusetts who based their design on one developed for the X-15 experimental rocket plane that flew to the edge of space. Throughout Gemini, the detailed construction of the suit changed to meet the demands of the program but all were based on a basic design, the G3C model which flew on Gemini 3. Next to the crewman was a layer of nylon followed by a pressure bladder made from neoprene-coated nylon. The outer layer was a

CENTER Prior to becoming a Gemini and Apollo astronaut, Neil Armstrong flew the X-15 rocket-powered research aircraft on seven occasions. He is pictured here next to X-15 aircraft #1, dressed in a pressure suit that became the starting point for the Gemini suit. *(NASA)*

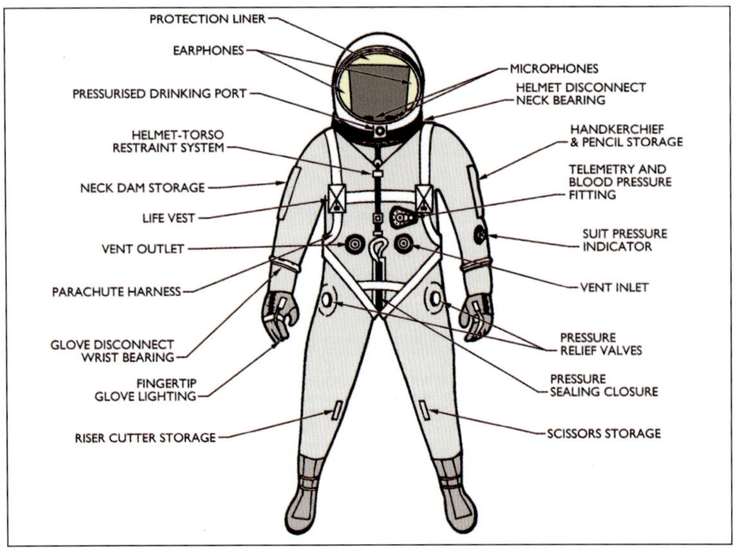

LEFT Diagram of the major components of the Gemini spacesuit. *(NASA)*

heat resistant cloth called Nomex. Between the two, a link-net material controlled any tendency of the bladder to balloon.

A long zipper ran down the back to the crotch to allow the astronaut to don the suit, and two connectors at the front provided inlet and outlet ports for the oxygen supply. The bladder was automatically pressurized at 3.7psi. Since the oxygen flow was also used to cool the occupant, a series of ducts ensured that it passed around the whole body, including the extremities, before exiting along with carbon dioxide, water vapor, and excess heat.

The suit incorporated a bioinstrumentation system to measure the astronaut's vital signs. This generated signals which indicated the heartbeat and respiration rate from a series of electrodes affixed to the body, blood pressure via a manually operated cuff, and body temperature from an oral thermistor.

A helmet with a Plexiglas visor and built-in communications equipment was attached to the suit via a neck ring that allowed for easy removal. Likewise, the gloves were easily detachable so that although the suit had to be worn at all times, an astronaut could work in the cabin without helmet and gloves in the knowledge that in the event of a cabin breach, he could seal himself into his suit in a matter of seconds. The gloves included fingertip lights to allow a crewman to scan the cabin instruments over the night-time hemisphere of Earth without losing his adaptation to the dark.

The G4C suit

For Gemini 4, modifications were made to produce a suit capable of withstanding the harsh space environment. Primarily, the single outer layer was replaced by multiple layers which, from the inside out, consisted of two layers of Nomex for micrometeoroid protection, seven layers of aluminized Mylar for thermal insulation, a layer of felt to act as a spacer, and an outer layer of Nomex. A second zipper was added to relieve strain on the pressure zipper. The commander, who did not exit the spacecraft, wore a simpler version with fewer layers. Apart from Gemini 7, these G4C suits were worn for the rest of the program with minor modifications for EVA.

Ed White's helmet was adapted to support a double external visor. The outer Plexiglas visor had a gold film which inhibited transmittance by 88% to reduce glare, restrict the inward passage of solar infrared in daylight and reduce heat loss through the faceplate in darkness. The inner polycarbonate visor filtered out the harmful ultraviolet sunlight and provided protection from micrometeoroids. Additional thermal gloves were worn over the suit gloves to minimize heat loss from the fingers.

AiResearch of Los Angeles, which was making the spacecraft's environmental control system, supplied a ventilator unit for the spacewalker to wear on his chest in order to regulate the flow of oxygen from an umbilical. The Manned Spacecraft Center devised a *hand-held maneuvering unit* (HHMU) which, by squirting a jet of cold gas (in

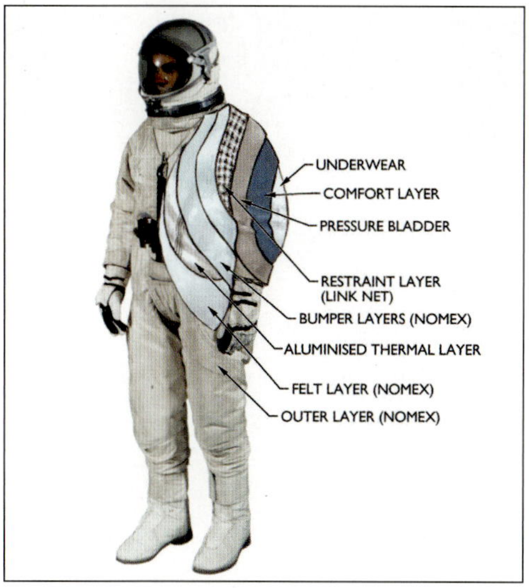

LEFT A cutaway illustration to show the various layers of the G4C suit used for EVA on Gemini. *(NASA)*

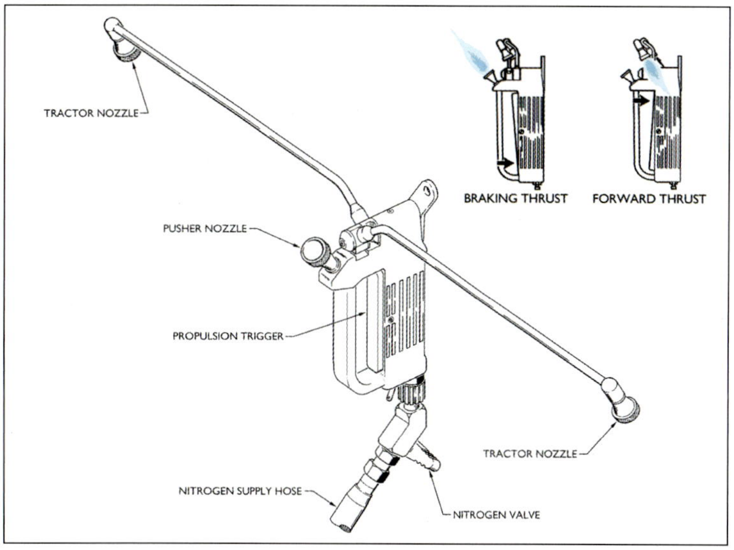

BELOW Diagram of the HHMU. *(NASA)*

White's case oxygen from small canisters that were attached to the unit but other gases on later flights) would enable a spacewalker to control his position and orientation.

The crews for Geminis 5 and 6 had no plan for an EVA and so wore the more basic version of the G4C suit. This comprised a cotton undergarment, a blue nylon layer for long-term occupancy, a pressure garment of neoprene-coated nylon, a restraining net of Dacron and Teflon, and finally, a Nomex outer layer.

RIGHT Immediately prior to entering the Gemini spacecraft, one of the mission's crewmen is given a presentation by the ground crew. He is wearing a lightweight G5C suit which is inflated by the air supply he is carrying. *(NASA)*

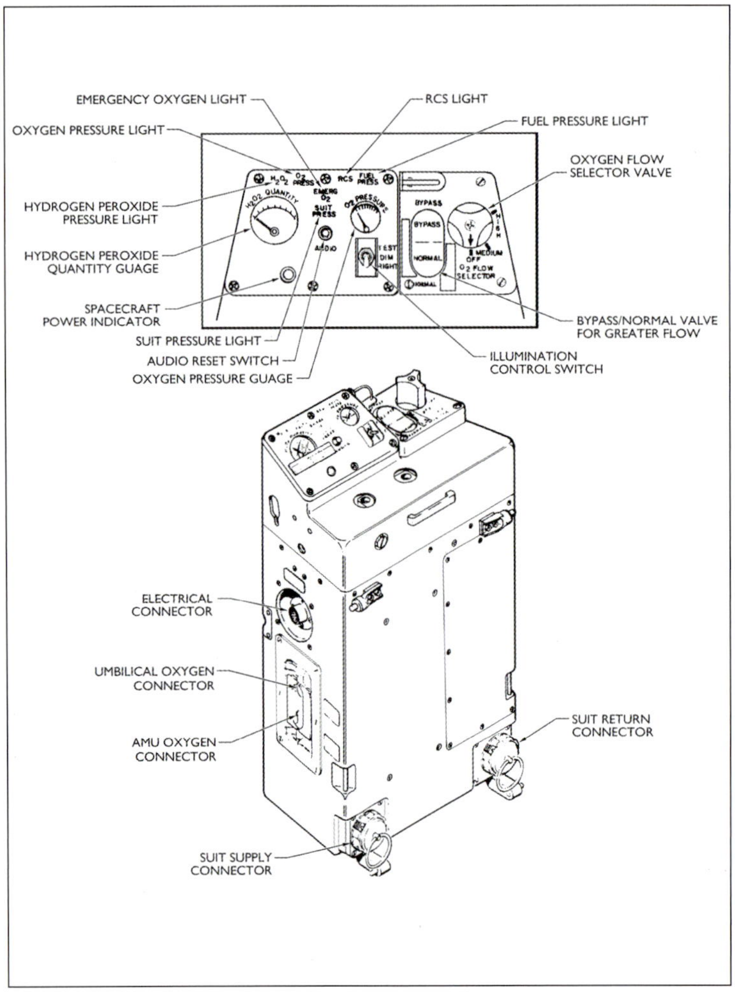

BELOW Diagram of the extravehicular life support system with inset to show control panel. *(NASA)*

The G5C suit

A specialized suit, the G5C, was developed for the long duration flight of Gemini 7. It was felt that 14 days was too long to expect a crew to wear the rather restrictive full pressure suit, yet the astronauts still required protection not only from the possibility of decompression in the cabin but also in case they had to endure the blast caused by use of the ejection seats.

The G5C suit was a lightweight two-layer garment intended for use within the cabin only. It comprised an inner bladder of neoprene-coated nylon and an outer layer of Nomex. One of the major changes for long duration comfort was to replace the rigid neck ring and helmet with a large soft helmet that could be unzipped and rolled back to form a headrest. This cover had a polycarbonate visor built into it, beneath which the crew wore a conventional aviator's crash helmet.

Suiting up for EVA

Until Gemini 8 was forced to return to Earth early, pilot David Scott had intended to make a demanding spacewalk wearing an EVA suit identical to Ed White's except that the gloves had thermal protection built in rather than as separate items. Additional equipment included a new chest-mounted pack for life support and a backpack with extra consumables.

The *extravehicular life support system* (ELSS) was a 19kg box worn on the chest. It contained a pump to ensure oxygen circulation throughout the suit, a heat exchanger to keep the supply cool, plus controls and warning systems. In case of problems with the oxygen supply, the pack had an emergency oxygen bottle that would give the astronaut 30 minutes to get back into the cabin.

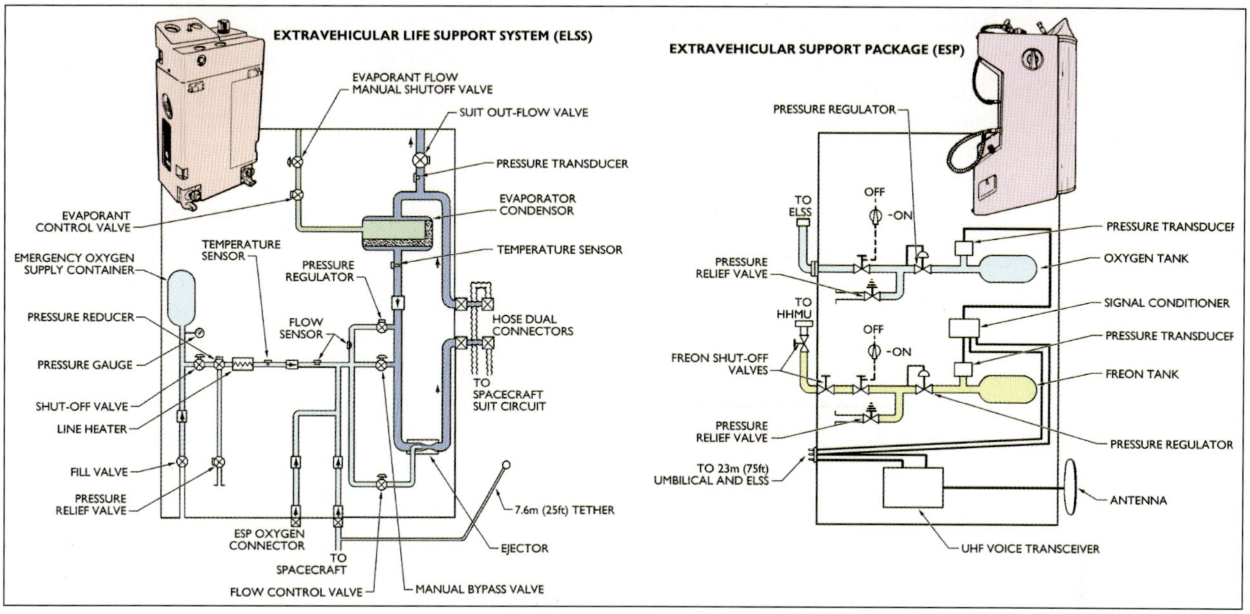

ABOVE Schematic of the ELSS. *(NASA/David Woods)*

Scott's plan had been to exit the cabin and make his way to the rear of the adapter module where he would find the *extravehicular support pack* (ESP). This was a 42kg backpack that contained extra consumables including 3.2kg of additional oxygen for 79 minutes of independent use. It also carried 8.2kg of Freon propellant to power Scott's HHMU, offering a total velocity change of 16.5m/sec. Scott was to use two nylon tethers; one short and one long. The short 7.6m tether included an oxygen feed that would either be plugged into the spacecraft or to the ELSS, and the requisite wires for communications and biomedical measurements. Once hooked up to the ELSS, he was to switch to the longer 23m tether which lacked the oxygen supply. But the mission was cut short prior to his spacewalk and the task of developing advanced EVA techniques passed to Gemini 9.

As part of an agreement with the Air Force, NASA installed the *astronaut maneuvering unit* (AMU) on Gemini 9 to be evaluated by Eugene Cernan. At $12 million, this "Buck Rogers" backpack was the single most expensive Air Force experiment in the program. It had been developed for the MOL space station program in order to permit the servicing of satellites, including the possibility of inspecting enemy satellites.

The AMU was built by the Chance Vought Company in Texas and designed to allow an astronaut to fly independently of his spacecraft.

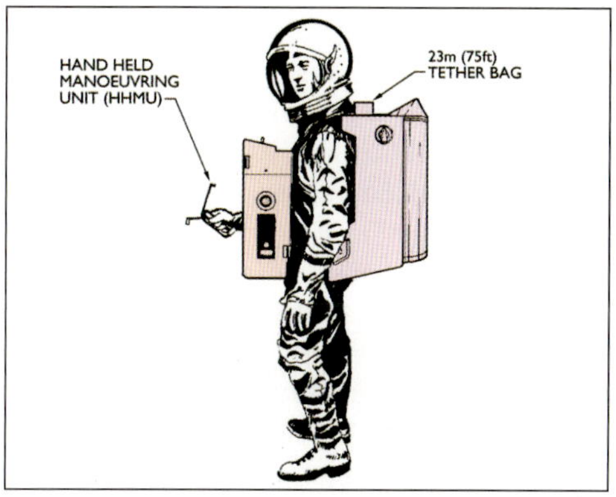

LEFT Diagram to show how Gemini 8's David Scott would wear the ELSS on his chest and the extravehicular support package on his back. *(NASA)*

LEFT Test subject Fred Spross wearing the full EVA kit for Gemini 9. On his back is the AMU. Note the metal cloth leggings to protect him from the unit's hot exhaust. *(NASA)*

It had systems for communications and life support as well as monopropellant thrusters for propulsion and attitude control. Monopropellant thrusters work by passing hydrogen peroxide across a catalyst, which causes it to break down at high temperature into water vapor and oxygen gas. To protect the astronaut from the extremely hot exhaust, extra layers were added to the legs of Cernan's suit, including an outer layer of Chromel R metal cloth.

Cernan discovered the hard way that EVA is far more difficult than it first appeared to Ed White. Exhausted and overheated, the Gemini 9 pilot returned to his seat without riding the AMU. It was slated for Gemini 12, but NASA decided instead to devote the final mission of the program to nailing the basic techniques of EVA.

The final three flights of the program continued the use of two slightly different versions of the G4C suit for the two crewmen with the pilot using the thicker EVA version for his spacewalk. On Gemini 10, Mike Collins used a so-called Siamese tether/umbilical in which different parts had differing lengths: a 15.2m nylon tether, a 16.5m oxygen supply hose, and an 18.3m nitrogen hose to provide propellant for his HHMU from a tank in the adapter module. This arrangement for the handheld jet gave Collins enough propellant to change his velocity by a total of 26m/sec. Richard Gordon also used the HHMU on Gemini 11. However, Buzz Aldrin did not have it on Gemini 12 because he was to focus on evaluating mobility and stability aids such as handholds and foot restraints.

Cabin interior

The cabin of the Gemini spacecraft was dominated by a large winged instrument panel that was built around the two astronauts. More than either Mercury or even Apollo, the Gemini interior had a look and feel that indicated it had been designed by and for pilots. Directly in front of each crewman was a panel that reflected his role. For example, it was usually up to the commander to actually fly the spacecraft and so he had an *incremental velocity indicator* (IVI) that allowed him to monitor the effect of the engine burns he made, a range/range-rate display for monitoring the progress of rendezvous, and an altimeter to allow him to monitor the final stages of their descent through the atmosphere.

The pilot had responsibility for the computer, so on his side were two units that comprised the *manual data insertion unit* (MDIU), essentially the keyboard and display for the machine.

On the central panels were controls and displays that both astronauts could directly access. In particular, a centrally located control stick meant either man could take control of the ship's attitude. Translation maneuvers were always carried out manually using one of two controllers, one on either side of the cabin.

For times when one astronaut was resting or otherwise occupied, a so-called swizzle stick, stowed overhead, enabled either man to reach any control in the spacecraft. Other elements of the cabin interior included stowage pouches on either

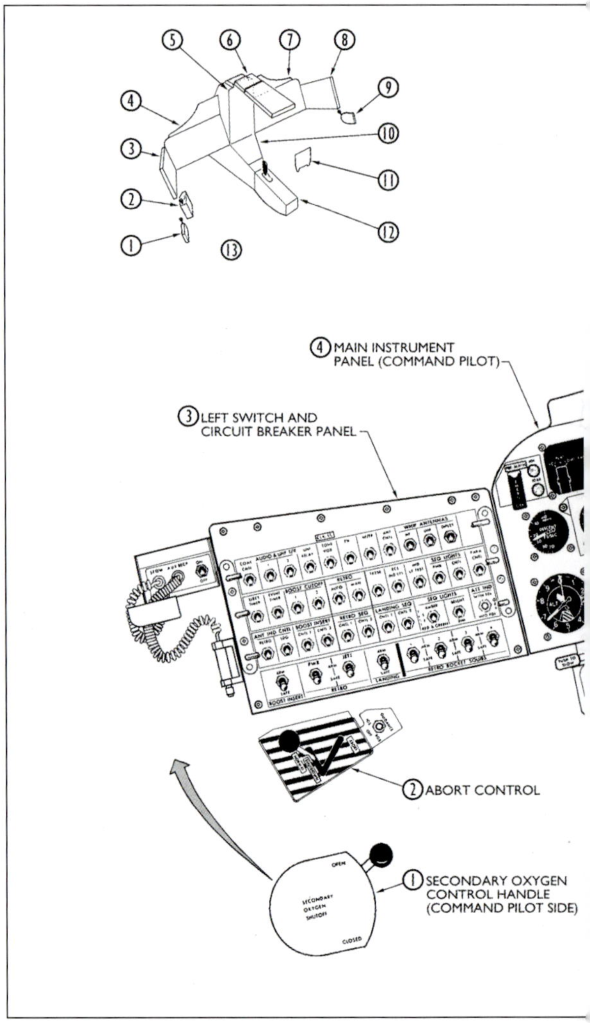

side of the astronauts, containers built into the side wall of the cabin to hold apparatus and large containers at the back for equipment, food, and eventually for waste as the mission progressed. There were two sets of floodlights that could be dimmed as required. One set were mounted centrally behind and above the seats to provide general illumination. In addition, white and red floods were mounted above each instrument panel with a switch to select for bright conditions or preserving the astronauts' adaptation to the dark.

Communications/tracking

From a communications standpoint, the world of the mid-1960s was very different to that of the 21st century. Whereas modern space travellers have near-continuous communications with their mission control centers, the Gemini astronauts had only a scattering of ground stations located around the world. Owing to their altitude and orbital speed, and the line-of-sight nature of their radios, direct communication with any particular ground station was limited to a maximum of ten minutes, but longer periods of contact were possible as the spacecraft transited the United States from Hawaii to Bermuda owing to overlaps between stations.

Space flight was one of those activities that stretched the state of the art. Worldwide satellite-based communications are now ubiquitous because Earth is circled by a belt of hundreds of geostationary satellites, yet the very first of these, Syncom 3, reached its station over the Pacific in August 1964, just prior to

BELOW Diagram of the typical layout of the Gemini spacecraft's instrument panel. Note the maneuver controller sited beneath the commander's main panel. This allowed control of the spacecraft's fore and aft thrusters whereas the joystick was for manual attitude control. *(NASA)*

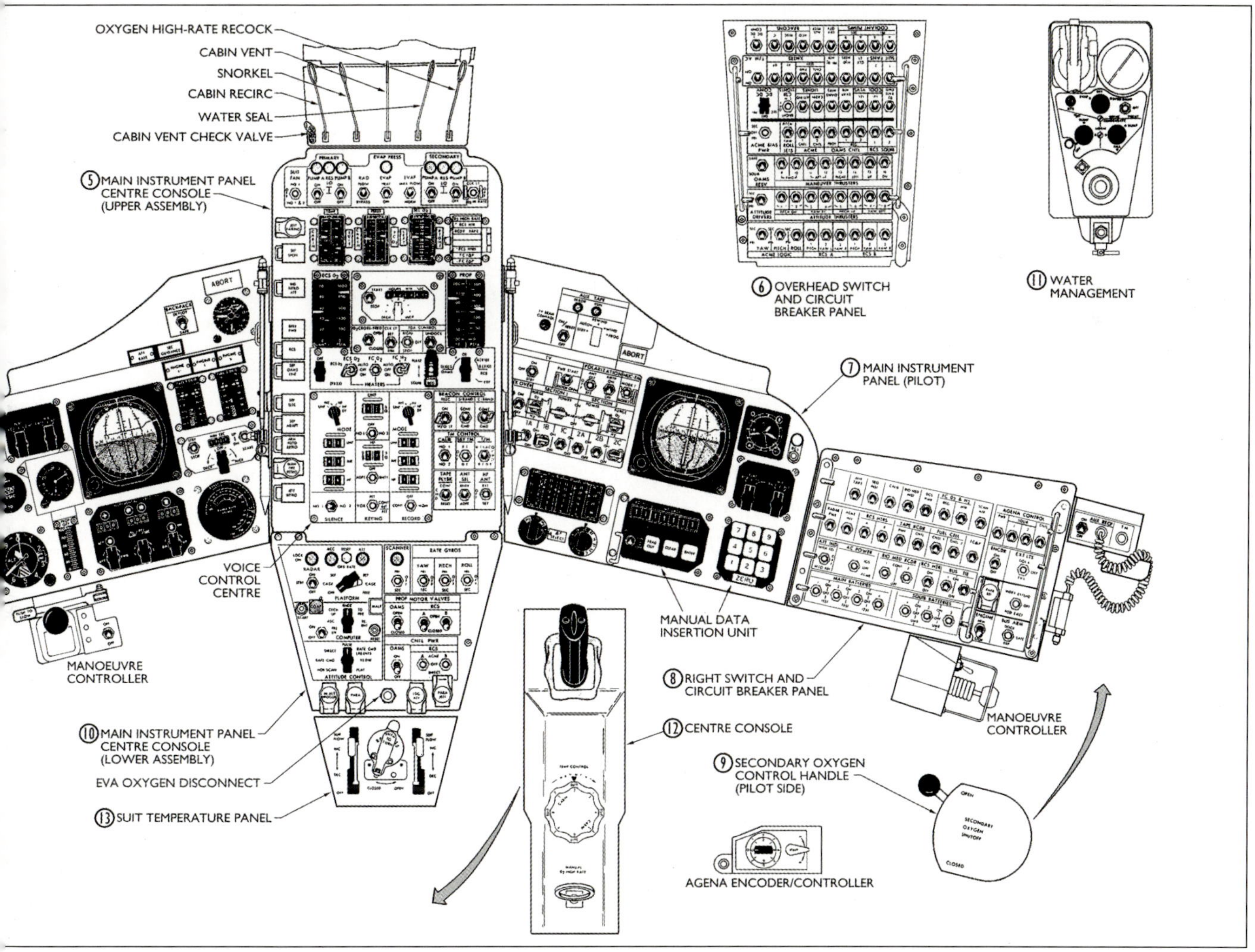

Gemini, and its capabilities were rudimentary. Most long distance communication still used analog telephone lines which were prone to interference and had a poor bandwidth.

The Gemini communications systems permitted two-way voice between the spacecraft and the ground, and between the two astronauts when they were suited. It provided a digital command link from the ground for remote operation of some spacecraft systems, and a telemetry link to allow engineers on the ground to monitor the health of the vehicle. It also included beacons to help ground stations track the vehicle and measure its orbit.

Radios

Two frequency bands were used for spacecraft-ground voice communication; UHF and HF. The UHF link came through a 3W transceiver to provide direct line-of-sight voice communications at 296.8MHz. Limited "over-the-horizon" contact could be made by a 5W HF transceiver working at 15.016MHz and this could also act as a direction-finding beacon after splashdown. All voice communications were handled through the *voice control center* (VCC) panel mounted between the two astronauts.

Additionally, there were three telemetry channels available at 230.4MHz to transmit real-time spacecraft data, 246.3MHz to play back data from a tape recorder, and 259.7MHz as a standby channel. These were early examples of digital transmission, then called *pulse code modulation* to distinguish it from other methods of placing information on a radio signal. Measurements within the spacecraft were converted to binary numbers which were streamed onto the radio carrier as a series of pulses. An accurate and robust means of information transmission, this forms the basis of most modern radio communication.

Other radio systems included a set of beacons. An acquisition aid beacon operated at 246.3MHz to help tracking stations acquire the spacecraft's C-band beacon. Once the C-band beacon had been acquired successfully, the acquisition aid beacon was switched off for the rest of the pass.

There were two C-band beacons, one on the adapter and the other on the re-entry module. They functioned like a transponder in that upon being interrogated by the ground on 5,690MHz they would reply on 5,765MHz with information about the spacecraft's position, thereby permitting ground stations to accurately track the spacecraft.

Finally, a beacon at 243MHz aided the recovery forces in locating the spacecraft on the ocean when it did not come down in direct view.

An important lesson learned from Gemini that informed Apollo was not to implement separate

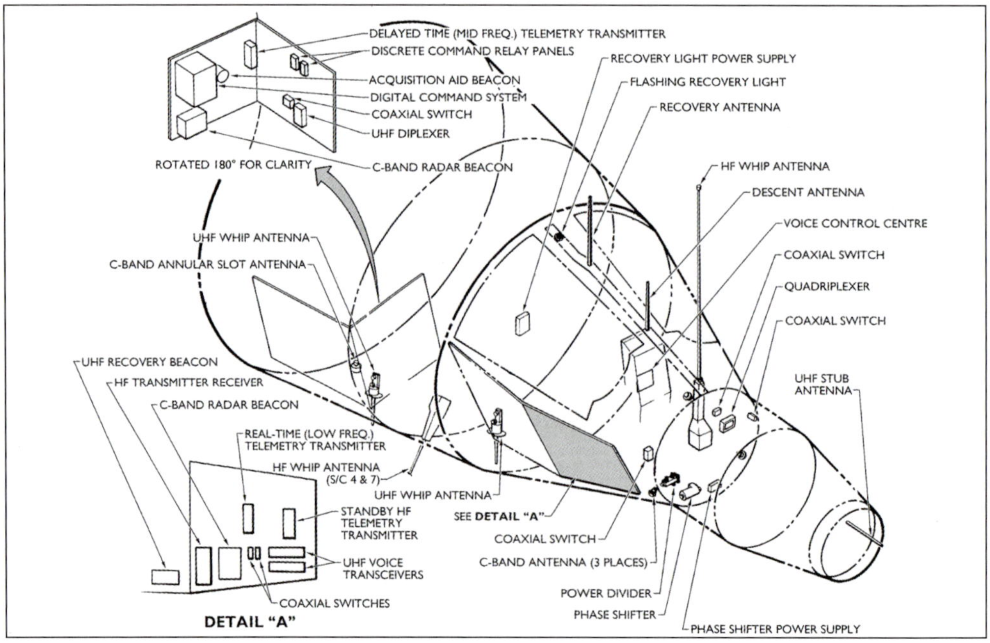

RIGHT Diagram showing the location of the spacecraft's communications equipment. *(NASA)*

systems for each communications task, but rather to combine them. Apollo flew with a more sophisticated communications system in which the needs of voice, television, and telemetry for science and engineering were combined with the requirements for measuring distance and speed as a single powerful radio signal known as *unified S-band* (USB). The ranging abilities of USB were later developed for satellite navigation, now a crucial infrastructure in the modern world.

Antennae

To support this range of radio communications, the Gemini spacecraft sprouted a suite of 11 antennae. A stub UHF antenna emanated from the nose of the spacecraft next to the radar unit to permit communications during ascent and re-entry. In such an exposed position it was subject to knocks during docking maneuvers and parachute deployment, so it was configured to rebound under spring action. Once in orbit, two spring-loaded UHF whip antennae made from beryllium-copper strip were deployed. These were mounted in each of the adapter sections. A longer whip antenna, between 4 and 4.8m long, depending on the flight, was also deployed from the adapter module for HF communications. After splashdown, the astronauts could deploy this antenna for long-distance voice communications and direction finding.

Two further UHF antennae permitted communications for the final moments of the flight after the parachute had changed from a one-point suspension arrangement to two points. The release of the second parachute bridle cleared the trough between the hatches and allowed these gold-plated sprung steel blades to pop up. At 46cm, the longer one broadcast a recovery beacon. The shorter 41cm antenna supported voice and telemetry.

Four C-band antennae supported the radar tracking of the spacecraft and were flush-mounted in various positions. A single antenna on the adapter section faced the ground during orbital flight when the spacecraft was in its heads-up attitude. Three antennae distributed around the narrow end of the re-entry section gave the beacon all-round coverage as the spacecraft undertook roll maneuvers during its return to Earth.

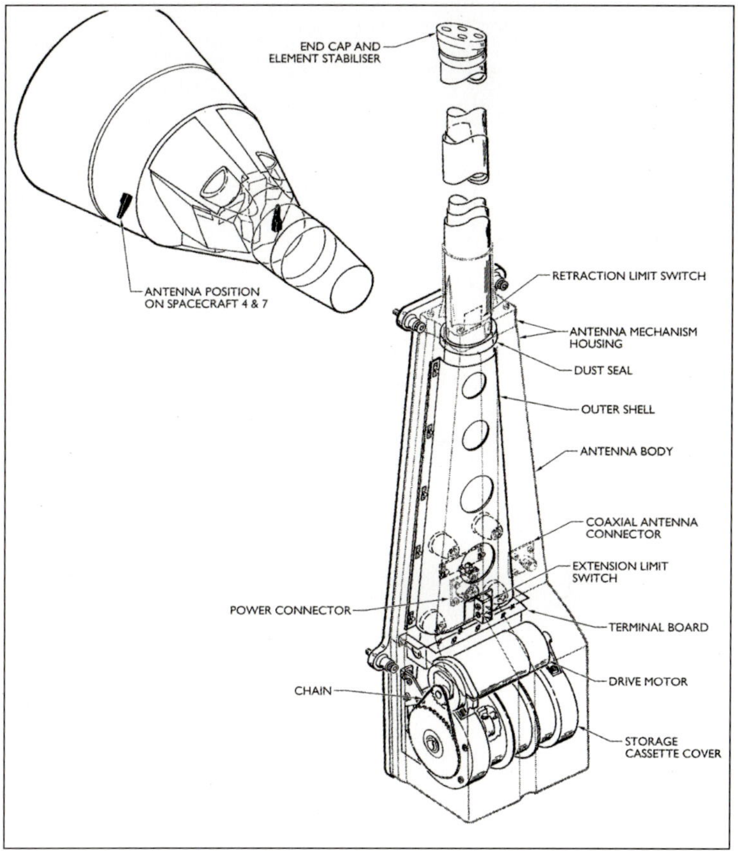

ABOVE In a manner similar to a handyman's steel tape measure, the long HF antenna was a curved metallic strip that was fed out under motor power from a set of reels. *(NASA)*

BELOW Diagram of the descent and recovery antennae. These were stowed in the parachute bridle trough between the hatches. They deployed under spring action when the spacecraft changed to two-point suspension. *(NASA)*

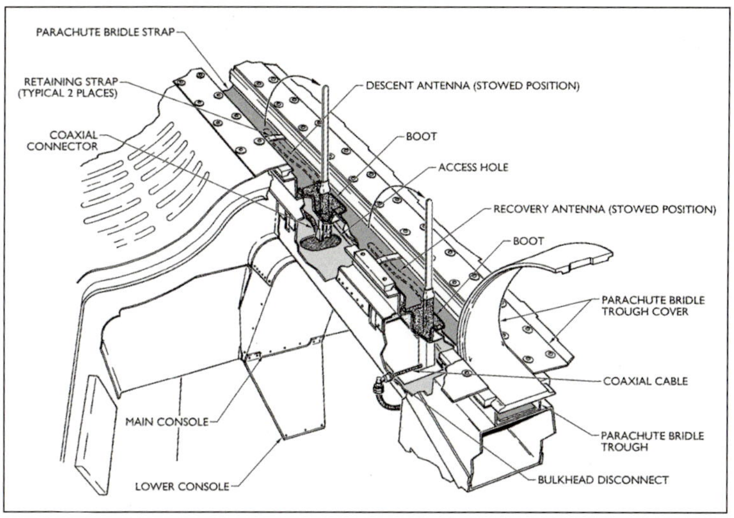

Chapter Ten

Launch and endurance

Every one of the manned Gemini-Titan flights began with a launch from Complex 19 at an Air Force station on Cape Canaveral, Florida. At T-10 minutes, with the crew in the spacecraft and the mission ready to proceed, the astronaut serving as the *capsule communicator* (CapCom) at the launch site would relay a "Go" for launch.

OPPOSITE Gemini 6 departs from Launch Complex 19, part of "Missile Row." Dome-shaped concrete blockhouses are visible on the left. *(NASA)*

ABOVE Jim Lovell (left) and Buzz Aldrin seated in the Gemini 12 spacecraft. A blue cover protects Buzz's EVA visor. *(NASA)*

Cooling water deluged the pad at T-2 minutes as the first stage's twin-chambered engine swivelled to test its ability to steer the vehicle in flight. Once ignition was commanded, a check ensured that the engine had reached at least 77% of its rated thrust. If that was the case, then the bolts that held the Titan to the pad were pyrotechnically released.

Liftoff was generally so smooth that the astronauts found it difficult to tell when they became airborne, but the spacecraft's *mission event timer* was started by a plug being pulled out from the launch vehicle's tail. As it ascended on an almost transparent flame, the rocket rolled around its long axis to align itself with its intended heading, then began to pitch over to fly the prescribed arc out over the Atlantic.

During the ascent, various abort procedures were available in case the crew or the *malfunction detection system* (MDS) found a non-recoverable fault in the vehicle. These

LEFT The launch of Gemini 10 is captured in this image along with the lowering of the erector tower; an effect created by combining multiple exposures in the darkroom. *(NASA)*

BELOW A pad perspective of the Titan II's twin thrust chambers as Gemini 9 accelerates past the launch tower. *(NASA)*

ranged from the use of the ejection seats during the first 50 seconds to the separation of the spacecraft and either splashing down in the ocean or limping into orbit under its own power.

As the vehicle went supersonic, the increasing aerodynamic pressure rattled the structure. On reaching 40,000ft at 1min 20sec, this rattle reached its peak and then rapidly tailed off. The next event was the lamp on the digital command system illuminating to show that the Cape had sent a navigational update based on radar tracking by the Eastern Test Range. This was soon followed by the second such update. The acceleration had increased to 3.3*g* when the first stage shut down at 2.5 minutes.

The efflux from the "fire in the hole" ignition of the second stage's single-chambered engine was directed out through a ring of vents in the interstage, creating a characteristic "ring of fire." Then the spent stage was pyrotechnically jettisoned. To the crew, for whom the sky had already turned black, the brilliant orange-yellow flash of staging was startling.

The job of the first stage had been to climb above the "sensible atmosphere" as efficiently as possible. The second stage then had to correct any trajectory errors inherited from the booster as it accelerated to orbital velocity. Flight controllers in mission control scrutinized a display of the desired and actual trajectories.

LEFT A cleverly planned long shot of Gemini 10 ascending on its nearly transparent flame with the Apollo-Saturn facilities test vehicle, 500-F, some miles in the distance and more than three times taller. *(NASA)*

When CapCom called "Point 8," this meant the Titan had attained 80% of the speed required for orbit. As it continued to consume its propellants, it became lighter and rapidly accelerated, subjecting the crew to a peak of 7.2*g*.

The spacecraft was carried to orbit "right side low" by the Titan, with the result that whereas the mission commander in the left seat saw only black sky out of his tiny window, the pilot on the right had an awe-inspiring view eastwards across the Atlantic. Only as the

BELOW Stills from a film of a Gemini-Titan space vehicle ascending on its first stage. After shutdown, the characteristic orange efflux of propellants are visible as the second stage engine is started prior to separation. As the stage pulls away, the interstage can be seen to fragment. *(NASA/David Woods/ Courtesy of Mark Gray – spacecraftfilms.com)*

Operational Units and Terms

Although by the mid-1960s many engineering groups within NASA were using metric units of measurement, the astronauts and their mission controllers measured altitudes in *nautical miles* (nmi), separation distances in *feet* (ft), and orbital velocities in *feet per second* (ft/sec) reflecting their aviation background. We will do the same. One nautical mile is approximately 1 arc-min along any terrestrial meridian line. By convention it is 1,852m, or about 6,076ft. For convenience, astronauts considered it to be 6,000ft.

The subject of orbital mechanics has its own jargon. Orbits are never perfectly circular. For an orbit around Earth, the lowest point is called the *perigee* while the highest is the *apogee*. The point where two orbits cross, or where an orbit crosses the equator is called a *node*. The angle that the plane of an orbit makes with the equator is called its *inclination*.

When discussing velocities with respect to orbits, they may be described as being "in plane" or "out of plane." Imagine throwing scrunched-up waste paper across a room into a wastepaper basket and missing the target. If you miss by being too short or long, then you got the direction correct but the strength of your throw was out. The curve of the throw defines a plane, and the plane is required to coincide with the basket. In this case the throw was "in plane." If the paper falls to the left or right, then your throw was "out of plane."

The distinctive shape of the Gemini spacecraft yielded two terms to describe which way it was pointed with respect to its direction of travel; *sharp end forward* (SEF) and *blunt end forward* (BEF).

RIGHT Wally Schirra leads Tom Stafford up the ramp to board an elevator that will take them to the top of Gemini-Titan 6 on what would prove to be an aborted attempt to launch for a rendezvous with Gemini 7. In their left hands, both astronauts carry portable oxygen ventilators to purge nitrogen from their blood. *(NASA)*

upper stage made its final trajectory refinement by dipping the spacecraft's nose below horizontal did the commander gain a view of the horizon. After smoothly thrusting for three minutes, the second stage's engine shut down.

Floating bits of detritus emerging from the nooks and crannies of the cabin indicated the onset of weightlessness, but the crew remained strapped into their seats. Within 30 seconds of shutdown, the pilot detonated a pyrotechnic strip to separate Gemini from the Titan. Then the commander fired the aft-facing OAMS thrusters for 15 seconds in order to move well clear. In the case of Gemini 3, the first manned mission, the insertion orbit had a perigee of 87nmi and an apogee of 125nmi in a plane inclined 32.6° to the equator.

The next task was to achieve precisely the desired orbital parameters. The *incremental velocity indicator* (IVI) showed the variance between the desired and actual velocities in three axes, and the discrepancies were eliminated by firing the OAMS thrusters. Roughly speaking, every extra 2ft/sec of forward motion would add 6,000ft or 1nmi to the apogee.

"No liftoff!"

An extraordinary situation developed during the attempt to launch Gemini 6 on December 12 1965. The Public Affairs Officer at the Cape counted down the final ten seconds, called "Ignition!" and handed the commentary over to his colleague in Houston. Fire, smoke, and steam belched from the trench beneath the rocket. In the spacecraft, commander Wally Schirra felt the shudder as the engine ignited. He observed the thrust-light flicker and then fade, just as it was intended to do as the engines built up to full thrust, and saw the clock start as would occur when a plug was pulled from the base of the vehicle as it lifted off.

In Houston, Chuck Harlan, the flight controller monitoring the booster saw the engine thrust build up and then, to his amazement, diminish. If he decided to call an abort, he was required to verbally announce that fact and throw a switch. Launch was a fast-moving situation and Harlan trod a narrow line between calling a false abort and ruining a mission, and failing to call out a valid abort and perhaps losing a crew. Throwing the switch would illuminate a

red light in the spacecraft. To guard against a malfunction illuminating the light, Schirra would act only if this was accompanied by a verbal call. The starting of the clock supposedly meant the vehicle had lifted at least 1.5in off the pad, but Harlan's instincts told him it had not moved, so he instead called "No liftoff!"

In response, the Cape began to *safe* the launch vehicle by isolating its pyrotechnic systems.

Meanwhile in the spacecraft, Schirra, who had ridden an Atlas and witnessed the "fizzle" on the first attempt to launch Gemini 2, trusted his pilot's instincts, which told him the vehicle had not moved. In the simulator, when the regime was to "prime" a crew to abort, he surely would have yanked on the ejector seat's "D" ring, but in real life he did not. The irony was that he had been assured that the clock couldn't start until the vehicle had left the pad. Tom Stafford awaited his commander's decision on whether they would eject. Their boss, Deke Slayton, who was in the blockhouse near the pad, expected to see a blast of smoke as the crew "punched out."

Kenneth Hecht, head of the Gemini Escape, Landing and Recovery Office, was also surprised that the crew stayed with the vehicle. However, he was well aware that unless it was clearly a matter of risking possible death in order to escape certain death, pilots were reluctant to suffer the 20*g* impulse of the seats' firing. Besides, on one test of the ejection system, the doors had failed to release and the suited mannequins had been shredded as the seats punched through. Furthermore, because the cabin contained pure oxygen there was a fair chance that if Schirra chose to eject then he and Stafford would emerge as flaming candles.

Once the Titan had been "safed," the erector was raised alongside so that the crew could be extracted. An investigation concluded that the vibration of the engine ignition had caused the electrical plug to prematurely disconnect from the booster, prompting the MDS to initiate the shutdown. But analysis of the engine telemetry revealed this to have been a blessing in disguise. The engine had stalled before the MDS issued the shutdown signal. A physical inspection found a rogue dust cover. It had been placed in the oxidizer inlet of the gas generator by the manufacturer during engine assembly, and had never been removed, thereby obstructing the flow. About the only good news was that the installation of the MDS by NASA had been money well spent.

Even so, as Schirra later observed, the fact that there had been a man in the abort "loop" had saved the spacecraft for another day; an automatic launch escape system like that of Mercury would have whisked the spacecraft away at the first sign of trouble, even though liftoff had not actually occurred. If the plug had not fallen out, the failing Titan may well have lifted off and fallen back onto the pad several seconds later when the engine failed. The plug had fallen out 1.2 seconds after engine ignition. The nuts holding the vehicle to the pad were to fire when the engine attained 77% of its rated thrust. This

ABOVE A cloud of orange smoke drifts away from Gemini-Titan 6 in the aftermath of its aborted launch. *(NASA)*

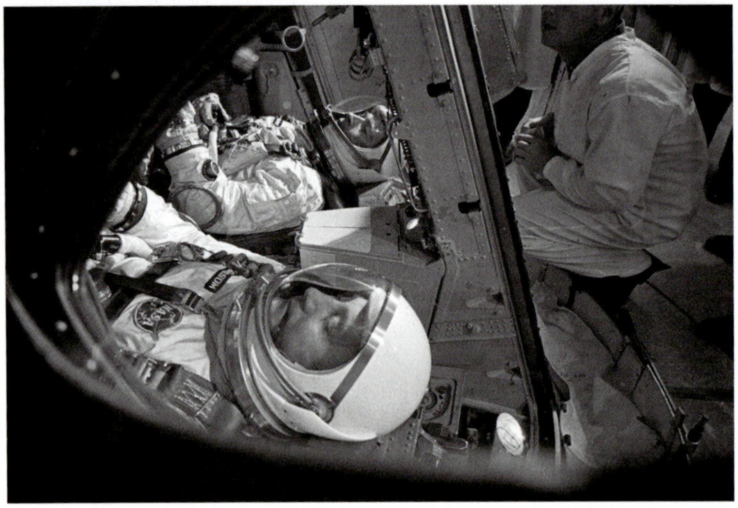

ABOVE **A view through the window of the opened hatch of the Gemini 3 spacecraft as technicians help prepare Gus Grissom (foreground) and John Young for their three-orbit shakedown mission.** *(NASA)*

ABOVE RIGHT **A chirpy Ed White and a bearded Jim McDivitt stride across the deck of the USS *Wasp* after their four-day space flight. Interestingly, the Gemini 4 crew were the first NASA astronauts to wear the Stars and Stripes on their suits.** *(NASA)*

normally took two seconds. If the MDS noticed the slow start and issued the shutdown prior to this, the pyrotechnics would have been inhibited. In the event of the engine failing after the vehicle had lifted off, the crew would have had no option but to eject. And when the vehicle fell back and exploded, it would have severely damaged the only pad set up for Gemini-Titan missions, which would have thrown the remainder of the program into doubt. The program had had a very narrow escape.

Flight duration

When planning began in 1963 for the first manned Gemini flight, its duration was to match that of the final Mercury one, which had yet to launch and was expected to last at least a day. In the event, Gordon Cooper finished Mercury with a 34-hour flight in May 1963. But Charles Mathews, the program manager, decided the new vehicle must remain within the coverage of the World-Wide Tracking Network, which translated to no more than three revolutions of Earth. In 1964 the Astronaut Office argued for an "open ended" inaugural mission that would remain in space either as long as the final Mercury flight or until a serious fault obliged a recall, but this was ruled out. Gemini 3 began the manned phase of the program with a successful "shakedown" flight that lasted just under five hours.

In the expectation of a successful inaugural flight, the plan in 1964 was for the second mission to last a week in order to test the innovative fuel cell system that was to provide electricity during prolonged periods in orbit. Owing to development problems this test was slipped to a later flight. As a result, the duration of the second mission of the program would be limited to four days, which was the maximum capacity of conventional batteries.

When Jim McDivitt and Ed White returned after a flight lasting just a few minutes short of 98 hours, the medical expectation was that they would be incapacitated as gravity drew the blood into their legs, but they walked unaided across the deck of the recovery ship. Post-flight tests did reveal a surprising reduction in blood plasma volume (cardiovascular capacity) in both men, but Charles Berry, NASA's chief physician, was very satisfied with the mission. "It was far, far better than anything we could have expected. We have knocked down an awful lot of "straw men." We had been told we would have unconscious astronauts after four days in weightlessness; well, they're not!" In view of this, Berry agreed to a "doubling up" in which the week-long mission scheduled for Gemini 5 would be extended by a day.

Gordon Cooper and Pete Conrad adopted the motto of "eight days or bust" and, with the introduction of a patch for their spacesuits, they reinforced the pioneering spirit with a covered wagon of the type used by the settlers who had opened up America. They had wanted to place the motto on the canopy of the wagon, but James Webb, the administrator of the agency, ruled this out because it would tempt the press to deride the mission "a bust" if it had to return early.

FAR LEFT The first ever NASA crew patch was introduced by Gemini 5 and featured a Conestoga wagon to reinforce the pioneering nature of their week-long mission. *(NASA)*

LEFT Pete Conrad and Gordon Cooper on the pad a few days before their Gemini 5 mission. *(NASA)*

Although a fault in the fuel cell system early on meant the spacecraft had to spend most of the week in an essentially powered-down state, a great amount of useful data about the system was obtained and in the end it proved possible to achieve the desired duration. To the public at large, flying in space was exciting and glamorous, but the reality of spending so long in an inert craft was an ordeal in boredom. A major milestone was achieved at 119hr 6min when they beat the record that had been held since June 1963 by cosmonaut Valeri Bykovsky. When Cooper and Conrad returned to Earth after almost 191 hours, the United States held the endurance record by a wide margin.

On reaching the aircraft carrier some 90 minutes after splashing down, some of the medics expected them to be so weak that they would require to be carried, but they were able to walk; albeit with their arms linked for mutual support because their legs were rather wobbly. "There is absolutely nothing wrong with them," was the immediate medical report. Nevertheless, further observation found both men to be dehydrated and somewhat weakened. There was a more pronounced loss of blood plasma and bone calcium than on previous missions, but these deficiencies were readily rectified.

This duration was significant, because if the Soviet Union looked likely to win the race to the Moon one option available to NASA was to send an early Apollo spacecraft on a "free return" loop around the far side of the Moon and straight back to Earth, a voyage that would take eight days.

Frank Borman and Jim Lovell were to attempt the program's maximum endurance target of 14 days during the Gemini 7 mission.

Because the cabin of the spacecraft was too cramped to enable an astronaut to don a spacesuit which had a metal collar ring, and spending two weeks in a pressure suit would be taxing, NASA had a lightweight pressure suit developed with an integrated hood that zipped

FAR LEFT Pete Conrad at work in the cramped confines of his spacecraft during the Gemini 5 mission. *(NASA)*

LEFT Conrad teases Cooper about the length of his beard after their splashdown. *(NASA)*

ABOVE To permit greater comfort during a 14-day mission, the Gemini 7 astronauts wore "soft" suits. Here, Jim Lovell is sealed behind the suit's zippered helmet in preparation for launch. *(NASA)*

ABOVE RIGHT Gemini 7 commander Frank Borman during training wearing a conventional aviator's helmet within the "soft" suit. In space, the suit's helmet could be unzipped and pushed back as a headrest. *(NASA)*

into place instead of attaching a fiberglass-shell helmet onto a neck ring. For communications, the astronaut would wear a conventional pilot's helmet inside the hood. This "soft" suit would be able to be removed in space. Tests showed that the environmental control system of the spacecraft operated more efficiently with the crew unsuited. The plan was that if the spacecraft was healthy at the end of the first full day, both crewmen would strip to their longjohns and don jackets, but prior to the flight it was decided they would take turns so that one man was suited at all times in case of an emergency.

Borman and Lovell soaked up the lessons learned by their predecessors. On Gemini 5, for example, storing trash had become a serious issue. It was decided to discard the first week's food packaging by stuffing it behind Borman's seat and the second week's trash behind Lovell's seat. Another lesson was that no one knew how long any given task, including preparation and clear-up, would take in weightlessness so there was little point in drawing up a detailed timeline. An "outline" flight plan was developed instead that allowed non-time-critical tasks to be interleaved with the time-critical events as conditions permitted. This flexibility was deemed likely to keep this crew in a better psychological state than their predecessors who, upon finding themselves "behind," had grown frustrated trying to "catch up" on an unrealistic schedule.

RIGHT Frank Borman near the end of the long duration flight of Gemini 7. *(NASA)*

Then there was the issue of sleep. The alternating sleep cycles employed by their predecessors had been a disaster, since in such a cramped cabin it was difficult for the off-duty man to sleep while his colleague maintained communication with Earth. But Gemini 5 had established that even an ailing vehicle could safely be left untended. With confidence in the spacecraft, Borman and Lovell decided to start out on the same cycle, synchronized with Houston time, and see how things progressed.

To fill their day, Borman and Lovell carried out 20 experiments that included studies of the radiation environment in space, Earth's magnetic field, and a variety of photographic tasks. Many were biomedical in nature to evaluate the human body's reaction to space. One assessed whether inflatable rubber cuffs compressing Lovell's thighs would stimulate his autonomic nervous system, reduce his reaction to weightlessness, and hasten his recovery upon return to Earth. Another utilized an in-flight exerciser to test its benefits by noting heart rate before and after a specified number of calibrated pulls, then measuring the time required for the heart to recover its previous state. An in-flight phonocardiogram studied possible fatigue of the heart muscles.

There were elaborate experiments to measure loss of fluids in the body and the demineralization of the bones. The astronauts' calcium intake and output prior to, during, and after the flight was carefully noted, and it was bookended by X-rays of their heels and the bones in the little fingers. Urine, faeces, and perspiration, including the sweat soaked into the longjohns, were returned for analysis, creating a significant imposition on the crew.

In addition, Borman had EEG electrodes glued to his scalp to document his brain activity while awake and asleep in the space environment. The final biomedical experiment studied the sense of balance provided by the otoliths of the vestibular system of the inner ear which, being gravity sensors, are unable to function in weightlessness. Some astronauts resented the medical "fishing trips" and did not envy Borman and Lovell their two weeks as lab rats for the medical community.

At least if their mission turned sour, they had a book each to read; *Roughing It* by Mark Twain for Borman and *Drums Along The Mohawk* by Walter Edmonds for Lovell.

In the event, things went well and, although it was tedious, they returned to Earth in much better physiological condition than their predecessors despite extending the record to 330hr 35min. As Dr Berry observed, "Apparently, there had been enough time for an adaptive phenomenon to take place." Borman had lost 10lb of body mass and Lovell had lost 6lb. Lovell's pulsating thigh cuff had had no measurable effect. Borman's EEG waves showed he had slept fitfully for only a few hours on the first night (which proved to be the worst night from the standpoint of sleep) but this experiment had been curtailed when he inadvertently disconnected the sensors. Nevertheless, he had slept well thereafter.

"Our watches were set on Houston time," Borman said. "We had a regular work day, three meals a day, and then at night we went to bed. We put up light filters in the windows and didn't look out."

As measured in terms of heart rate induced by exercising using a bungee cord, their stamina had not decreased appreciably. The bone density data was surprising: at 3%, the bone loss was one third of that suffered by Cooper and Conrad on their shorter mission.

The "soft" suits were a major factor in maintaining the psychological state of the astronauts. As Borman put it, if they had worn the normal suits "it would have been a matter of survival rather than a matter of operating efficiently." Nevertheless he likened the ordeal to spending two weeks in the front of a Volkswagen and they counted the days by scratching marks on the control panel. Lovell said it was like living in a men's room. When he lost his toothbrush early on, they shared for the rest of the flight.

The marathon of Gemini 7 demonstrated that astronauts would be able to endure weightlessness for the times envisaged for the Apollo lunar surface missions.

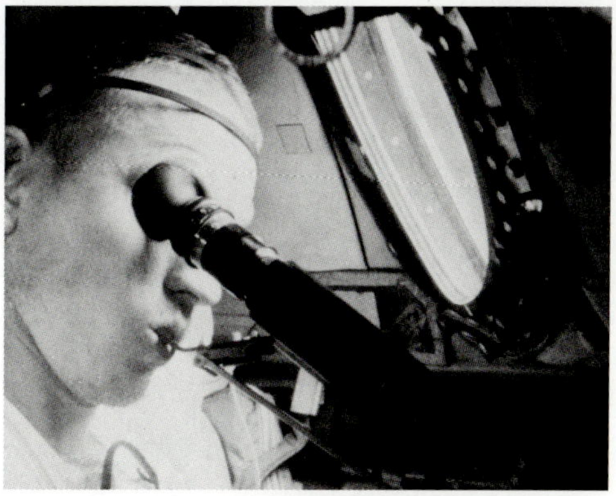

LEFT Frank Borman performing a visual acuity test. The apparatus is held steady by use of a bite board inserted into the mouth. *(NASA)*

LEFT Frank Borman with EEG electrodes glued to his scalp while suiting up for the Gemini 7 mission. *(NASA)*

BELOW After the Gemini 7 splashdown on December 18 1965, Jim Lovell is hoisted into a helicopter while Frank Borman in the life raft awaits his turn. *(NASA)*

Chapter Eleven

Orbital operations

The main technical challenge of the Gemini program was to demonstrate that one spacecraft could rendezvous and dock with another in orbit, a capability that required orbital maneuvering. Gemini 3 offered the first opportunity to demonstrate such maneuvers.

OPPOSITE Gemini 10 approaches its Agena target vehicle. *(NASA)*

RIGHT The Gemini 3 crew of Gus Grissom and John Young standing beside a spacecraft simulator. *(NASA)*

Its Titan launch vehicle had inserted the spacecraft into an elliptical orbit whose apogee was on the opposite side of the planet. Upon completing their first revolution, Gus Grissom aligned the spacecraft *sharp end forward* (SEF) and burned the OAMS thrusters to act as a brake, lowering their apogee and almost circularizing the orbit. It was a historic moment for manned space flight. Gordon Cooper, the CapCom in the control room, joked that if they caught sight of the expired upper stage of the Titan they should proceed to rendezvous. Their bosses, Robert Gilruth and his deputy, George Low, heard this and decided that it would make an interesting experiment on the next mission.

An exercise in *station-keeping* was added to the Gemini 4 flight plan. As soon as the spacecraft had separated from the second stage, Jim McDivitt fired the aft-facing OAMS thrusters to move clear at 10ft/sec. After 30 seconds, he cancelled this motion and yawed around 180°, ready to assess the controllability of his spacecraft. A pair of flashing lights had been added to the Titan stage to aid visibility over Earth's night side.

As they passed over the Bermuda station at the far end of the Eastern Test Range, he informed Gus Grissom in Houston that they were about 350ft from the stage and it was tumbling at a rate of 30°/sec. McDivitt then aimed his vehicle's nose directly at the stage and thrust towards it at 5ft/sec. Surprisingly, it receded. He added another 3ft/sec, and was astonished to observe the range open further. Strange! Furthermore, immediately after separating from the stage he had been out in front and now he was off to one side and above it.

Over the Indian Ocean they were contacted by Carnarvon on the western coast of Australia and McDivitt explained that he had not been able to close in on the stage, whose lights he could still see at a distance of "probably around half a mile." As the spacecraft crossed the United States at the end of its first revolution, he was directed to terminate the experiment because roughly half of the available OAMS propellant had been expended without achieving anything significant. McDivitt had been caught out right from the start.

When the upper stage shut down it was aligned along the velocity vector (their direction of travel) which, since the orbit was elliptical, was inclined slightly upward. By separating, McDivitt had entered an orbit with a higher apogee. As the orbits diverged, the stage seemed to draw ahead and descend. As no one had warned him otherwise, he had expected to be able to

BELOW The spent Titan second stage alongside a Gemini spacecraft, in this case Gemini 7. Unused propellant is venting from one side, causing it to tumble. *(NASA/David Woods/ Courtesy of Mark Gray – spacecraftfilms.com)*

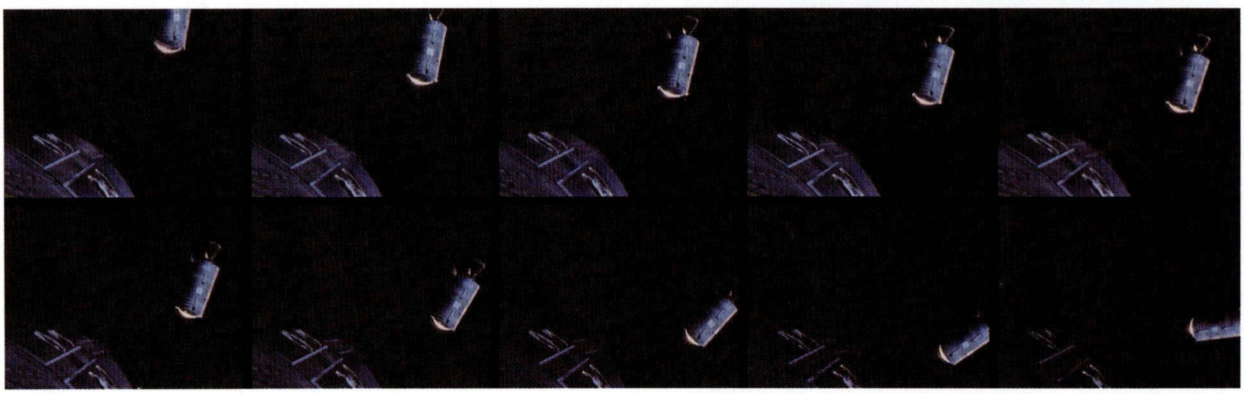

ABOVE The multi-colored splendor of an orbital sunset photographed from Gemini 4. *(NASA)*

fly in formation with the spent stage using his seat of the pants instincts as a pilot. When he tried to return by propelling himself towards his target with his craft's nose angled down towards the target, he actually increased the divergence between the orbits. The subtlety of orbital dynamics had come as a surprise. As André Meyer, a trajectory specialist, sympathized, McDivitt "just didn't understand." But the purpose of a test flight was to learn. "Frankly," Deke Slayton reflected, station-keeping "wasn't an operation that had been too well thought out."

The next spacecraft to roll off the production line had radar but the Agena target vehicle was not yet ready. Instead, a *radar evaluation pod* (REP) with a transponder would test the ability of the radar to determine the range, range-rate, and bearing angle to a target. The radar was expected to be capable of locking on at a range of 200nmi. Its data would be fed to the onboard computer, which would compute the orbital maneuvers required to perform a rendezvous.

The plan for Gemini 5 was to deploy the pod, let it drift away, then use the radar to return. But the fuel cell system began to misbehave shortly after the pod had been released, and the radar experiment was

ABOVE The radar evaluation pod stowed in the rear of Gemini 5's equipment section. *(NASA)*

LEFT Gordon Cooper (foreground) and Pete Conrad in training for Gemini 5. *(NASA)*

How to Rendezvous

The means by which Gemini should undertake a rendezvous had been intensely debated. In the 1920s Walter Hohmann in Germany discovered that the most efficient means of rendezvousing involved flying a *transfer orbit* in which the chase vehicle travelled one-half-leg of an elliptical orbit that intersected both orbits tangentially. This would require two engine burns, the first to enter the transfer orbit and the second to leave it. When Gemini planning began it was presumed this method would be used, but further study led to a more cautious technique called *co-elliptic* rendezvous.

BELOW **A minimum-energy Hohmann transfer orbit.**

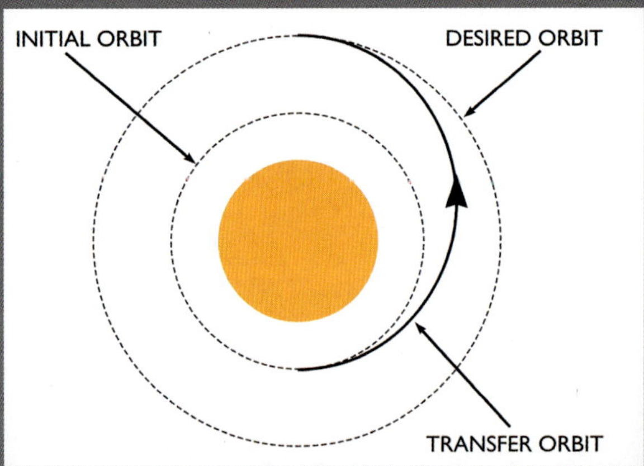

Co-elliptic rendezvous

This required that the chase vehicle be placed in an orbit that was co-elliptic with the target's orbit (the same shape and alignment) so that it maintained a specific difference in height below. Starting off behind the target, the chase vehicle would slowly catch it up by being in a lower and therefore faster orbit. By careful timing, this catch-up could be made to occur at any point in the orbit. Specifically, the planners wanted to execute the final climb to intercept the target, known as the *terminal phase*, over the night-time side of Earth.

The reason for flying the terminal phase in the dark was that as the chase vehicle rose from its lower orbit, the commander would see the target against the background of stars. Furthermore, if everything was occurring as it should, the target would appear stationary with respect to the stars. Any apparent movement of the target against the stars would be immediately obvious and hence readily and rapidly corrected. It was a method that ignored the Earth below. All the commander cared about was what appeared to be a straight-line approach to the Agena. This was a powerful technique for ensuring that the terminal phase was flown accurately, and for a co-elliptic height difference of 15nmi it was achieved over about 130° of travel around Earth. The terminal phase began shortly after orbital sunset with an engine burn to set the chase vehicle on its slow rise to the target. This burn was called *terminal phase initiation* (TPI). If the geometry was established correctly, the final approach would occur shortly after sunrise. On closing within a few miles, and continuing to maintain the target fixed, the commander would brake according to a profile designed to halt alongside the target.

Starting at launch, the Titan's second stage would attempt to insert the Gemini spacecraft into an elliptical orbit with its apogee 15nmi below that of the target's orbit. At the end of the first Earth revolution the spacecraft would improve the height of the apogee. Half a revolution later, at that apogee, there would be an opportunity to raise the perigee. The height that was chosen affected the relative timing (or phasing) of the two orbits and thereby arranged the desired timing for the co-elliptic maneuver.

If the planes of the two orbits were out of alignment, then a burn could be made at one of the nodes to align them. For Gemini, the largest out-of-plane error that could be handled was about half a degree.

Finally, with the two orbits coplanar and with their apogees aligned, a burn would be made to raise the perigee of Gemini's orbit to establish a constant difference in height below the target's orbit. This would be done when the Gemini reached its third apogee, defining the conditions for the terminal phase of the rendezvous.

It was decided to make the interception on the fourth revolution because this would allow time for the World-Wide Tracking Network to measure each orbit and compute the next maneuver, and also allow the astronauts a significant period in the co-elliptic orbit to prepare for TPI. In the terminology of the flight dynamics specialists, this rendezvous was referred to as "m=4." After this case had been perfected, it would be possible to tighten up the timing for faster procedures.

cancelled. When the situation improved later in the mission, the pod's battery had long-since expired. Nevertheless, flight controllers in Houston had the spacecraft carry out a series of maneuvers typical of a rendezvous, albeit without the satisfaction of closing in on the pod. Engineers did manage to exercise the radar by mounting a transponder on a tower at the Cape and have the spacecraft track it.

A meeting in space

A setback was turned into an opportunity when the Agena intended for Gemini 6 exploded at ignition during its ascent to orbit. While the problem was being investigated, NASA decided to have Gemini 6 rendezvous with Gemini 7 instead. This would be considerably more satisfying than drawing alongside an unmanned target vehicle.

After an aborted launch attempt Gemini 6 set off in chase of Gemini 7, patiently waiting in the desired target orbit and some 1,200nmi ahead. The insertion orbit of 87 by 140nmi was a little short of the intended apogee. The height adjustment burn made at perigee at the end of the first revolution raised the apogee to 146nmi, which was about 15nmi below the apogee of Gemini 7. By that time, as a result of being lower, Gemini 6 had reduced the separation to 635nmi.

At apogee on the second revolution, a phasing burn raised the perigee to 121nmi

LEFT An Atlas rocket lifts off with the GATV intended for the Gemini 6 rendezvous. *(NASA)*

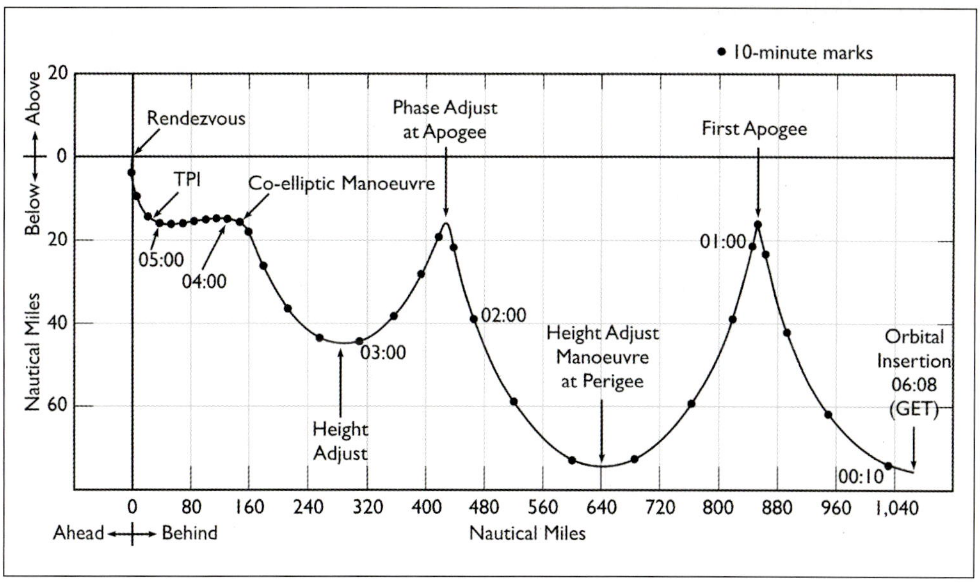

BELOW A graphical representation of the "m=4" rendezvous carried out by Gemini 6. This type of diagram indicates the position of the chase vehicle with respect to the target. In this case, the peaks and troughs of the curve represent the apogees and perigees of successive orbits as it closes in, showing the effects of the various maneuvers. Note how the co-elliptic maneuver causes the chase vehicle to adopt a parallel orbit just below that of the target, and the TPI maneuver begins the final approach. *(NASA/ David Woods)*

RIGHT The crew patch for Gemini 6 depicts the final stage of the rendezvous with the target viewed against a stylized starfield including Orion and the twins of Gemini; Castor and Pollux. Although the patch shows an Agena target, in the event, the rendezvous was made with Gemini 7. *(NASA)*

to control the timing of the rendezvous. On reaching the node or crossing point between the two orbits, Wally Schirra yawed 90° right to fly sideways and made a brief burn to adjust the plane of his orbit by 0.07° in order to match that of the target. At perigee at the end of the second revolution, a burn of 0.8ft/sec raised the apogee by several thousand feet to precisely 15nmi below that of the target.

As Gemini 6 set off across the Atlantic on its third revolution, its radar was successfully tracking the target's transponder at a range of 200nmi. They made the co-elliptic burn at their next apogee to raise the perigee by 28nmi. Their orbit of 146 by 148nmi was the desired 15nmi below the 161 by 163nmi orbit of the target. Now Schirra used the needles on his panel fed by the radar to keep the nose of his vehicle facing the target.

Once within 100nmi, Tom Stafford used the radar every 100 seconds to measure the range and range-rate, and began to plot the range against the elevation (the spacecraft's pitch angle) on a graph to verify that the height difference was constant. With Gemini 6's nose pitched up at 19° facing the target, the Sun was behind the adapter module and the windows were in shadow as orbital sunset loomed. Schirra saw the target illuminated by the last rays of the Sun. It was between Sirius and the two brightest stars in the constellation of Gemini, Castor and Pollux, just as depicted on the patch for the mission.

As Gemini 6's lower orbit brought it in beneath Gemini 7, Schirra kept the nose facing the target and Stafford monitored the increasing pitch. As the angle approached 25°, the onboard computer processed three measurements to calculate when the terminal phase should begin. As a backup, Houston provided its estimate. The key parameter was the geometry; they had to make the burn when their pitch angle was 27°, at which time the range would be 33nmi. Stafford was sure

BELOW The Gemini 7 spacecraft seen during a fly-around by Gemini 6. The two objects sticking out of either side of the retrograde section are deployed acquisition lights. *(NASA)*

BELOW RIGHT Gemini 7 seen broadside during close maneuvers by Gemini 6. *(NASA)*

of their trajectory because his graph continued to confirm co-ellipticity.

Gemini 7 passed into the Earth's shadow and disappeared. As Gemini 6 followed it in, Schirra discovered that he could not see its acquisition lights. Nevertheless, when the angle was right, he initiated the transfer by firing the aft thrusters for 41 seconds to speed up by 33ft/sec. He reduced the illumination on his optical sight to its minimum and three minutes later finally saw a speck of light close to the center. Frank Borman blinked his spacecraft's acquisition lights several times for positive identification. Now that he was sure of his target, Schirra momentarily dropped the nose to the horizon to verify the calibration of the inertial platform. It was now crucial that he maneuver to maintain the target fixed with respect to the background stars.

Although the approach appeared straight in with respect to the stars, looked at from the point of view of two objects orbiting Earth they were pursuing different curves around a 130° arc. Seen from the ground, Gemini 6 seemed to pass under Gemini 7 as Schirra's pitch angle reached 90°. As the vehicles emerged into sunlight, Gemini 6 was leading, and presenting its rear to the Sun with its windows still in shadow.

With the separation down to 1,000ft, the reflection from the white adapter of Gemini 7 was so bright that Schirra, his eyes dark adapted, was blinded. As Stafford called out the diminishing range, Schirra fired the thrusters to slow down in a programed manner. By the time they were 120ft apart, the two spacecraft were stationary with respect to one another. By the nature of the process of pitching to maintain its nose facing the target, Gemini 6 ended up "heads down," so the final step was to roll the right way up.

With the vehicles so close together and in precisely the same orbit, it was possible to use seat of the pants flying. Having been in space so long, Gemini 7 had no propellant to spare. Gemini 6 had half of its load still aboard, so Schirra closed in to make a fly-around inspection of the other spacecraft. They were not to make contact, because flying in the ionosphere might cause an electrostatic discharge, but in a superb demonstration of controllability Schirra maneuvered so that the vehicles were directly facing one another. With their noses only a foot apart, the two crews waved at each other.

After several hours of formation flying, Gemini 6 returned to Earth, leaving Gemini 7 to finish its marathon mission.

ABOVE Nose to nose: Gemini 6 and Gemini 7. The former is seen here against Earth's horizon and is recognizable by the white radar unit with its three radomes installed in the spacecraft's nose. *(NASA)*

RIGHT Neil Armstrong leads David Scott up the ramp to the Gemini 8 launch vehicle. *(NASA)*

ABOVE The Gemini 8 crew patch shows a prism splitting light from Castor and Pollux of the constellation Gemini into a spectrum of colors, indicating that this was to be the first full spectrum mission, combining rendezvous, docking and EVA. *(NASA)*

RIGHT The launch of Gemini 8's Agena target vehicle, boosted by an Atlas rocket. *(NASA)*

The perils of Gemini 8

Having resolved the problems with the Agena target vehicle, NASA dispatched Gemini 8 to perform a rendezvous on 16 March 1966 with a sequence of maneuvers almost identical to those of Gemini 6.

After a period of station-keeping, Neil Armstrong lined up his vehicle with the Agena's docking apparatus, closed in, and docked just as they entered the Earth's shadow. It was almost routine.

The next step was to assess the integrity of the linkage mechanism using the Agena's thrusters to yaw the docked combination through an angle of 90° at a rate of 1.5°/sec. However, as they flew on in darkness, preoccupied with tasks in the cabin, Dave Scott noted that they had rolled 30° to the left according to their attitude indicator. Neither man had felt it.

Suspecting an Agena problem, Scott issued commands to switch off its attitude control system, deactivate its horizon sensor, and inhibit the function designed to maintain its orientation fixed relative to the Earth. Then Armstrong reactivated the OAMS and restored the desired attitude. When the docked combination began to drift again, Scott reactivated the Agena's attitude control system to damp out the spurious motion, but this proved ineffective. By this point they were approaching the dawn terminator.

On spotting a 25ft persistent plume projecting from one of the Agena's pitch thrusters in the growing light, Scott realized the Agena was rapidly consuming its propellant and he shut off its attitude control system again. As the Agena appeared to be malfunctioning, the logical action was to undock. Once Armstrong had slowed the rates, Scott commanded the docking mechanism of the Agena to release them and Armstrong applied a five-second burst of the forward-firing thrusters to rapidly withdraw.

Immediately, Gemini 8 began to spin up at an even faster rate than before. Armstrong realized that the fault was in his own vehicle and

RIGHT Gemini 8 blast off to give chase to its target vehicle. *(NASA)*

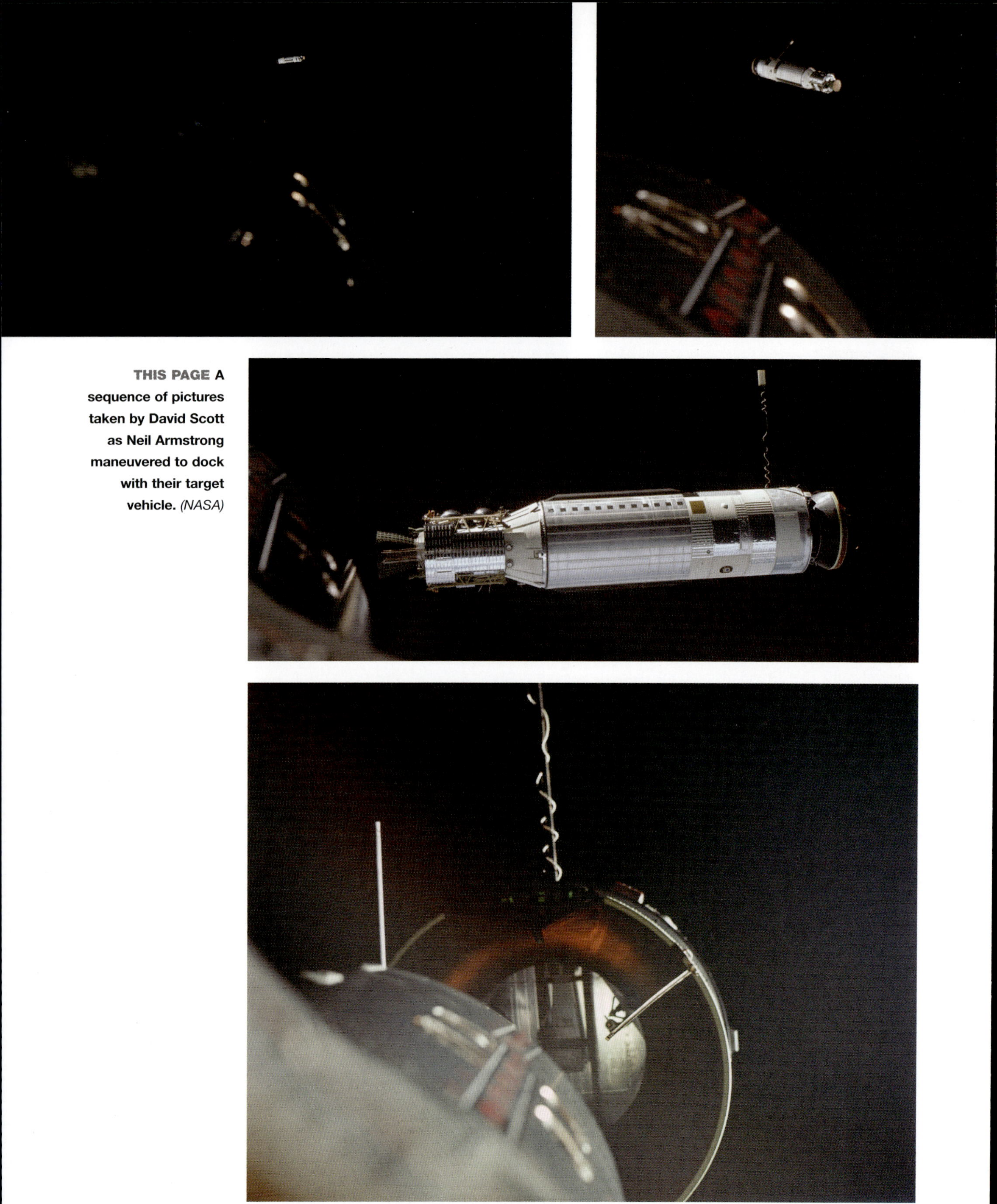

THIS PAGE A sequence of pictures taken by David Scott as Neil Armstrong maneuvered to dock with their target vehicle. *(NASA)*

it appeared that a single thruster was misfiring. As he struggled to regain control, he saw that they were rapidly running out of propellant.

The flight controllers at the next station of the World-Wide Tracking Network expected the astronauts to be progressing through the maneuvers listed in the flight plan, and were shocked to discover that the vehicles were undocked. "We have a serious problem," announced Scott and then Armstrong tried to explain their situation, but the transmission was intermittent because the vehicle was tumbling. There was nothing the ground could do to assist. The astronauts were on their own with their vehicle spinning once per second and accelerating. They had severe tunnel vision and were near to blacking out.

Recognizing that they were fast running out of time, Armstrong decided on drastic action. He cut the power to the OAMS and pulled the circuit breakers for all of the thrusters, then armed the *re-entry control system* (RCS) mounted in the nose. However, whereas the propellant in one ring was deemed sufficient to control the vehicle during re-entry and the second provided a healthy degree of redundancy, there was a risk that stabilizing the rapidly spinning ship would consume so much propellant that there would be insufficient left for re-entry.

Having stabilized his spacecraft using the RCS, Armstrong then powered up the OAMS and pushed in the circuit breakers one by one to identify the faulty thruster; it was one of the yaw thrusters on Scott's side. The valves of the thrusters were activated by electrically powered solenoids which were held at high potential and "grounded" when selected. The OAMS had been serviced three days prior to launch, and it was surmised that one of the wires had come loose, causing the thruster to fire erratically when not selected, and not to fire when commanded. Because the "ground to fire" logic had allowed the thruster to "fail on" while "logically off," Armstrong's only option in the very short time available was to power off the entire OAMS, which in turn meant activating the RCS to stabilize the vehicle. For later missions the OAMS was revised for "apply power to fire."

The mission rules specified that in the event of activating the RCS, the flight must be terminated as soon as possible, so the mission

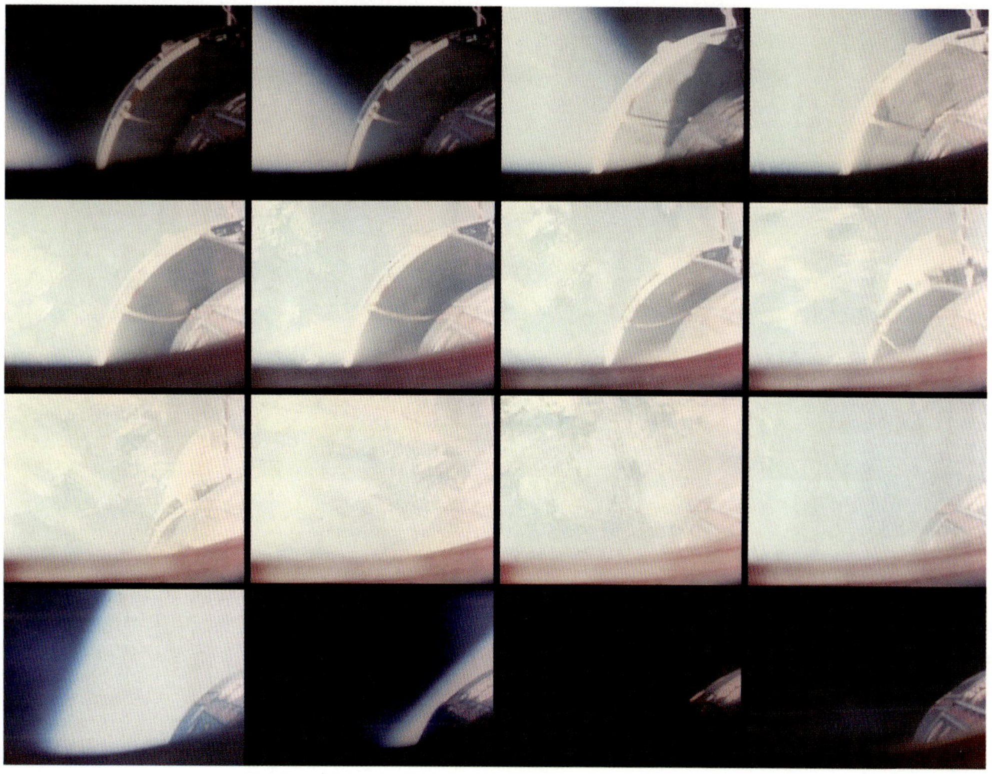

LEFT After the docked combination began to tumble, Neil Armstrong undocked Gemini 8 from the Agena. This sequence of stills captured from film footage shows the wild gyrations at the moment of undocking. *(NASA/David Woods/ Courtesy of Mark Gray – spacecraftfilms.com)*

ABOVE Neil Armstrong (in the left seat) and David Scott await recovery of their spacecraft after an emergency splashdown in the western Pacific Ocean. *(NASA)*

ABOVE RIGHT Neil Armstrong and David Scott pose with the Air Force pararescuers Glenn M. Moore (standing), Eldridge M. Neal (left) and Larry D. Huyett aboard the USS *Leonard F. Mason*. *(NASA)*

transformed from a celebration of the historic docking to an emergency return to Earth. Meanwhile, flight controllers sent commands to the Agena to stabilize its attitude and park it in a 220nmi circular orbit in which it could serve as an inert "target of opportunity" for future use.

The angry alligator

In the summer of 1966, having demonstrated the "m=4" case of orbital rendezvous on Geminis 6 and 8, the plan was for the next two missions to attempt the faster "m=3" scenario because Apollo planners wanted a lunar module to rendezvous with its mothership on the third revolution after lifting off from the Moon. To compress the timescale, single maneuvers would be designed to achieve multiple goals.

Rather than simply firing the aft thrusters to move clear of the Titan's second stage immediately after separating, Gemini 9 would make an *insertion velocity adjustment routine* (IVAR) burn that would correct the launcher's in-plane velocity error. A phase adjustment at the first apogee would raise the perigee to set up the general timing for the rendezvous. Then a combination burn at the start of the third revolution would refine the timing, tweak the apogee, and eliminate any out-of-plane error. The co-elliptic maneuver performed 90° later was to set up the reduced differential height of 12nmi. The terminal phase would be initiated later in that revolution.

Additionally, Gemini 9 was to use its Agena as a target to test out optical rendezvous techniques that would be used as contingencies on Apollo. The originally assigned crew of Elliot See and Charles Bassett had died in an aircraft accident in February 1966 and the flight passed to their backups: Tom Stafford and Gene Cernan.

Gemini 9's Agena was lost at launch due to the failure of its Atlas booster. Nevertheless, it was decided to push on and launch a stand-in, the *augmented target docking adapter* (ATDA) that had been built following the loss of the Gemini 6 Agena for precisely this situation. Having no propulsion, it would be inserted directly into the required orbit by its booster. If it too was lost, Gemini 9 would not have the necessary propulsion to reach the inert Agena from Gemini 8 so instead it would be launched on time and carry out such tasks as could be undertaken in the absence of a target vehicle.

The Atlas placed the ATDA into a circular orbit at 161nmi, but the telemetry was contradictory.

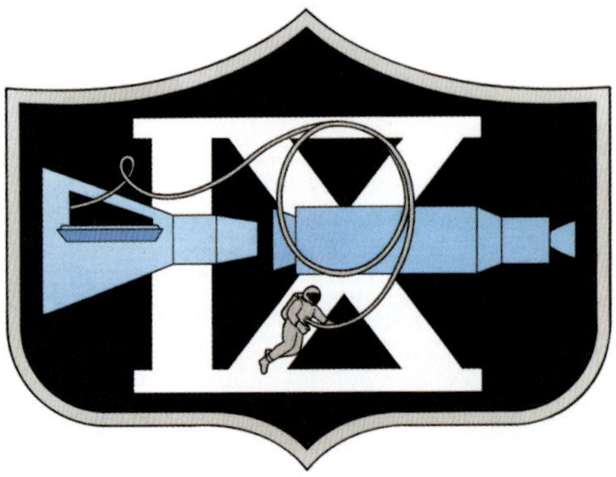

RIGHT In the crew patch for Gemini 9, the spacewalker's umbilical forms the numeral 9 against a docking Gemini and Agena. *(NASA)*

ABOVE After the original prime crew of Gemini 9, Elliot See and Charlie Bassett, were killed in an aircraft accident, the mission went to their backups, Tom Stafford and Gene Cernan (standing). *(NASA)*

The command to jettison the aerodynamic shroud that had protected the docking system during the ascent had been issued but the signal to verify its release had not been received. Worse, the vehicle was consuming attitude control propellant at a prodigious rate, leading flight controllers to switch off that system to save the remaining propellant. It was decided to launch Gemini 9 to rendezvous with the ATDA and report its condition.

Gemini 9 set off on June 3 1966 to attempt the "m=3" rendezvous using its new procedures. All went well until the lamp to indicate that the radar had locked on merely flickered. The target vehicle was meant to maintain its transponder facing the inbound spacecraft, so the intermittent lock was not good news. But there was nothing anyone could do about it. As they closed within 100nmi the radar improved, but now the computer was being confused in its attempt to calculate the details of the TPI burn. It appeared that every time they alternated the computer between its "Rendezvous" and "Catch-Up" modes, it restarted its sequence of measurements and calculations.

As the spacecraft slowly caught up, the elevation of the target increased. At a range of 75nmi it was 8° above the local horizon and Cernan began to take sightings. Meanwhile, mission control calculated the best time for the astronauts to place the computer into the "Rendezvous" mode so that if it proved able to make only one attempt at a solution, this would be delivered just in time to execute the maneuver. The recommendation was to activate "Rendezvous" at an elevation of 15.3°. The pitfall, of course, was that a single bad data point would ruin the computation.

Heading across the Atlantic on the third revolution, Stafford caught sight of the target as a faint speck against the stars. The result delivered by the computer disagreed with that calculated by mission control, so it was decided to make the maneuver based on the ground solution. When the target flew into the Earth's shadow, the astronauts were delighted to see its flashing beacon, because that implied that the shroud had separated to expose the docking system. But then they realized the beacon was intermittent. Worse, as Stafford tried to hold the target fixed against the stars, moonlight interfered with his dark adaptation and some 20 minutes into the transfer, with only 5nmi to go, he was still unable to see any stars. A two-day launch delay had placed the Moon in his field of view for the interception. Using the radar needles to maintain the spacecraft facing the target was not as accurate.

Once they could make out details of their quarry in the moonlight, it was seen to be fairly stable; rolling but not tumbling. "We've got a weird looking machine here," reported Stafford as he saw that the two halves of the shroud had opened but were fouled.

LEFT This "augmented target docking adapter," seen here during pre-flight checkout at Kennedy Space Center, was used for Gemini 9 after the loss of the Agena intended for the mission. *(NASA)*

BELOW As Gemini 9 closed in on the ATDA, it found the spacecraft to be tumbling, its shroud having failed to jettison giving it the appearance of an "angry alligator." *(NASA)*

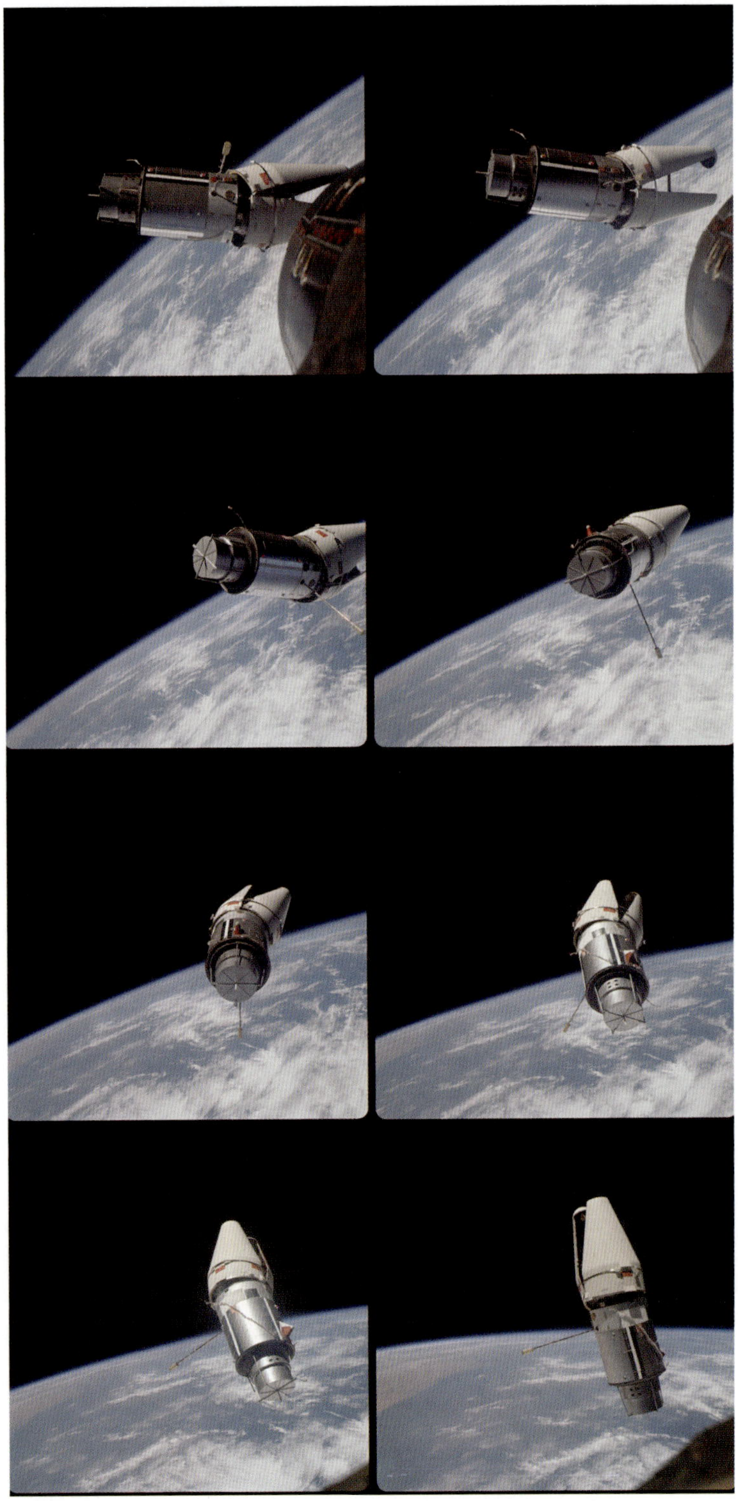

Pistons in the shroud had tried to force the halves apart but a strap at the base had prevented the sections from clearing the rim of the docking collar. After drawing to a halt alongside the target, he made a fly-around inspection and compared it to "an alligator" whose jaws were open in an asymmetric configuration which had evidently confused the attitude control system.

In an effort to shake the shroud loose, mission control decided to cycle the docking mechanism, extending and retracting the collar. Stafford moved off to observe as the ATDA's thrusters fired to counteract the disturbance. The motion of the collar animated the alligator's jaws and pitched the vehicle, but the strap held the shroud. The effort was called off. Stafford's suggestion that he try to release the shroud by nudging it with the nose of his craft was declined. The docking would later be cancelled.

As Gemini 9 started its fourth revolution, and barely 45 minutes after drawing up alongside its target, it was ordered to withdraw and proceed with the second rendezvous, originally planned for the second day. This involved maneuvering into an elliptical orbit which had the same period as their current circular orbit, a preliminary to testing whether the TPI burn could be calculated by tracking the target optically.

The plan was to make a burn away from Earth's center, a so-called radial burn. The resulting equi-period elliptical orbit would have an apogee 90° around from the point of separation and some 2.5nmi above it. Its perigee would be a similar distance below. When Gemini 9 was above the ATDA it would travel more slowly and slip behind and when it was lower it would catch up. By the time it reached the opposite side of the orbit from the point of separation, the spacecraft would be trailing the target by 11nmi. This arrangement meant that at perigee, Gemini 9 would be able to set up for TPI as if it had just made the co-elliptic burn, although because the altitude difference was only a few miles the transfer would subtend a much smaller central angle. This time the spacecraft was to maintain a horizontal attitude and Cernan would measure the target's elevation using a sextant to enable the computer to calculate the time of TPI for a rendezvous shortly prior to orbital sunset.

Because their prospects were strongly dependent on the purity of this vertical separation burn, Stafford aimed his spacecraft's nose directly at Earth and then used the forward-firing thrusters to impart a purely radial impulse. Sunset was eight minutes later, so while they still had sunlight Cernan lined up the sextant and tried to track the ATDA as it slipped away beneath them. He found that keeping track of the bright speck moving against the backdrop of clouds was extremely difficult. After sunset, however, he was able to follow its acquisition lights against the dark planet below. As a check, Cernan took note of when the target passed through the local horizontal, which was within 20 seconds of the nominal time.

As they started to catch up with the ATDA in daylight, Cernan took sextant sightings but airglow made the horizon indistinct, complicating measuring the angle of elevation. Nevertheless, they were successful. Since they had a significant amount of propellant remaining, it was decided to attempt a third type of rendezvous.

Just 30 minutes later they were off again. This time they adopted a lower orbit which would cause Gemini 9 to draw ahead of the ATDA. Once clear, the spacecraft was powered down and the astronauts had supper.

When they awoke eight hours later, the spacecraft was 60nmi ahead of its target. Two burns were made half an orbit apart, the first for phasing and the second to create an apogee 7nmi above the orbit of the ATDA. As their radar would be tracking the target, they oriented BEF for the co-elliptic maneuver to raise the perigee. This ensured they would not lose radar lock. The burn was made without incident. One item of good news was that the computer problem that had impaired the initial rendezvous was no longer present. Being lower, the ATDA was catching up, but from the astronauts' perspective it was they who were approaching it.

For this test the terminal phase was to be flown in daylight, so the TPI burn would be some time close to sunrise. But as they tried to get sightings of the target in the dark, they could not see the ATDA's acquisition lights at all. Their first sighting of it was in reflected moonlight at a range of 20nmi. Meanwhile, Cernan began to feed the radar data into the computer. Starting the terminal phase, they lost sight of the target when it crossed the terminator into daylight. Stafford switched to the radar needles to maintain the nose alignment while the computer continued to process the pitch angle, which was below the horizon because they were aimed at an object in a lower orbit. Towards the end of the transfer, they were looking down at the Sahara. This had been arranged to enable them to view the target against the dunes and dark lava flows of the desert, the bleakness of which, it was believed, would be a fair approximation of the Moon's surface.

Stafford knew where the target ought to be, because his optical sight was boresighted

BELOW LEFT Tom Stafford, commander of Gemini 9, in space. *(NASA)*

BELOW A graphical representation of Gemini 9's third rendezvous in which they approached the target from above. The loops along the bottom represent the spacecraft's orbital rise and fall during their sleep period as they drifted away from the ATDA. The height adjust burn initiated the rendezvous. *(NASA/David Woods)*

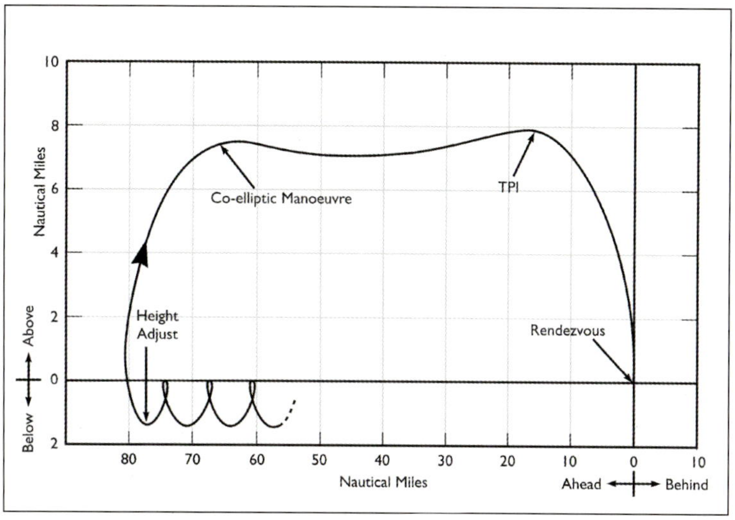

with the radar, but he could not see it. An Apollo mothership trying to rescue a lunar module which was stranded in low orbit would not have radar, so the point of the test was to assess optical tracking. Finally, at a range of 3nmi he spotted the target. But it was difficult to hold because the terrain below drifted so rapidly across the field of view of his optical sight and the variation in albedo was striking.

As they set out across the Indian Ocean, Stafford was readily able to see the ATDA as a white dot against the blue water, but lost it while over cloud formations. Closing within 6,000ft, he started to brake. As the target loomed in his optical sight he reckoned he was coming in too fast and, in over-braking, attained a negative range-rate which cost a lot of propellant to correct. On making contact with Carnarvon he was able to report that they were station-keeping.

From the point of view of evaluating rendezvous methods, Gemini 9 was a remarkable success. It had not been possible to dock, but this was a minor issue because the ATDA could not have supplied any propulsion. Once the photographs of the fouled shroud were examined, the error was identified. Technicians from one company had been briefed by a supervisor from another. When they installed the shroud, the supervisor had been called away and his verbal instructions for how to finish the job had been misunderstood. Lanyards had been taped in place when they ought not to have been. It was just one of those things that can happen with a one-off item like the ATDA.

RIGHT Gemini 10's mission patch shows the spacecraft's orbital pursuit of its Agena. *(NASA)*

One mission, two Agenas

The baton was passed to John Young and Michael Collins on the Gemini 10 mission. Thus far, "m=4" and "m=3" had been demonstrated but not without massive help from mission control. As NASA sought to stretch its capabilities, Collins was to perform an exercise in optical navigation on the first revolution to assess the scope for using a sextant to measure the elevations of stars above the horizon in order to determine the spacecraft's orbit. This done, he would compute the sequence of maneuvers for an "m=3" rendezvous. In parallel, mission control would calculate the maneuvers in the usual way. If the sequence computed by Collins seemed reasonable then that would be used, otherwise the ground solution would be used.

Furthermore, if all went well, Gemini 10 was to use its Agena to set up a second rendezvous with the Agena from Gemini 8, parked in high orbit. This would demonstrate docked maneuvers by having Gemini 10 ignite the *primary propulsion system* (PPS) of its Agena in order to reach this second target. Moreover, because the battery of the old Agena would long-since have expired, its transponder would not be operating and the terminal phase would have to be performed without radar tracking.

Planners decided this second rendezvous would use a phasing orbit with an apogee at 400nmi, almost twice that of the target and a record-breaking altitude for any human. This introduced the issue of exposing the crew to the trapped charged-particle radiation in the van Allen Belt. It was decided to orient the apogee to avoid the South Atlantic Anomaly, a zone off the coast of Brazil where the electrons and protons trapped by the Earth's magnetic field dipped down towards the ionosphere.

On July 18 1966, both the 10-Agena and Gemini 10 were inserted into the 8-Agena's orbital plane with the 10-Agena entering a 160nmi circular orbit. Gemini 10's launch vehicle left it 26ft/sec short in velocity so Young corrected this with the IVAR burn. The resulting 145.1nmi apogee was off by a mere 0.1nmi. Its Agena was 900nmi ahead, and the 8-Agena was 100nmi above that and trailing by about 500 miles.

ABOVE John Young and Mike Collins enjoy a hearty low-residue pre-launch breakfast of steak and eggs. *(NASA)*

As they flew out over the Atlantic and the evening terminator loomed, Collins used a Kollsman sextant to take a few sightings of the brightest star in the constellation of Cassiopeia. He found that measuring the elevation of a star above the horizon was more difficult than in the simulator. With no Moon to illuminate the Earth the boundary between the dark limb of the planet and the black sky was ill-defined. But as his eyes adapted to the darkness, he was able to discern a line along the horizon. He had just over 30 minutes of orbital darkness in which to carry out a series of sightings of two stars, one directly ahead and the other behind, with Young turning the vehicle around to face each star in turn. As Collins measured the brightest star in Aries he realized that what had seemed to be the limb was actually the top of the airglow layer. In the final minutes of darkness he followed Vega, the brightest star in Lyra, to what he presumed was the horizon and timed its disappearance, only to observe it momentarily reappear before finally fading away for good.

Collins entered each sighting into the computer, but he did not reckon the orbit calculation would be worth much because the measurements had too much variability. As he passed over the US at the end of the first revolution he reported his solution for achieving co-elliptic orbit, and mission control said to use the solution based on radar tracking.

Once in the co-elliptic orbit, 15nmi below that of the 10-Agena and 100nmi behind but catching up, Collins ran the computer through its calculations for TPI. His solution called for a forward component of 41ft/sec. Houston said 34ft/sec and decided that Collins should use his own result. On entering the Earth's shadow Young spotted the light beacon on the target. On closing within 2nmi it became evident that something had gone awry, because they ought not to have reached this point until shortly after sunrise. It meant he would have to brake in darkness. Then Collins said that they were at 600ft and holding. For some reason, they had drawn to a halt far from the target.

Young thrust forward to resume moving towards the target, only to draw to a halt once again at about 300ft. Then the range began to open, and he had to fight to close to 120ft. A glow on the horizon presaged sunrise. Young fought his way in and then docked.

As would be determined after the mission, when Gemini 10's inertial platform was initialized, it was slightly misaligned, meaning that the spacecraft was not flying in quite the plane that its platform implied. Instead of reducing the range and range-rate to zero simultaneously, their solution had brought the vehicle to a halt some 600ft to the left of the target. Then, with the vehicles travelling in slightly inclined orbits, the range had varied as Gemini 10's trajectory traced a helical arc in to the target. They had seen such a situation in simulations when they were out-of-plane, but

LEFT Gemini 10's Agena at the top of its Atlas booster during preparations for launch. Its aerodynamic shroud has yet to be installed. *(NASA)*

ABOVE **Mike Collins takes a picture out of his window as John Young maneuvers Gemini 10 into position to dock with its Agena target vehicle.** *(NASA)*

this time their instruments had misled them into thinking they were in-plane. Such a large amount of propellant had been consumed in eliminating this out-of-plane error to complete the rendezvous that there was insufficient left to pursue the mission as it had been planned. However, the 10-Agena had plenty of propellant. It was about to get used to take Gemini 10 up to their high apogee as they began their overnight chase of the 8-Agena. Mission control decided that instead of discarding the 10-Agena after that task, they should hang onto it to husband what was left of their own propellant.

At 16,000lb of thrust, the Agena's PPS was expected to deliver a real kick when it lit, and with Gemini 10 flying BEF it would be an "eyeballs out" maneuver for the crew. Since there was a significant risk of the big engine

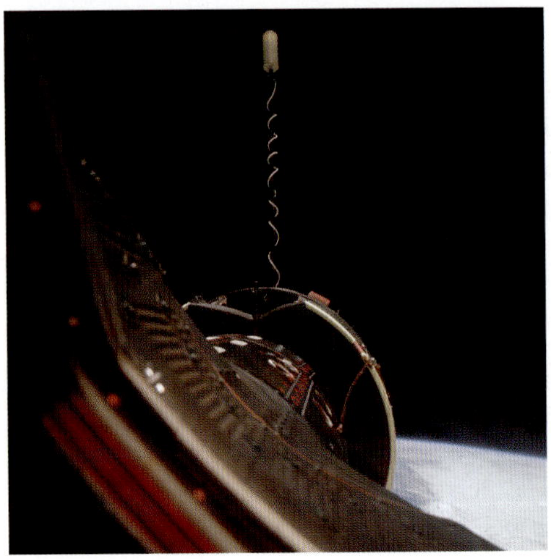

RIGHT **Gemini 10 moments after docking. The index bar on the spacecraft is fully nestled within the V-shaped groove in the docking collar.** *(NASA)*

misfiring, there was tension in mission control, and indeed in space, as the moment of ignition approached. The burn was to be made while in contact with Hawaii so that the performance could be monitored. To initiate the maneuver, the low-thrust engines of the secondary propulsion system fired briefly to settle the propellants in their tanks. Then the PPS fired for 14 seconds.

No one had ever seen a large rocket motor fire in space and, by facing backwards, Young and Collins had a magnificent view. If they detected any indication of instability in the combustion, they were to shut down the engine using a specially installed switch that was wired through the docking adapter directly to the Agena's engine controller. All went well. After the engine shut down, it continued to vent propellant and made a spectacular sight.

Given that the objective was an apogee at 410nmi, the resulting 160 by 412nmi orbit was excellent. As they climbed towards their unprecedented apogee, attention turned towards the dosimeters. The readings were amazingly low, barely 10% of the expected level. Since the PPS burn had been made at sunset, they made the climb in darkness and did not receive their first high view until apogee at sunrise, but because the Agena maintained a horizontal configuration its bulk allowed them only a sliver of the horizon out to either side.

Next day, on awakening, the chase continued. Overnight, the 8-Agena in its 216nmi circular orbit had caught up with and drawn ahead of the

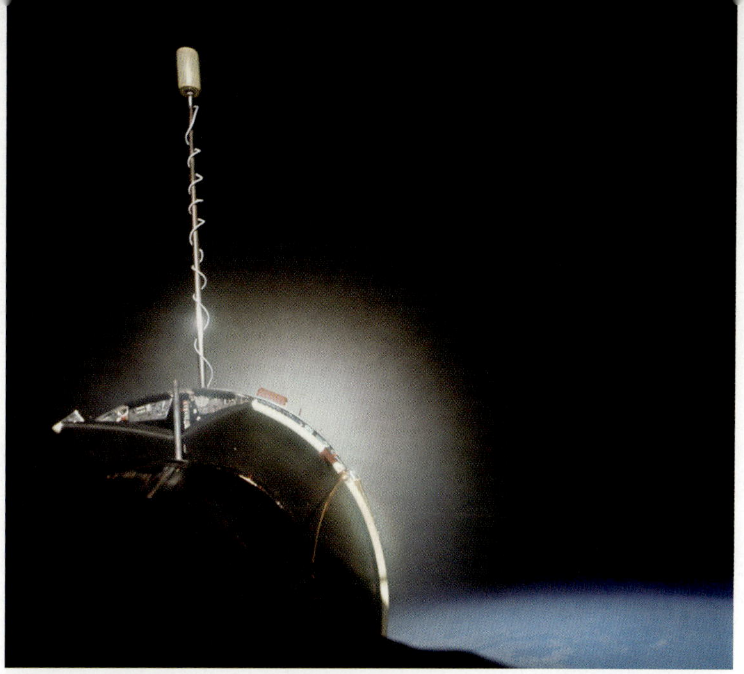

ABOVE The exhaust plume of the Agena's primary propulsion system during the first ever docked maneuver. *(NASA)*

docked combination. Using the Agena's PPS, they lowered their apogee to 206nmi. Then at apogee one-and-a-half revolutions later, their co-elliptic burn raised the perigee to circularize at this altitude. At that point, the astronauts retired for their second sleep period.

On awakening, Young and Collins were told to proceed with the second rendezvous. The first task was to use the secondary propulsion system of the Agena to correct a slight out-of-plane error imparted by the first PPS burn. With only ten minutes to go, upon seeing northern constellations out of his window, Young realized that they were pointing in precisely the wrong direction for the northward correction. They managed to yaw through 180° just in time to perform the burn. The final phase adjustment was executed about 20 minutes later. The 8-Agena was 246nmi ahead.

Although it was being conducted rather higher than usual, this rendezvous had been routine thus far. However, the catch-up was being pursued slowly in order to establish the required lighting for the terminal phase, which would be the really demanding part of the exercise. The 8-Agena's radar transponder was unavailable, so mission control intended to steer Gemini 10 precisely to the TPI point. Thereafter the crew would have to rely on visual sightings, which meant making the transfer in daylight.

Furthermore, since their target had no lights, the braking phase would have to be finished prior to sunset, lest the two spacecraft collide in the ensuing period of darkness. If all went well, Young would then hold the 8-Agena in the beam of his docking lamp while Collins prepared to start a spacewalk at sunrise. Given the meager amount of OAMS propellant, there was little margin for error. After a tweak of the phasing by the secondary propulsion system of the Agena, Gemini 10 undocked, moved clear, and performed a burn to optimize the lighting in the terminal phase.

Then the orbit was adjusted to maintain a differential of precisely 7nmi beneath the target. At sunrise, the target was 29nmi ahead and at an elevation above their local horizontal of 13.5°. At TPI, 23 minutes later, the range had halved and the angle was 33°; some 5° higher than the canonical case owing to the smaller differential height. Young rolled his vehicle inverted to place the Sun behind its nose so as to enable him to view the target in daylight without his optical sight being flooded with light. Lacking radar to measure range or range-rate, Collins was to use his narrow-field sextant to estimate the apparent size of the target and then calculate its range. He was not optimiztic of his chances.

When he estimated they were 2nmi out and closing at 50ft/sec, Young started to brake.

BELOW A graphical representation of Gemini 10's rendezvous with the inert 8-Agena. 1. A phasing maneuver performed by the 10-Agena PPS to place the spacecraft in an orbit with an apogee nearly 200nmi higher than the target. 2. Height adjust burn to reduce the apogee in order to play catch-up with the target. 3. Plane change maneuver. 4. Co-elliptic maneuver to achieve an orbit at a constant height just below the target. 5. TPI burn to initiate the terminal phase of the rendezvous. *(NASA/David Woods)*

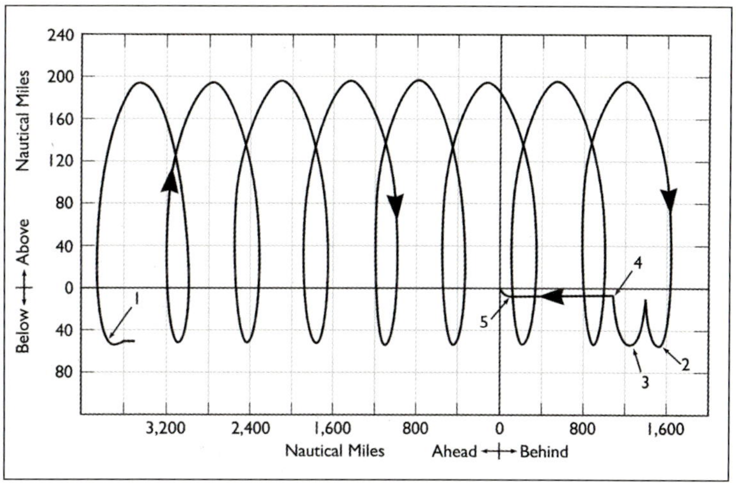

ABOVE Shortly prior to TPI as Gemini 10 rendezvoused with the 8-Agena, the crew announced that they had their target in sight. "Ninety-five miles is pretty long range," teased CapCom C.C. Williams because it was actually the recently discarded 10-Agena just a few miles away. *(NASA)*

Soon after Collins had estimated they had about 1,000ft to go, the range-rate tailed off. It appeared, as previously, that they were drawing to a halt short of their target. Judging he had the propellant, Young continued to bore in and achieved a station-keeping position with the OAMS supply at only 12% of its initial load; the cutoff point had been 10%, the amount that they would require to conclude the mission.

Several hours after Collins performed a spacewalk to retrieve a meteoroid package from the 8-Agena, Gemini 10 broke out of its high circular orbit. The plan called for a burn of 100ft/sec, but the system would peter out when the regulator fell below its minimum operating pressure and the engineers predicted they would achieve only 75ft/sec. However, the astronauts reported that they got the full 100 and still had propellant left. The resulting perigee at 158nmi would ensure a de-orbit even if one of the four solid rockets in the retrograde section of the adapter module failed to fire. Gemini 10 returned to Earth a remarkable success.

Rendezvous in one

Gemini continued to test possible scenarios for Apollo. In particular, how might an Apollo lunar module abort its descent to the Moon and perform a rapid return to its mothership. The primary objective for Gemini 11 was therefore to attempt an intensive series of maneuvers designed to achieve interception barely one hour after launch.

To achieve this "m=1" rendezvous, the post-separation IVAR burn would correct the inclination and a second burn executed 90° around from the insertion point would make the orbit coplanar with the Agena. Hopefully the out-of-plane error would be trivial if the liftoff was on schedule and the Titan's upper stage steered true, but the launch window would be open for a mere two seconds.

Pete Conrad, the commander, cast around for something to do with his Agena's propulsive power that would capture the imagination. One idea was to rendezvous with a Pegasus satellite, named after the mythical winged horse because it had unfolded two long thin panels bearing sensors to report strikes by micrometeoroids. Spanning nearly 100ft, these wings would be a spectacular sight, but this proposal was rejected.

RIGHT The Gemini 11 crew of Dick Gordon and Pete Conrad preparing for water egress training in the Gulf of Mexico. *(NASA)*

FAR RIGHT The mission patch for Gemini 11 included a representation of their first-orbit rendezvous and the subsequent very high apogee orbit that would be provided by the Agena. *(NASA)*

RIGHT An artist's rendering of a Pegasus satellite with its meteoroid-detecting wings deployed. *(NASA)*

At that time, NASA's meteorological satellites orbited at 675nmi and transmitted monochrome television imagery. However, the Weather Bureau was considering using a color camera on its next generation of satellites. Conrad convinced the meteorologists that if Gemini 11 employed its Agena to raise its apogee to that altitude, it would be able to take pictures on film for comparison with the television from the satellites in order to assist in assessing the value of color in such work. When Gemini 10 found the radiation to be less intense than predicted at 412nmi, Conrad was given permission to go higher with the safety proviso that he could make only two passes at high altitude.

Gemini 11 lifted off only 0.5 seconds late, well within the window for an "m=1" rendezvous. The Titan left them with a 39ft/sec shortfall, so after a brief burst of the OAMS to move clear of the spent stage Conrad pitched the nose down to the horizon to burn the forward component of the IVAR and correct the apogee to that required for initiating the terminal phase of the rendezvous. Then he burned the 5ft/sec radial IVAR correction that established an 87 by 151nmi orbit. The 1ft/sec out-of-plane error was so minor that he opted to incorporate it into the 90° correction.

As Gemini 11 left the Eastern Test Range behind, it was off to an excellent start. On spotting the Agena visually at a range of about 50nmi, Conrad activated the radar but got only intermittent returns. After yawing around for the 3ft/sec northward plane change he resumed SEF to give the radar another look, and this time obtained a solid lock-on. The plan was to initiate the terminal phase just after apogee, when 18.9nmi behind and 8.6nmi below the target. For this differential altitude the shorter transfer would subtend an angle of only 120°.

Approaching sunset, Conrad maintained his vehicle pitched up at the Agena. As soon as

RIGHT Gemini 11 heads for space, its launch photographed from inside the lowered erector tower. *(NASA)*

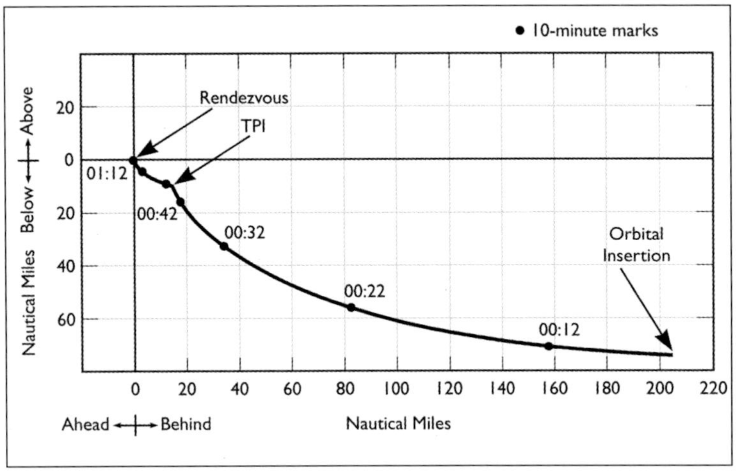

ABOVE A graphical representation of Gemini 11's single-orbit rendezvous with its Agena target vehicle, a task that at the start of the program had been deemed impossible. *(NASA/David Woods)*

his eyes adapted to the darkness he centered the beacon in his optical sight. Meanwhile, Dick Gordon used the computer to obtain a result for their upcoming TPI and compared this to his own calculations and those of mission control. Since they were in close agreement, Conrad decided to accept the computer's values of 140ft/sec forward, 27 down and 5 left. The climb to the target began while passing over Western Australia.

After 12 minutes, Conrad made the first mid-transfer correction calculated by the computer. Then the radar needles started to stray, as if the strength of the radar signal was inconstant. But the target was not drifting relative to the stars so he omitted the second correction and began to brake at a range of 6,000ft. A moment later, the Agena emerged from the Earth's shadow and the sunlight reflecting off it dazzled his dark-adapted eyes. As they approached 500ft, he was able to judge range and range-rate visually by the size of the target in his optical sight.

Their report that they were station-keeping at 50ft raised a round of applause in mission control. Even though they had flown the "brute force" rendezvous, they had consumed no more propellant than Gemini 6 had during its long and careful chase of Gemini 7. To wrap up, they closed in and docked.

As Gemini 11 headed out over the Atlantic Ocean on its second revolution, Conrad undocked for an experiment in which he was to fly around the Agena while a sensor measured how the charged particles of the ionosphere flowed around that vehicle. The redocking was performed by Gordon. As they ate lunch, mission control gave the go-ahead for docked maneuvers. A preliminary burn to calibrate the PPS was made above Hawaii, where its telemetry could be monitored. This was done out-of-plane in order not to disturb the circular orbit. The next item on the busy flight plan was to repeat the undocking/docking in darkness to determine whether it was more difficult than in daylight.

The highlight of the third day in space was lighting the big engine. The apogee-raising burn was to occur close to their existing perigee, which would remain unchanged at 155nmi. The Agena was programed to achieve 912ft/sec, and although the tail-off of the thrust gave an overshoot of 6ft/sec, this was of no concern. The 750nmi apogee occurred above eastern Australia to avoid the South Atlantic Anomaly. The dosimeter readings were slightly less than for Gemini 10 flying at half that altitude. After making two high passes, they were to resume their low circular orbit. The prospects for photography were excellent because the Horn of Africa was fairly clear, there was mixed cloud over the Indian Ocean, and although Jakarta was socked in, almost the entire Australian continent was visible.

Unlike Gemini 10 they were oriented for Earth observation. As they climbed to apogee Conrad had India out of the left window, and Gordon had Australia out of the right window, with the sunset terminator just beyond. Once in the Earth's shadow, they took pictures of the horizon to document the airglow which occurs in layers of varying intensity up to an altitude of about 150nmi. Previous missions had photographed it from just above its ceiling, but from their high vantage point Conrad and Gordon were able to observe it on a grander scale. After the perigee pass over the US they headed up again for more photography, and then, back at perigee, the Agena was burned to resume the low circular orbit.

Conrad had endorsed another experiment which, if they managed to pull it off, promised to be spectacular. In late 1965 it had been suggested that a spacewalker could hook up a tether to the Agena for two engineering tests. For one, the Gemini would position itself directly above the target and test the ability of the tether to maintain the vehicles stable in the

RIGHT As Gemini 11 climbed towards its high apogee, its crew had an unprecedented view of their planet. In this case, we see the Horn of Africa and across the Gulf of Aden to the Arabian peninsula. *(NASA)*

CENTER A view of the Indian subcontinent as Gemini 11 continued its climb towards apogee. *(NASA)*

gravity gradient. In the second test, inspired by the popular perception of a space station as a "wheel in space," the tethered system was to be set rotating around its center of mass to assess the scope for creating artificial gravity.

After Gordon had attached the tether, Conrad aligned the docked combination with its long axis oriented vertically and the Agena on the bottom, then undocked and slowly opened the range to draw the tether out of its container. But things did not go to plan. In the weightless environment of action and reaction, various dynamics set in and worsened as the tether approached its 100ft length and soaked up more energy.

Realizing that it would be very difficult to establish the static configuration required for the gravity gradient experiment, Conrad moved on to the rotational experiment. But every time he withdrew, to pull the tether taut, the two vehicles rebounded and the tether went slack. At one point it had a pronounced bow and rotated in the manner of a skipping rope. Nevertheless, he was able to set the system rotating with a period of about 10min/cycle, half of the planned rate, and observe the resulting centrifugal force slowly drive a loose object inside the cabin. After passing through the Earth's shadow in this state, they jettisoned the tether, leaving the Agena inverted and the tether stretched out horizontally.

The tether experiments had consumed rather more fuel than expected, but plenty still remained and mission control suggested a new kind of rendezvous. As the spacecraft's

RIGHT A view of the northwestern coast of Australia taken as Gemini 11 neared its 750nmi apogee. *(NASA)*

ABOVE The 11-Agena during tether experiments over Baja California. The Agena is directly below Gemini 11 as a test of the gravity gradient effect. *(NASA)*

radar was still in the anomalous state that it had assumed during the later stage of the initial rendezvous, radar tracking by the World-Wide Tracking Network would be used to steer Gemini 11 to a position from which the crew would be able to rendezvous. After resuming station-keeping, Conrad performed a prograde/up separation burn to achieve an elliptical orbit with an early apogee. At the intersecting node about 75 minutes later they made a retrograde burn to resume the Agena's orbit and maintain station a few miles behind it. Then Conrad and Gordon rounded out their day with a cold supper and went to sleep. Because the cancellation burn had not been exact, the range opened to about 25nmi during the night.

The purpose of the rendezvous was to use ground radar tracking to maneuver in such a manner as to simulate arriving at the apogee of a Hohmann transfer orbit, at which time the crew were to brake based on optical tracking. This was to be achieved by establishing a condition in which, as the range to the Agena reduced, the relative velocity approximated that at one of the midcourse corrections of the canonical 130° transfer. One option was to descend sufficiently far to produce a fast catch-up and execute the interception early on, but this would not provide much time for tracking. The other option was to allow the radars time to determine the ideal moment to initiate the braking phase and only then establish the desired relative velocity. Since it was to be initiated from the same orbit as the target, the flight controllers referred to it as a stable-orbit rendezvous, but to fighter pilots like Conrad and Gordon it was a ground-controlled interception.

Conrad made a retrograde/down burn to enter an elliptical orbit with its perigee 5nmi below the orbit of the target vehicle in order that after subtending a central angle of 258°, with Gemini 11 rising again, its trajectory would mimic both the ascent to the apogee of a Hohmann transfer and the point in a canonical transfer 34° prior to initiating braking. If they braked successfully, they would draw alongside the Agena some 292° from their starting point. Houston's willingness to try such a rendezvous indicated its mastery of orbital operations.

The sequence was initiated approaching Australia. Radar at Woomera checked the result of the burn. Half a revolution later, they were nearing perigee and about 4nmi below the orbit of the target, with ground radars monitoring so that the final maneuver could be calculated. Gordon was to calculate this burn independently on the basis of his optical tracking. In Earth's shadow, Conrad found that he could not track the Agena by its lights because the view through his sight was obscured by a grease spot on his window. As the target entered daylight, it was blindingly bright. The midcourse correction of a simulated terminal phase transfer was to be executed six minutes later, over the Atlantic. As they reached the end of the Eastern Test Range, mission control gave its estimate as 6ft/sec forward and 2.4ft/sec to the right.

The fact that Gordon had a viable solution was encouraging. After the burn, he used the rate of increase of pitch to calculate their range and range-rate until the range was approaching 6,000ft, at which point, as had Mike Collins, he switched to estimating its angular size in his sextant. At 1,000ft they were closing at 15ft/sec, and Conrad started to brake. In their absence, the gravity gradient had realigned the Agena vertically with its engine down and drawn the tether straight upwards.

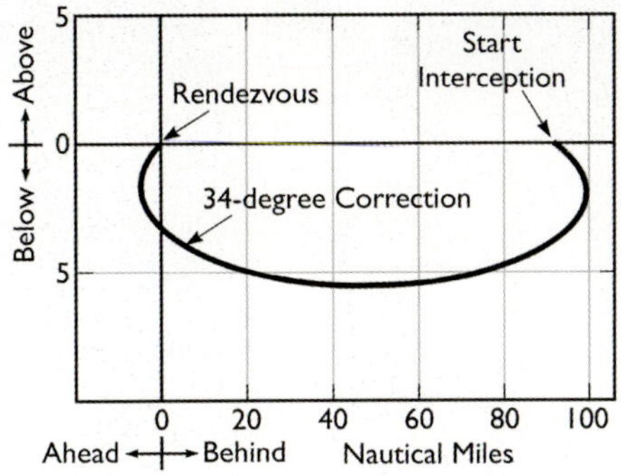

LEFT **A graphical representation of Gemini 11's stable-orbit rendezvous in which the spacecraft started off 90nmi behind the target but in the same orbit. It then dropped down in order to catch up.** *(NASA/David Woods)*

Station-keeping once again, Conrad and Gordon, both familiar with the practice of extending a sortie by in-flight refuelling, joked that if NASA were to send up a tanker, they were willing to push on with some more orbital operations.

Gemini 12

By the final mission of the Gemini program, and with all the flight-worthy Agenas used up, it was necessary to refurbish the one which had been used for ground testing. Planners decided that Gemini 12 should perform the standard "m=3" rendezvous, then use the Agena to achieve an orbit with a 400nmi apogee above the continental United States to obtain unprecedented photography of the nation.

BELOW **The 11-Agena is photographed during station-keeping. Parts of its surface are heavily blistered and flaking off.** *(NASA)*

RIGHT Lovell and Aldrin walk up the ramp of Launch Complex 19 for Gemini 12 symbolizing the end of the program with messages attached to the back of their suits. *(NASA)*

The crew of Jim Lovell and Buzz Aldrin arrived at the launch pad with cards on their backs, one saying "THE" and the other saying "END." No sooner had the pad cooled down after launch than a salvage team arrived to start the decommissioning process by stripping it of anything useful.

Their Titan left them 24ft/sec short, so Lovell rectified this with the IVAR burn followed by a series of burns that brought them into a co-elliptic orbit 10nmi beneath the Agena. They got a radar lock-on at the record range of 236nmi and Aldrin sighted it with his sextant at a range of 85nmi. Then a gremlin struck.

RIGHT The Gemini 12 mission patch. *(NASA)*

As Aldrin prepared the computer to monitor the radar during the ensuing catch-up phase, the range-rate became nonsensical. In fact, the lock-on light had gone out as well. Deciding not to rely on the radar, Aldrin retrieved the backup optical tracking charts. He had earned a PhD in rendezvous from MIT prior to becoming an astronaut, and had helped to develop the backup procedures. Now he could put theory into practice and calculate the maneuver himself.

Lovell kept the Agena centered in his optical sight and at the required pitch angle he initiated the terminal phase. The fact that the target remained fixed relative to the stars meant the corrections were very small. On the nominal rendezvous they would have waited for sunrise before starting to brake, but as they slipped within 10,000ft he began a braking sequence. As they slowly closed within 500ft, he held the Agena in the spacecraft's spotlight. A few minutes after they drew to a halt, the Sun rose. A year earlier, losing the radar/computer interface prior to the terminal phase of a rendezvous would have been a "show stopper."

Once they had docked, Aldrin issued commands to the Agena to perform yaw maneuvers for a stress test of the docking collar. The next item on the checklist was

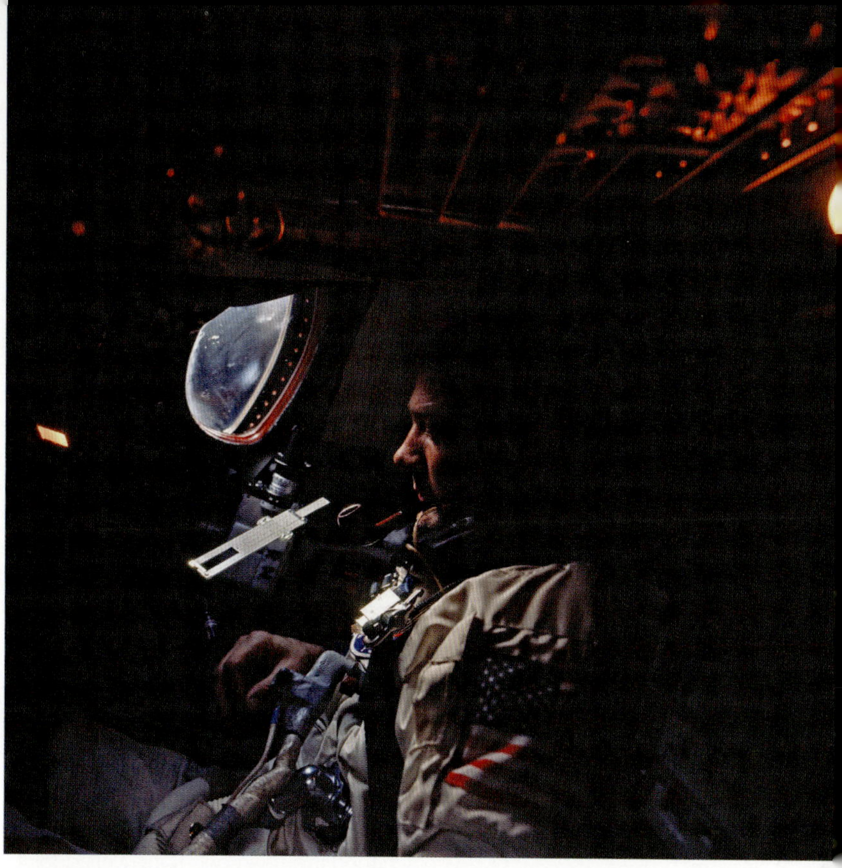

ABOVE Gemini-Titan 12, the final flight of the program, heads for space and an "m=3" rendezvous with its Agena. *(NASA)*

ABOVE Buzz Aldrin, unlit pipe in his mouth, consults his weightless backup computer, otherwise known as a slide rule. *(NASA)*

BELOW The 12-Agena prior to docking. This shot nicely shows the PPS which had suffered an anomaly during orbit insertion thereby preventing it from being restarted to achieve a high apogee. *(NASA)*

BELOW A dramatic shot of the 12-Agena prior to docking. *(NASA)*

a series of undocking and redocking trials, so Lovell withdrew. On entering the Earth's shadow he turned on his spotlight and prepared to redock. As he drove his nose into the Agena's collar, the two vehicles were not correctly aligned and only one of the three latches triggered, inducing an unexpected motion and jamming the spacecraft in the conical docking adapter. Repeatedly firing the fore/aft thrusters in order to break free produced an awful grating vibration. After the Agena had restabilized itself, further tests confirmed that there was no problem with the hardware; it had been an unfortunate misalignment in darkness.

Once redocked, mission control passed up some real bad news. As the Agena had climbed to its operating orbit, radio telemetry had indicated an anomaly in its big engine. An overspeed in the fuel pump had caused fluctuations in the thrust chamber pressure. The engineers recommended against reigniting the PPS. Although this ruled out maneuvering for a high apogee, it would be possible to pursue an alternative by using the secondary propulsion system to enter an orbit that would enable the spacecraft to pass directly between the Moon and Earth during a solar eclipse.

When they yawed around for the preliminary phasing burn, Lovell was surprised that the Agena overshot by 40°. Its attitude control system took a while to line it up correctly, and even then the vehicle had a tendency to roll. The likelihood that the rapid turn had left the propellants sloshing around in their tanks raised concern in Houston about the vehicle's stability during the burn. If this had been the first mission to attempt a docked maneuver using the Agena, NASA would probably have cancelled the burn, but Lovell was given permission to proceed at his discretion. In the event, the Agena never strayed more than a few degrees from the desired attitude during the maneuver.

As Lovell and Aldrin began their first sleep period, the flight controllers revised the schedule to take account of the fact that the PPS was not available. On awakening, they performed another burn to optimize the timing of their passage through the Moon's shadow cone. With just eight seconds of totality available, there was feverish activity. The plan required them to shoot three photographs at various exposures in the hope of documenting the solar corona projecting around the lunar disc, then yaw around to use a 16mm movie camera to record the shadow of the Moon racing across the face of the Earth. In the event, the yaw maneuver was performed slowly to preclude upsetting the Agena, and by the time they were facing the Earth the spot of the Moon's shadow had receded over the horizon.

During a spacewalk, Aldrin had connected a tether between the spacecraft and its Agena so that they could further investigate the gravity gradient phenomenon. With the docked combination in a vertical orientation and the Agena below, Lovell undocked and eased back to start to draw out the tether. One issue, which had also affected Gemini 11, was that the tether was connected to a short rod that projected sideways from the Gemini's nose and when the tether was pulled taut it jerked the vehicle around. This was a particular problem for Lovell because two of his thrusters had malfunctioned; whenever he tried to yaw or pitch up to cancel the rotation imparted by the tether, he gained an anomalous roll.

Over time, the tethered system slowly traced out an arc of a circle. Having begun directly above the Agena, Gemini 12 had first drifted ahead of it and then to one side. Whenever the tether went taut it gently drew the vehicles back and relaxed again. Eventually they achieved a configuration in which the vehicles were stationary with the tether taut between them. The system oscillated slowly 60° to either side of vertical, but it was evident they had been captured. Given sufficient time, the oscillations would have damped out. Satisfied, Lovell undocked and shortly thereafter returned to Earth.

When the lunar orbit rendezvous mode was selected for Apollo in 1962, people questioned whether orbital rendezvous was feasible. But by the end of the Gemini program in 1966, NASA had demonstrated its mastery of bringing two spacecraft together, with and without technological aids.

LEFT The 12-Agena on a tether which Lovell successfully managed to straighten out in the gravity gradient, seen here passing over Baja California. *(NASA)*

LEFT High altitude clouds straddling the River Nile and the Red Sea, as seen by Gemini 12. *(NASA)*

Chapter Twelve

Spacewalking

When studies for *extravehicular activity* (EVA), or spacewalking as it is popularly known, started in 1962, there were no plans for such activities on Apollo lunar missions. Nevertheless, it offered a contingency procedure in the event of a lunar module which had just lifted off the Moon being unable to dock with its mothership. And longer-term projects were already being investigated in which Apollo vehicles would be used to assemble facilities in orbit around Earth.

OPPOSITE In what was perhaps the most influential and terrifying spacewalk in NASA's history, astronaut Gene Cernan struggles with a looping umbilical and the unfamiliar Newtonian environment of weightlessness during the mission of Gemini 9. *(NASA)*

ABOVE **Astronauts Ed White (left) and Jim McDivitt two days prior to the launch of their Gemini 4 mission.** *(NASA)*

BELOW **Soviet cosmonaut Alexei Leonov made history on March 18, 1965 by leaving his Voskhod 2 spacecraft for a 12-minute spacewalk.** *(Getty Images)*

In January 1964, planners began to consider assigning the first EVA investigation to an early Gemini mission but this was not a high priority and was contingent on the development of the requisite apparatus and operational procedures. The step-by-step plan called for a preliminary experiment in which an astronaut was simply to swing open the hatch and poke his head and shoulders above the casing to assess exposure to the space environment. The objective was to demonstrate that this could be done and clear the way for a subsequent crew to don the special apparatus and attempt a full egress.

Clearly, both crewmen had to be suited because the cabin would be exposed to vacuum. It was decided the mission commander would remain strapped into his seat and look after the vehicle while his colleague went out. There was a significant risk involved, because if the spacewalker were to become incapacitated then his colleague could only unplug the umbilical and close the hatch.

At a press conference in July 1964 to announce that Jim McDivitt and Ed White were to fly the Gemini 4 mission, the possibility was raised of White opening the hatch. Behind the scenes, White argued that he should don the chestpack and, after standing in the hatch to assess his reactions, egress to test a mobility aid, but managers refused to commit to such an ambitious initial foray. In November, while Gus Grissom and John Young were in training for Gemini 3, they voluntarily extended a test in a vacuum chamber to establish that a spacesuited astronaut could open and close the big, hinged hatch, and reported that it was difficult to close. Although this cleared the way for an EVA on one of the early missions, the special apparatus was still under development and there was no guarantee that White would egress.

On March 12, 1965 a vacuum chamber test was conducted using the spacecraft assigned to the Gemini 4 mission, whose hatch had been modified to make it easier to close. But still there was no decision. NASA medics, always fearful of human frailty, were concerned that if a floating spacewalker lost sight of his vehicle he might suffer vertigo. This concern was dispelled on 18 March when Alexei Leonov made a spacewalk. Several days later Gemini 3 made its brief but trouble-free proving flight. On May 25, Administrator James Webb gave the go-ahead because spacewalking was a program objective, the special apparatus was available, and White was enthusiastic. Behind Webb's endorsement of the plan was a recognition that the development of the Agena target vehicle was running so late that progress would not be able to be made towards rendezvous until later in the year, and extravehicular activity would be "something spectacular" to motivate the troops.

As Gemini 4 passed over the Atlantic on its second revolution, White set to work on the 40-item EVA checklist. It took longer than he expected to strap the *ventilation control module* (VCM) onto his chest harness and to unpack the 25ft umbilical and the *hand-held maneuvering unit* (HHMU) but he was in no hurry. Once he was on the umbilical, he was to disconnect from the spacecraft's environmental control system. His final act prior to venting the cabin would be to check his emergency apparatus. The cabin was to be depressurized from its 5.2psi norm slowly, in order that if one of the suits leaked it would be possible to repressurize the cabin rapidly.

There were three time constraints in force. The first was that they must be in communication with Hawaii when opening the hatch, so that mission control would know if something went awry. Secondly, the spacewalk must occur in daylight and while over the continental United States to provide near-continuous communications. And White must ingress before they flew beyond the Eastern Test Range and the hatch be closed before entering Earth's shadow.

On establishing contact with Hawaii, McDivitt announced that they had decided to postpone the activity to the third revolution because White had become hot and sweaty. White switched back onto the cabin systems to wait.

As White opened the lock of the hatch its ratchet was impeded by a faulty spring, but because he had disassembled a hatch in the factory he was familiar with its mechanism and used brute force to overcome it. The hatch was stiff to open, but after he had swung it wide he mounted a guard on the sill to prevent his umbilical from becoming snagged.

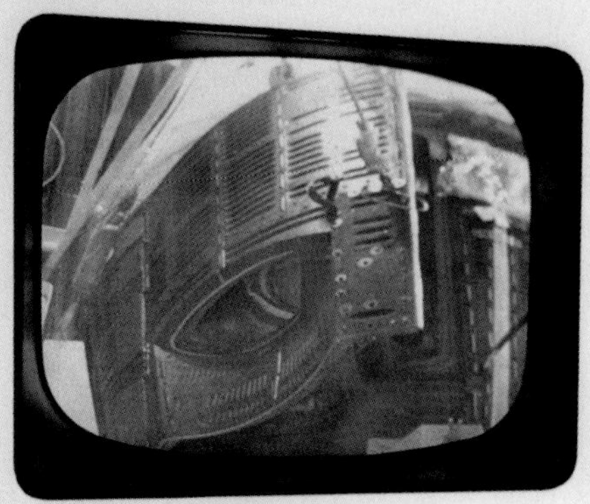
HATCH OPENING

EQUIPMENT OPERATION

STAND UP

HATCH CLOSING

LEFT Four photos from a CCTV monitor showing Ed White taking part in a simulation of his EVA in an altitude chamber at McDonnell on 24 March 1965. *(NASA)*

ABOVE A frame from the 16mm movie camera footage looks past Gemini 4's open hatch to Ed White floating above the California coast at Santa Barbara. He has his HHMU in his right hand. *(NASA)*

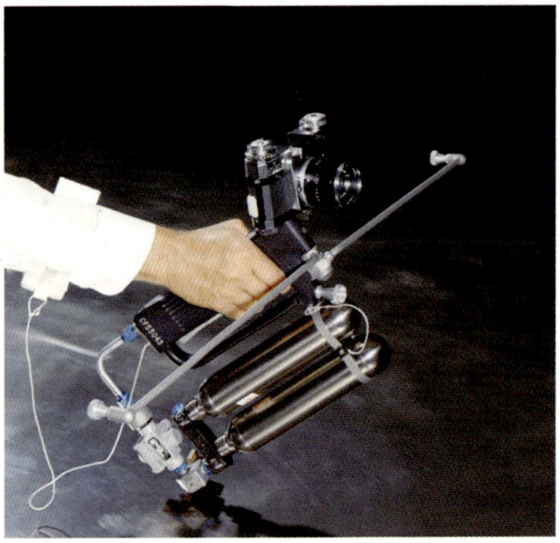

ABOVE The HHMU in which two oxygen canisters fed three thrusters to help Ed White maneuver in space. A Maurer 35mm camera was attached. *(NASA)*

LEFT One of a sequence of 70mm photographs taken by Jim McDivitt as Ed White performed his 21-minute EVA over the United States. *(NASA)*

Standing up, he installed a 16mm movie camera facing forward to record his excursion. There was no indicator to show that the camera was operating and its motor was impossible to sense through the outer thermal gloves, so he took one glove off and checked the camera three times before satisfying himself that it was properly configured. Deciding that he did not have time to put the glove back on, he tossed it into the cabin. At six frames/sec, the camera had an endurance of about 15 minutes. McDivitt was to snap still pictures out of his window whenever the opportunity presented itself.

White assembled the HHMU by fitting the vent tubes onto the hand unit, which integrated the trigger and a pair of oxygen canisters, then tethered the unit to his right wrist so as not to lose it.

McDivitt set the communication system to *voice activation* (VOX) to allow the ground to listen to White on the intercom circuit. They had left Hawaii behind by the time he was ready to exit.

White gently pushed himself up out of the hatch and then used a squirt of HHMU gas to move over the nose of the spacecraft and into the field of view of the movie camera. To attain a pure translation motion, he had to aim the gun in such a manner as to direct the impulse through his center of mass. If he did not line it up accurately, the offset force would impart a rotation as well as a translation. There was no specific test sequence; he simply had to evaluate as many control inputs as the small amount of gas available would permit.

After halting, White turned around and started back towards the spacecraft. Crossing over the top, he tugged on the umbilical to evaluate whether he could use that to control his movement, but in weightlessness the reaction set him tumbling and before he could regain control using the HHMU he had drifted all the way back over the adapter module and out of the movie camera's field of view. After stabilizing himself using the HHMU, he moved forward again.

Now out of propellant, he had to resort to trying to control his movements by swinging the umbilical but, as previously, this was ineffective. McDivitt had to fire the thrusters to hold the vehicle stable against the forces transmitted by the umbilical.

As White slowly tumbled, he relaxed, admired the view, and shot several frames using a 35mm camera mounted on the HHMU.

Not having heard from mission control for some time, McDivitt switched the communications system to push-to-talk. The ground had been repeatedly calling while they were on the intercom circuit, but those calls had passed unnoticed.

With contact established, Chris Kraft, the flight director, who rarely spoke directly to a crew, told White to get back in because there were only a few minutes left before the spacecraft would head out over the Atlantic and, because the exercise had been postponed for one revolution, the sunset terminator was about 20° closer than it otherwise would have been.

White was readily able to return to the hatch by pulling himself along the umbilical, but then had difficulty bending his waist and legs in the inflated suit to ease himself down into his seat. After forcing his knees under the instrument panel and using the resulting leverage to force his bottom onto the seat, he drew the hatch shut without too much difficulty but the fouled ratchet made the mechanism difficult to lock. Because applying torque merely rotated White in his seat, McDivitt held him in place as he operated the mechanism.

By the time White had the hatch locked, his exertion had overwhelmed the suit's environmental system, his faceplate had misted up, and he was drenched in sweat. He was to revert to the cabin air supply and then swing the hatch open to jettison the special apparatus, but McDivitt decided instead to find room for the stuff in the cabin for the remainder of the mission.

The lesson learned from this experiment was that although the hatch required attention, White had not suffered any disorientation and had been able to maneuver using the HHMU.

Overall, it seemed that working outside would be straightforward. Also, as NASA delightedly noted, America now held an endurance record because, at 21 minutes, White had been outside for almost twice as long as Leonov.

The next spacewalk was assigned to Dave Scott on Gemini 8. The plan was for the spacecraft to undock from its Agena target vehicle and fly in formation. Scott would then exit and evaluate his mobility and stability using the HHMU, in this case drawing Freon from a backpack tank which contained 15 times as much gas as was available to White.

As it would be impossible to accommodate this bulky *extravehicular support package* (ESP) in the cabin, it was to be stowed at the rear of the adapter module and Scott was to retrieve and don it. Given White's experience, this was not expected to pose a problem. To

LEFT Test subject Fred Spross is kitted out with the gear that David Scott was expected to don in carrying out his EVA. The smaller unit on his chest is the EVA life support system and the large unit on his back is the EVA support package. *(NASA)*

RIGHT The air-bearing floor was one of the many ways NASA tried to prepare their crews for the purely Newtonian environment of EVA even though it could only permit motion in two dimensions. Here, David Scott practices use of the HHMU. *(NASA)*

BELOW The only means of producing true weightlessness without going into space is during the few seconds that an aircraft makes a parabolic dive. David Scott floats beside a Gemini mockup as he practices for his planned EVA during Gemini 8. *(NASA)*

BELOW RIGHT The torqueless wrench that Scott was to test during his EVA. *(NASA)*

enable Scott to operate independently of his vehicle, an *extravehicular life support system* (ELSS) had been developed. This considerably bulkier chestpack was designed to enable him to switch to a tank of oxygen in the ESP and disconnect from the spacecraft. He was to don the ELSS and a 25ft umbilical prior to opening the hatch and then go to the rear of the adapter and strap into the ESP. After switching over to the backpack's oxygen supply, he would disconnect the umbilical and attach it to a 75ft tether which he retrieved from inside the adapter to create, in effect, a 100ft line. In the event of difficulty, Scott would have to switch over to the emergency oxygen tank in the ELSS and beat a hasty retreat to the safety of the cabin.

A series of tasks were assigned to test the utility of EVA. One experiment was to measure the radiation level, particularly in the South Atlantic Anomaly. Scott was to evaluate a torqueless wrench designed for use in weightlessness. The most spectacular task was to cross over to the Agena and retrieve a package which hopefully would have been struck by micrometeoroids in space, to give scientists their first direct samples of these particles.

But Scott never got the chance to venture out to fulfil these grandiose plans. His mission was curtailed after a stuck thruster spun the spacecraft and mandated an abort.

Jetpacks for Gemini

Although the spacewalking tasks assigned to Gemini 8 were not able to be carried out, they were not passed onto the next mission because its astronauts were already training to undertake their own tasks. The Air Force was hoping that its form of the Gemini spacecraft would operate with the MOL space station and possibly even inspect Soviet satellites.

There were two schools of thought on mobility in EVA: one favored the HHMU, which was simple to make but could induce rotations;

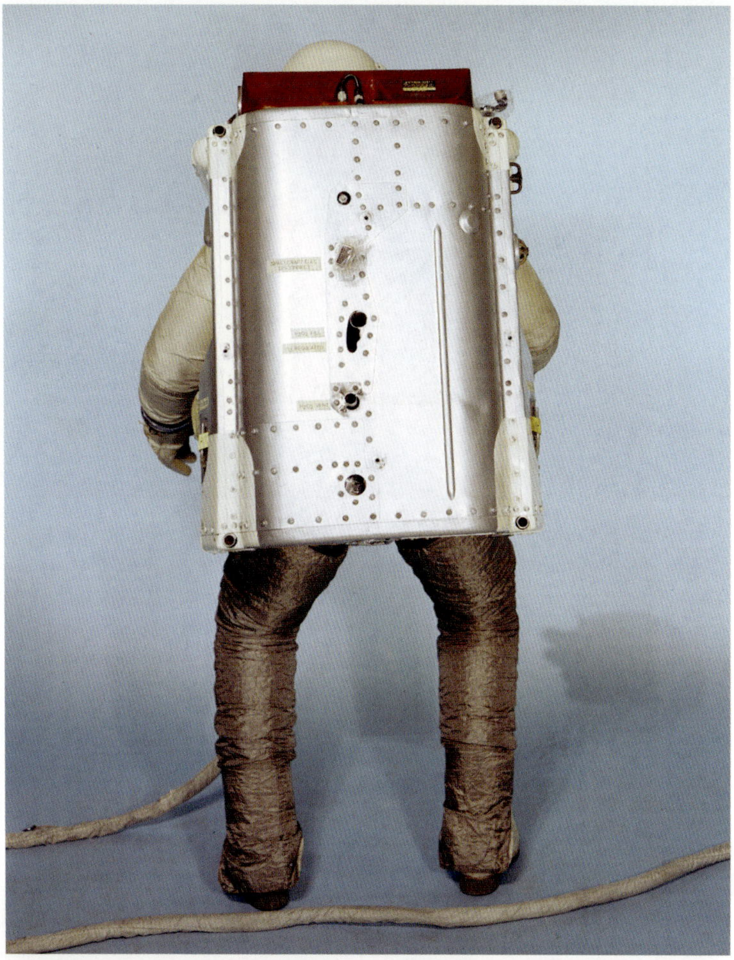

RIGHT **The back of the AMU. Thrusters are visible at the four corners of the unit. The wearer's legs are covered with protective metal fabric to guard against the hot efflux.** *(NASA)*

the other favored a backpack that was capable of imparting "pure" motions with five degrees of freedom by delivering its impulses through the wearer's center of mass. In effect, an astronaut equipped with such an *astronaut maneuvering unit* (AMU) would be able to fly as an independent satellite.

In August 1964, the Air Force awarded a contract to AiResearch in Los Angeles to incorporate the ELSS that NASA was developing for use as a chestpack into a backpack which had a system of thrusters. When tests found the 700°C efflux of the hydrogen peroxide thrusters damaged the Mylar insulation of the suit, the exposed sections were reinforced with 11 layers of aluminized polyamide as a thermal shield, and the legs were further protected by a woven stainless-steel cloth.

The Air Force wanted the AMU tested on two missions. The first opportunity was Gemini 9 and Gene Cernan of the prime crew and Buzz Aldrin, his backup, trained to use it. Although the Air Force wanted it to be flown freely, NASA insisted the astronaut be tethered in case of an AMU problem. Given the manner in which crews rotated from backup to prime, the second test would be on the final mission of the program and if all went well on the first test then Aldrin might fly it without a tether.

Cernan's terror

Early on the second day of Gemini 9, Gene Cernan began the three-hour preparation for his EVA. The checklist with hundreds of items occupied 11 pages of the flight plan. He was to drink a lot of water in order not to become dehydrated during the excursion, which was scheduled to last 2hr 40min. After donning

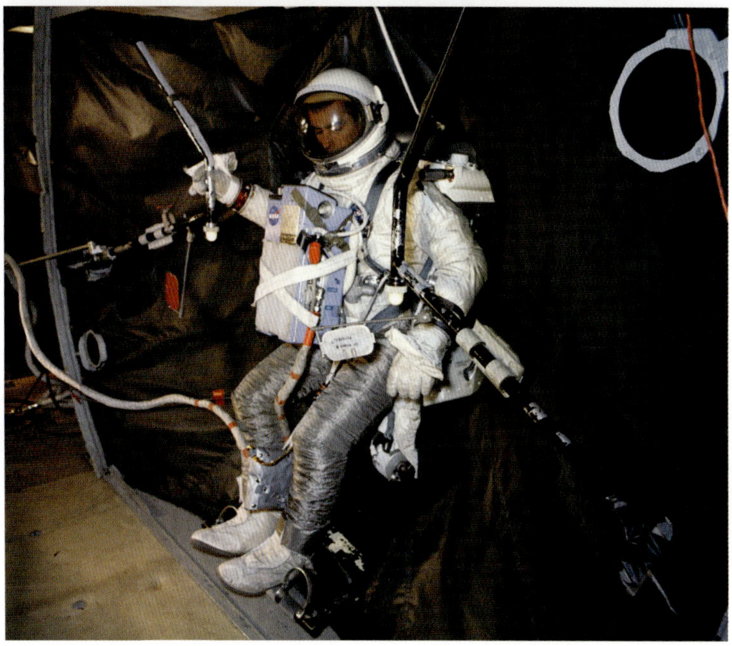

RIGHT **Astronaut Gene Cernan practices donning the AMU in a mockup of the rear of the adapter module mounted within a KC-135 aircraft flying parabolic arcs to reproduce short periods of weightlessness.** *(NASA)*

ABOVE **Cernan's spectacular view along Gemini 9's nose as he began his EVA.** *(NASA)*

the chestpack, he added the 25ft umbilical for a suit integrity check. They were right on the timeline. But then mission commander Tom Stafford discovered that a faulty thruster was imparting a 25°/sec roll. If this were to occur while Cernan was outside, the rolling spacecraft might wind up the umbilical, incapacitating him.

The problem was puzzling because after a stuck thruster had jeopardized Gemini 8, the OAMS was modified to prevent thrusters from failing "on." After further investigation, Stafford reported the fault appeared to be dependent on the mode of the flight control system. It turned out that a circuit breaker for the horizon scanner had been disturbed while they were unpacking apparatus, and resetting it eliminated the problem. But now they were running late.

Given that Ed White's spacewalk had lasted only 20 minutes or so and had not required carrying out any work, Cernan's assignment was very ambitious. But he had rehearsed each task during brief periods of weightlessness in a KC-135 flying ballistic arcs and was confident that the tasks were feasible. He got off to an excellent start. After twisting the large handle above his head to unlock the hatch, he swung it wide, stood on his seat, and ejected the trash.

They were still in darkness, but sunrise was imminent. He was the first spacewalker to witness an orbital sunrise and it was stupendous. Turning aft, he retrieved a micrometeoroid experiment and passed it to Stafford, verbally coordinating their actions to ensure that at no time was the package able to float away.

His first task completed, Cernan reached back to release the pop-out handrail recessed into the adapter module, but it was so far back that as he reached for it his feet lifted off the

RIGHT **The nose of Gemini 9, photographed by Cernan. This shows the white radar unit with its domed antenna covers, the stub antenna sticking forward and the two black covers of the drogue and pilot parachutes. The docking index bar is sticking up with the mirror attached to allow Stafford some vision of Cernan at work over the adapter module.** *(NASA)*

seat and he began to float out of the hatch. Stafford, in the process of stowing the package, grabbed one of Cernan's feet and restored it to the seat. It took longer than expected to deploy the handrail, as did the installation of a movie camera on the bracket just behind the hatch. These tasks had been straightforward in training but in space were awkward, especially if the task required the use of both hands because his body would float out of position when he tried to apply a force to some apparatus.

After taking a breather for several minutes, Cernan pulled out sufficient umbilical to enable him to reach the nose and went to affix a mirror to the docking bar to enable Stafford to monitor his progress while he was at the rear of the spacecraft.

With the mirror installed, he pushed himself off the spacecraft to start an umbilical-dynamics experiment, the purpose of which was to assess whether it was feasible to control his mobility and stability by pulling on and twisting the umbilical. To his surprise, the slightest change in posture twisted the umbilical, which perturbed him in return. It did not become evident until later, but as he performed these gyrations he tore open a seam in the back of his suit, with the result that his lower back got severe sunburn through the parted layers of thermal insulation.

On drawing the umbilical out to its limit, Cernan rebounded and the umbilical curled up as it remembered its stowed form. Then each time it twisted, it forced him in the opposite direction. On colliding with the spacecraft he inadvertently broke off one of its antennae. Attempting to control his movement using the umbilical was impractical and his actions were disturbing the spacecraft, which pitched, yawed and rolled inverted.

Drifting over the adapter module, Cernan grabbed the handrail and was finally able to anchor himself. His next task was an experiment to use Velcro pads on the surface of the spacecraft and on his gloves to provide stability. He discovered that although he was weightless his inertia tore him free. The test was a failure.

As he clawed his way along the length of the umbilical he discovered that the shorter it was, the better he could control his motion. But if he did not pull through his center of mass the induced rotations sent him tumbling.

ABOVE Cernan with his nemesis, the writhing umbilical, during his EVA. *(NASA)*

About 24 minutes after sunrise, and on schedule, Cernan took another breather and then retrieved the movie camera so that Stafford could load a new magazine of film. With the camera reinstalled, he swung the hatch until it was ajar only a few inches and then moved hand over hand along the handrail, pinching his umbilical into small rings along the way so that after he had disconnected from the umbilical it would remain tight against the vehicle.

At the lip of the adapter, Cernan got a nasty surprise: the ring that had been mated to the booster was a sawtooth of very sharp-looking metal. He gingerly slipped over the rim into the cavity at the rear. Although this excursion had been straightforward in training, Cernan's heart was racing by the time he reached the stowed AMU and he was sweating profusely. Stafford increased the oxygen flow rate through the umbilical in an effort to cool Cernan down. The schedule required Cernan to achieve this point by sunset because the only illumination available while in Earth's shadow would be the lights in the rear of the adapter. Although one of the lamps had failed, he slid his toes into the stirrups for stability and got to work. He was to be ready to start the AMU evaluation at sunrise.

Containing its own maneuvering, life support and communications systems, the AMU was a complex apparatus and Cernan had to work through a 35-item checklist. The procedure was complicated by the fact that most of the valves which he had to access were in out-of-the-way places. With gloves that provided little sense of

RIGHT **Gemini 9's backup pilot, Buzz Aldrin, practices donning the AMU on a mockup at the Manned Spacecraft Center in Houston.** *(NASA)*

touch, and in near-darkness, he had to feel for each valve and use a mirror on his wrist to verify its status.

Cernan had been able to set up the AMU rapidly during training, but the KC-135 had provided periods of weightlessness lasting for only 20 seconds. Performing the entire sequence in space in real time proved taxing. By the time he had set all the valves he was hyperventilating, and in the darkness he did not notice the accumulation of mist on the inside of his visor until it was almost opaque.

As he set about deploying the arms of the AMU, which had to be rotated down and extended in a telescopic fashion, his heart rate increased to 180 beats/min. It had been hoped that with his feet restrained he would have both hands free to work, but his boots kept slipping out of the stirrups. As a remedy, he placed one boot into a stirrup and used his other to jam it. He was able to relax only when he had buckled himself into the backpack.

After plugging the AMU's oxygen line into his chestpack, Cernan unplugged the umbilical. As this had provided power and communications in addition to oxygen, from this point he was to communicate by the UHF radio in the backpack but the reception from his location behind the adapter was poor and Stafford could barely hear what he was saying. So they waited in silence. Although Cernan rested, his faceplate remained fogged. The decision point would be at sunrise, which was when the attachment bolt was to be blown.

When Stafford decided that it would be irresponsible to proceed, Cernan restored the umbilical, unstrapped from the AMU, scrambled up over the rim of the adapter and groped his way along the handrail. Locating the hatch by feel, he swung it open. As soon as Cernan's feet appeared in the opening, Stafford drew them to the seat.

As Cernan rested in the sunlight, his visor gradually cleared. Once he had retrieved the movie camera, Stafford suggested that he fetch the mirror from the docking bar, but when he moved forward to do so his respiration rate rose and his visor fogged again.

Stafford decided that Cernan should ingress, instead of remaining in the hatch for the airglow photography just after sunset. Cernan slipped his feet beneath the edge of the instrument panel and began to force his body into his seat, but it was a struggle because the pressurized suit was inflexible at the knees. In fact, having been reinforced to protect against the AMU's efflux, his suit was even stiffer than the one that White had worn.

As soon as Cernan thought he was inside, he swung the hatch down only for it to bounce off his helmet. Stafford used the lanyard to draw the hatch down until the latch engaged, compressing Cernan in the process, whereupon Cernan used the ratchet to lock the hatch, completing what he would later call "the spacewalk from hell."

Stafford repressurized the cabin to collapse their suits sufficiently for Cernan to relax his posture. His face was bright red from the exertion. Having sweated 10lb, he was chilly for the remainder of the mission and, on doffing his suit following recovery, he poured several pints of water from his boots.

Although the Air Force was critical of the astronauts for cancelling the AMU test right at the point where it was to have begun, in truth Cernan had been the victim of ignorance of how to undertake extravehicular activity. His stability aids and training had been inadequate. But Gemini was a pathfinder to identify the limitations and, in overcoming them, advance the state of the art. Thus, in determining that EVA was not as straightforward as White's experience had suggested, Cernan had provided useful data. If Dave Scott had been able to go out on Gemini 8 he probably would have found donning the ESP backpack in the adapter to be more difficult than expected, and it may well have been possible to provide Cernan with better handrails and foot restraints. But in the lottery of life it was Cernan who learned this lesson.

As to the fogging of Cernan's faceplate, because crews developed their flight procedures more or less independently, he was unaware that Scott had intended to apply an anti-fogging agent to the inside of his faceplate prior to going out. This became standard procedure on future spacewalks. The overall conclusion from Cernan's ordeal was that the training regime for spacewalking had to be improved.

"A motion of stately grace"

On Gemini 10, Michael Collins was given two EVAs: the first to be performed standing in the hatch and the second a full egress alongside Gemini 8's Agena to retrieve the micrometeoroid package that Dave Scott had intended to get. Having concluded that Cernan's difficulties were specific to attempting to work in the rear of the adapter module, NASA deleted a backpack for Geminis 10 and 11. Instead, the HHMU would be fueled by nitrogen drawn from a tank in the adapter.

The objective of the first spacewalk was ultraviolet astrophotography, which had to be

ABOVE Gene Cernan safely back inside the Gemini cabin after the ordeal of his EVA. *(NASA)*

LEFT Astronaut Mike Collins practices for his EVA in the KC-135 aircraft. He is holding a mockup of the micrometeoroid package that he was to retrieve from their Agena. *(NASA)*

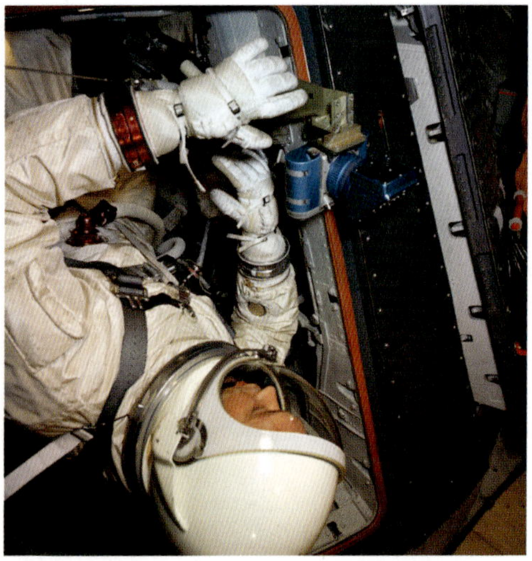

RIGHT Collins in the zero-*g* aircraft training to use a Maurer 70mm camera during his stand-up EVA. *(NASA)*

FAR RIGHT One of Collins' shots of the color chart. The same chart had been test photographed on Earth on the same roll of film prior to the flight in order to give consistent results. *(NASA)*

done in Earth's shadow, so the plan was to open the hatch at sunset and undertake the task standing on the seat.

After jettisoning the trash, he mounted a 70mm camera and a bracket. Because his eyes had yet to adjust to the darkness, he had to do this by feel. When he fired off a test exposure the camera became detached. As his eyes adapted to the darkness, Collins remounted the camera and took a sequence of 20 images manually, with John Young timing the exposures for him.

BELOW Collins practices removal of a micrometeoroid package from a mockup of the Agena in a zero-*g* aircraft. *(NASA)*

He passed the camera inside to have Young change the film for the next experiment, which was to take pictures of a color chart in full daylight to enable the photo lab to calibrate the film and render future space photographs in their true colors. However, following sunrise Collins' eyes began to water. On reporting this to Young he wondered whether it might be the chemical with which he had smeared his faceplate to prevent fogging, but Young said his eyes were watering too and so they curtailed the spacewalk.

Unlike his predecessors Collins was readily able to regain his seat, and because McDonnell had made the hatch mechanism operate at a lower force level he was able to close and lock it without difficulty.

Investigating possible causes of the eye irritation, engineers determined that it had arisen because (as directed in the flight plan) two compressor fans in the environmental control system had been active at the same time; the problem ought not to recur if a single fan was operated.

The second EVA began at sunrise, immediately after they arrived at the inert 8-Agena. Standing in the hatch, Collins released a pop-out handrail that he was to use while attaching the nitrogen hose for his HHMU. Then he fetched the micrometeoroid package that he would have retrieved on his first outing if that had not been cut short. The experiment was a slab about 6in wide and 12in long. He passed it to Young, but unfortunately at some point later in the EVA it floated out and was lost. With

Collins disturbing the spacecraft, Young was repeatedly maneuvering to keep the Agena in his window, each time making sure that Collins was clear of the hot exhaust from the thrusters.

Collins opened a flap to access the valve of the nitrogen tank. The hose connector was designed so that when he pushed it onto the valve, a cocked sleeve would slide down and engage. During weightless training he had been able to use one hand to hold himself stable on the rail and attach the hose using the other. However, the connector did not engage properly and he had to let go of the rail to reset the sleeve. When he swung his arm to reset the sleeve his body twisted, his legs bumped the spacecraft, and he tumbled. He had to keep grabbing the rail to stabilize himself as he worked to reset the connector. Fortunately, the hose engaged the valve at his second attempt.

Directed by Collins, Young carefully maneuvered close to the Agena, which was stable in a vertical orientation with its engine down. The micrometeoroid experiment was at the top, near the docking adapter. Pushing off gently so as not to build up too great a speed, Collins floated over. His aim was accurate and he managed to grab hold of the conical docking collar and halt his motion without destabilizing himself. He then worked hand over hand around the collar to where the package was located. Unfortunately, on reaching with one hand for the package, the twist of his body wrenched his other hand off the cone's smooth metal and he cartwheeled. His action set the Agena slowly tumbling and he had to grab the hatch of his spacecraft to stabilize himself.

Young relocated about 10ft from the now unstable Agena to give himself a wider field of view. Collins resumed his jump-off position and gave a squirt of the HHMU for his second attempt. However, his boot clipped the hatch and spoiled his trajectory, and when he tried to correct, a misdirected shot from the HHMU imparted a slow rotation. Nevertheless, he managed to grab a wire harness near the 8-Agena's docking collar to halt his flyby and stabilize himself. This time moving very slowly, he worked his way around the collar to the micrometeoroid package and released it. This was to have been retrieved within hours of launch, so the fact that it had been exposed to the space environment for three months was a bonus for the experimenters. Instead of using the HHMU, Collins tugged on his umbilical to start moving towards his own vehicle.

In contrast to Cernan's spacewalk, which was widely considered to have been a failure because he did not test the AMU, Collins' excursion was judged as a success because he retrieved the package from the Agena.

Unfortunately, the movie camera malfunctioned and Young was so busy maneuvering to avoid a collision with the 8-Agena that he was unable to take any still pictures through his window. As a result, Collins' adventure went completely undocumented.

Gordon's trials

After Gene Cernan's experience, NASA investigated the potential for neutral buoyancy training using a large water tank. Cernan had reported that it accurately reproduced the inertial aspects of being weightless. However, Collins had been too far advanced in his preparations for Gemini 10 to take time off to rehearse his procedures using this technique and Dick Gordon did not think it necessary in training for Gemini 11.

BELOW Astronaut Dick Gordon suiting up for his Gemini 11 mission during which he was to carry out EVA. *(NASA)*

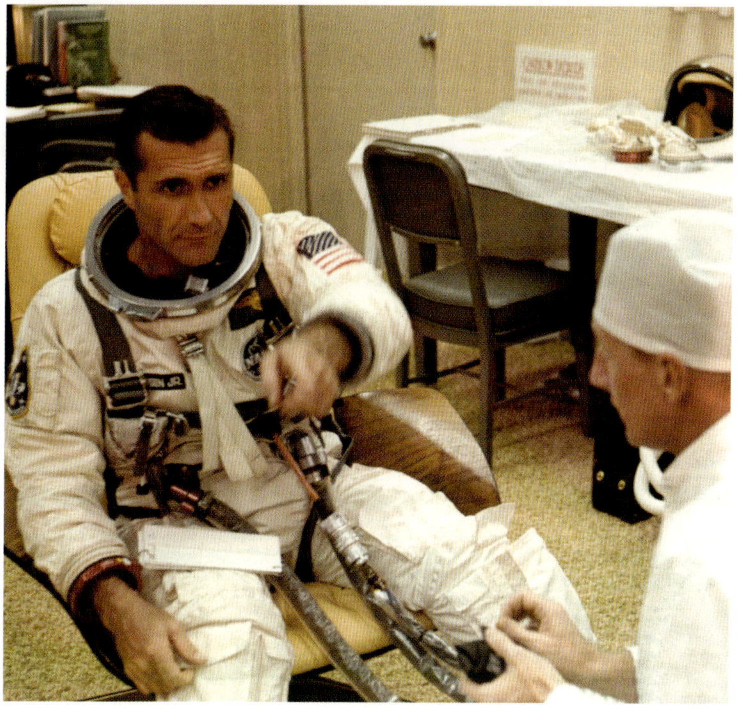

ABOVE Fully suited, visor down and with the Gemini 11 hatch open, Gordon prepares to exit at the start of his EVA. *(NASA)*

Pete Conrad believed in the maxim of "get ahead and stay ahead" to create a margin for dealing with unexpected problems, and they found themselves with 90 minutes to spare. Ironically, because they had missed a step on the checklist, Gordon had donned his gloves before affixing the outer visor to his helmet. As a result the task took over 30 minutes and he cracked the visor.

Over the Pacific heading for the United States they depressurized the cabin for a daylight pass. With the hatch open and Conrad holding his ankle strap to keep his foot on the seat for stability, Gordon performed some initial chores. He then exited the hatch and, when ready, had Conrad play out some umbilical.

This first EVA was performed with the Agena docked. As Gordon floated forward, he followed Cernan's advice and utilized the nozzle of one of the inert RCS thrusters as a handhold prior to reaching for the collar of the docking adapter. But when he set off again an unwanted sideways push sent him flying across the top of the Agena. Conrad tugged the umbilical to return Gordon towards the hatch, sending him flying past at high speed. On rebounding off the end of the line Gordon began to tumble, so Conrad reeled him in.

Back at the hatch, Gordon set off a second time for the Agena and managed to grasp the collar with the tips of his gloved fingers. His task was to extract the end of a tether from a dispenser on the side of the docking adapter. He had to attach this 100ft nylon strap to the docking index bar that projected up from the nose of the Gemini spacecraft, but first he needed to stabilize himself.

In training, he had simply sat on the nose of the spacecraft and jammed his boots in between it and the docking collar to hold himself in position. When suspended on a wire-rig trainer, it had been simple to reach down the side of the Agena to grab the end of the tether and connect it to the bar. He had also been able to do it in the weightless trainer, but in space it was much more difficult and when his boots slid out of the collar his legs floated off the vehicle.

Conrad joked that Gordon looked like he was riding a wild horse and told him to take a rest. On resuming his efforts, Gordon's heart raced and his respiration rate soared. In contrast to training, he had great difficulty screwing the clamp to connect the tether to the bar. Giving up on keeping his boots jammed in the collar, he stationed himself over the nose and held himself in position as best he could with one hand countering his body's reaction to the torque that was caused by his other hand manipulating the clamp.

By now they were nearing the end of the Eastern Test Range. After Stafford's endorsement of it on Gemini 9, Gordon was to affix a mirror to the docking bar to enable Conrad to monitor his activities at the adapter, primarily giving the HHMU a workout. However, due to his physical exertion his right eye had become flooded by sweat and was stinging so badly as to impair his vision, so Conrad ordered him back inside.

In effect, Gordon's exertions had overwhelmed the suit's environmental system. With the suit unable to cool him, sweat could not evaporate and in weightlessness it simply remained in place until surface tension drew droplets together and his eyes began to water, exacerbating the issue. An impromptu rest period had not really helped. It was no consolation that his faceplate had not fogged over.

A stand-up EVA later in the mission went well. Like Collins, he was to take ultraviolet pictures of stars, but with twice as many targets spread over two periods of orbital darkness. During the intervening daylight pass he was to snap pictures of cloud-free areas of the continental United States.

Out over the Atlantic with nothing to do until it got dark again to resume the astrophotography, both men dozed off and only awoke when mission control called via Madagascar to check on their progress. This awakened Conrad, who promptly discovered that Gordon, still standing in the open hatch, had also fallen asleep. Once done, Gordon resumed his seat and closed the hatch. In contrast to his exhausting initial excursion, he later described working in the hatch for 2.5 hours as an enjoyable experience.

ABOVE This still frame from Gordon's movie camera shows him astride Gemini's nose like he was riding a wild horse, as Conrad had joked. *(NASA)*

EVA licked

When Jim Lovell was assigned to command Gemini 12, the final mission in the program, he expected that it would be given the AMU to test because the agreement with the Air Force was for two flights. His colleague, Buzz Aldrin, had backed up Gene Cernan and was familiar with the apparatus. After Cernan's favorable report on the fidelity of underwater simulation, Aldrin used it as his primary training aid. It was certainly an improvement over the wire and pulley rig, and it facilitated integrated simulations with Houston that were not feasible using a weightless aircraft. Aldrin was confident that he would be able to move slowly and

BELOW Astronauts Jim Lovell and Buzz Aldrin during preparations for their Gemini 12 mission. *(NASA)*

ABOVE Aldrin practices with the AMU in an altitude chamber. Eventually, the AMU was deleted from the Gemini 12 flight to allow him to perfect the techniques of EVA. *(NASA)*

RIGHT NASA found that the best Earth-based training for weightlessness was by doing so in water. Aldrin extensively practiced his EVA in a pool at McDonogh School that NASA rented to test the suitability of neutral buoyancy training. Here he uses a telescopic pole to move between Gemini and the Agena. *(NASA)*

RIGHT Aldrin works around a mockup of the docked Gemini-Agena during neutral buoyancy training. *(NASA)*

deliberately to the rear of the adapter module to don the backpack.

But after Gemini 11 NASA felt that the difficulties of EVA was the one program goal that had yet to be mastered and, to Aldrin's dismay, deleted the AMU from the flight. Instead, the primary objective would be to perfect EVA techniques. It was evident that standing in the hatch bestowed sufficient stability to do useful work, but activities beyond the hatch which involved maintaining a given position were difficult since in weightlessness every physical act applied a force that induced a reactive force.

A convenient handrail could help an astronaut maintain position using one hand and work using the other, but not all tasks could be performed single-handed. The issue was stability to perform work and if the work needed two hands then stability would have to be achieved by some other means, such as by foot restraints. The long-term implication was that every spacewalking task would have to be thought out in advance and appropriate mobility and stability aids provided. Aldrin therefore devoted the rest of his underwater training to rehearsing moving purposefully around the docked vehicles and identifying the optimum placement for miscellaneous stability aids.

The individual tasks for this "back to basics" EVA seemed at first sight to be trivial, as indeed they were on Earth, but the objective was to provide leverage in weightlessness. By the time he set off, Aldrin was so much better prepared than his predecessors that if he was unsuccessful in space then NASA would have to rethink its ambitions for having astronauts assemble orbital structures.

The Gemini 12 plan followed the Gemini 10 model with the first EVA being undertaken in the hatch. This reflected the belief that an initial exposure would acclimatize Aldrin to working in weightlessness and better prepare him for more demanding activity when he egressed the next day. (The implication of this was that if Gordon's excursions had been switched around he may have been more successful.) An additional day was assigned to the mission to enable Aldrin to undertake a record-breaking three EVAs, the final one being another stand-up.

On his first outing, Aldrin stood in the open hatch for ultraviolet astrophotography during

LEFT An important aid to EVA stability is having somewhere to put your feet. Aldrin used foot restraints mounted at his work station when he had to perform various evaluation tasks. Here he is practicing their use in the pool. *(NASA)*

BELOW A frame from Aldrin's movie camera shows him in the open hatch of Gemini 12 with the Maurer camera he would use for ultraviolet photography. *(NASA)*

two night passes and a variety of other tasks in the intervening period of daylight. One experiment required him to exercise for 30 seconds by vigorously swinging his arms to move his hands between his waist and his helmet while his heart and respiration rates were monitored. He was to do this twice: first after depressurizing the cabin and still seated, and again when convenient standing in the hatch. He discarded the trash and then, once in Earth's shadow, started the astrophotography.

After sunrise, he dismounted the camera and handed it to Lovell to change the film, then turned around in the hatch to retrieve the micrometeoroid package from the adapter module. The next task was to install a telescoping pole between a hole in the Agena's

ABOVE Aldrin's view along the nose of his spacecraft and the 12-Agena. Running alongside Gemini's nose is the handrail he had installed to aid movement between the two spacecraft. *(NASA)*

RIGHT Another frame from Aldrin's movie camera shows him with the micrometeoroid package from the adapter module. *(NASA)*

collar and a fixture between the hatches to serve as a handrail to the Agena on his second spacewalk. When Lovell returned the camera, Aldrin took pictures of ocean currents, eddies, river outwash, and plankton blooms over the Pacific, then areas free of cloud over the United States.

Then it was astrophotography again. To his surprise, repeatedly holding the cable release for the two-minute exposures made his fingers ache. Also, once his eyes had fully adapted, he noticed that his gloves glowed. Experimenting, he found that rubbing his thumb against his index finger induced an electrostatic effect, evidently resulting from passing through the ionosphere; in effect, he was flying through a sea of electrons.

After sunrise Aldrin retrieved the camera, resumed his seat and closed the hatch. While working methodically through tasks that were manageable, his heart had hovered at 75 beats/min and his respiration rarely exceeded 18/min. He had been almost as relaxed as Lovell, who was hardly stressed at all.

Aldrin's second EVA the next day would take him completely out of the spacecraft. He opened the hatch at sunrise, set up a movie camera and then translated down the 6ft handrail which he had installed the previous day. He had two short tethers on the webbing harness at the waist of his suit. On reaching the docking adapter he hooked the left tether to the loop at the end of the handrail and the other to a ring on the docking bar, positioning himself as if swimming with his head above the collar and his feet near the open hatch; a considerably more relaxed posture in which to work than the cowboy stance astride the vehicle used by Dick Gordon. Like Gordon, Aldrin had to retrieve the end of the tether from its dispenser on the Agena and attach it to the docking bar, a task that proved straightforward. After exposing a micrometeoroid package that was to be left for possible future retrieval, he took a scheduled rest.

ABOVE Aldrin at work around the docking collar, taken by Jim Lovell. *(NASA)*

ABOVE Aldrin has his feet engaged in the "golden slippers" during underwater training. *(NASA)*

BELOW David Scott training on a zero-*g* aircraft with the torqueless wrench. Eventually it got an outing with Aldrin on Gemini 12. *(NASA)*

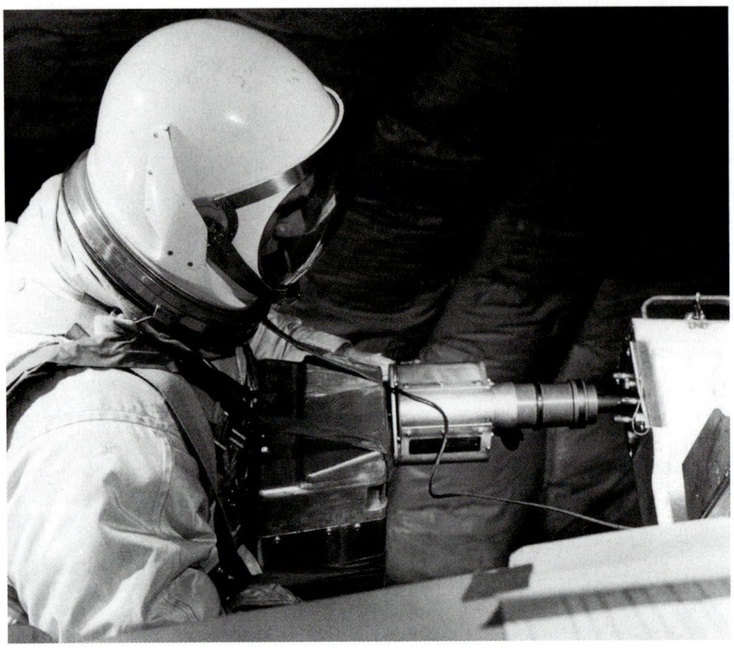

Aldrin's major goal was to prove that working in EVA was feasible. A series of tasks had been prepared at the rear of the adapter module, the place where Cernan had encountered his worst difficulties. Having already familiarized himself with the forces required to move purposefully, Aldrin readily made his way along the handrails. Once in the cavity at the rear of the adapter he clamped his umbilical to a tool so that it would not flex and disturb him. He then flipped himself right way up, faced forward, grasped two rails and eased his boots into the overshoe-style restraints that were sturdier than the stirrups provided for Cernan. These were painted gold to reflect sunlight in order not to damage his boots, and were therefore known as "golden slippers."

With both boots anchored, he was able to release his grip on the rails and let his body adopt the suit's neutral posture of slightly hunched forward with his arms in front of his chest. After some exercises to assess his ability to adopt various postures, he tied himself to the workstation using his waist tethers. The workstation tasks were to start at sunset. He had positioned himself with time to spare and his heart was relaxed. Lovell was to call out each task and log the time it took his partner to do it.

The objective was to evaluate the degree of difficulty associated with each task, undertaken in a variety of conditions. The tasks were deliberately not interdependent, so that if one task proved to be unexpectedly time-consuming he could abandon it and move on. And in addition to formal rest periods, he had the option of calling a time-out if he felt tired. In all, he had 17 numbered assignments that were deemed to be representative of space station missions. In particular, he was to test a torque wrench and measure the force needed to tighten and then release bolts. He would also test the torqueless wrench initially assigned to Gemini 8, compare one-handed with two-handed tasks, put plugs into sockets, and use a pair of shears to sever lengths of electrical cable. To assess dexterity using suit gloves, he was to link up sets of small hooks and loops. As an additional leverage test, he was to test the force required to tear off pre-positioned strips of Velcro of various widths. At one point he fumbled a bolt and washer, and as they drifted out of the field

RIGHT View aft from the open hatch of Gemini 12 in sunlight with the movie camera installed on the adapter module. *(NASA)*

of view of his helmet he leant backwards at the waist and caught them both.

As they progressed through the task list, Lovell told Aldrin that he was scheduled for a rest and should take a "banana pill." Because his workstation tasks had been derided as monkey work, a yellow Chiquita sticker had jokingly been placed beside his workstation.

Finished in the rear of the adapter, Aldrin made his way back to the Agena to carry out similar tasks on a workstation there. This time he tethered himself with his legs above the Agena. On finishing these tasks, he threw the loose items away and returned to the hatch. After passing the movie camera to Lovell, he jettisoned the telescoping handrail, resumed his seat, and closed the hatch.

The Agena had been discarded by the time of the third EVA. After tossing out the accumulated trash, most of which was food packaging, Aldrin stood on his seat and resumed the ultraviolet astrophotography of his first EVA. However, owing to a thruster problem it was impractical to have Lovell turn the vehicle to aim the camera at each star field for long exposures, so Aldrin held the camera and shot one-second exposures. As the Sun began to brighten the horizon ahead, he snapped a sequence of pictures for a scientist who had expressed a desire to study dust in the atmosphere, then lowered his protective visor and completed the astrophotography. When he closed the hatch, Aldrin had been outside for barely one hour and was totally relaxed.

During an accumulated 5.5 hours of external activity, Aldrin had certainly ticked the box for EVA as the last of the program's main objectives. Thanks to his training, he had been able to perform all of his assignments with ease. Ironically, if the AMU had been in the adapter, he would have been able to conclude the program with a spectacular Buck Rogers act.

RIGHT Buzz Aldrin took this selfie with his visor up in the hatchway during his final EVA. *(NASA)*

Chapter Thirteen

Returning to Earth

Leaving orbit and returning to Earth required a powerful retrograde burn to initiate the fall into the atmosphere, and the hypersonic re-entry required the vehicle to be capable of withstanding the extremely high temperatures created as it brutally compressed the air in its path. An Apollo spacecraft returning from the Moon would enter the atmosphere at a much higher speed than one from low orbit, and its heatshield would have to endure correspondingly greater thermal stress.

OPPOSITE Tom Stafford (left) and Wally Schirra on the deck of the USS *Wasp*. *(NASA)*

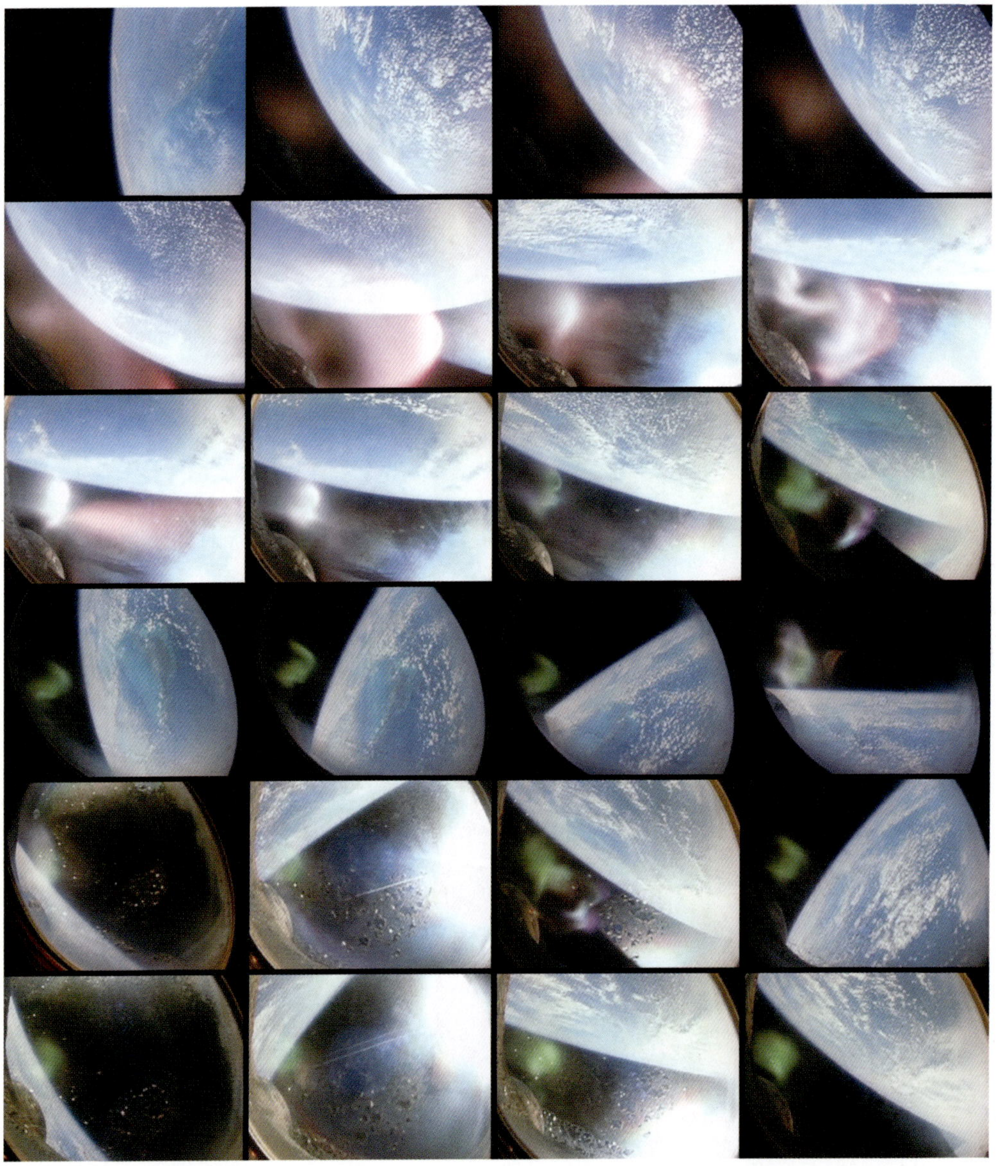

RIGHT **Gemini 12's spectacular view of re-entry. The rear-facing crew of a Gemini spacecraft were treated to a multi-colored display of greens and lilacs against a blue Earth as they barrelled in through the atmosphere. The horizon appears to rotate as the jets of the re-entry control system fire to steer the spacecraft's progress, disturbing the plasma as they do so.** *(NASA/David Woods/ Courtesy of Mark Gray - spacecraftfilms.com)*

This posed a challenge for Apollo's designers. One option was to slow down by dipping into the atmosphere at a shallow angle prior to pursuing a ballistic arc that would result in re-entry. Considering that the Mercury capsules had come down far from their targets, the very accurate navigation required for such a scheme appeared daunting.

Gemini was to develop techniques for *controlled re-entry*. The center of mass of the re-entry module had been deliberately offset in order to provide the blunt cone with some aerodynamic lift. By monitoring the trajectory, the onboard computer would predict the splashdown point and display this to the commander, who would use the nose thrusters to adjust the lift vector by rolling left or right of the neutral position and thereby steer towards the target.

Gemini 3 off target

For Gemini 3, the first manned mission, NASA headquarters had demanded that a fail safe burn be made using the OAMS thrusters in order to lower the perigee of the orbit to about 45nmi. This would guarantee re-entry even if the retrorockets failed, because

LEFT **The Gemini 3 spacecraft sits in the water after its short flight surrounded by divers and with its fluorescent dye coloring the water. Its HF antenna is fully extended to enable long distance communication, having landed well short of its target. John Young awaits a helicopter pickup from the life raft.** *(NASA)*

such a low perigee would cause significant aerodynamic drag. It seems this burn was prompted by a scenario depicted by Martin Caidin in his 1964 novel *Marooned*, in which a spacecraft was stranded in orbit when its retros failed to fire.

With the spacecraft flying BEF, the equipment section of the adapter module was pyrotechnically jettisoned. From now on, the attitude of the spacecraft would be controlled by the thrusters of the *re-entry control system* (RCS) on the nose. The de-orbit maneuver was achieved by firing four solid-rocket motors, one after the other. Then the retrograde section was discarded. The re-entry module maintained itself with its heatshield facing the direction of travel as it descended to the *entry interface*, defined to be 400,000ft altitude.

In the event, Gemini 3 came down 45nmi short of the USS *Intrepid*, the prime recovery ship, near Grand Turk Island in the Bahamas. Subsequent analysis revealed that the re-entry module had less lift than predicted, but in those days hypersonic flight characteristics were difficult to estimate because wind tunnels were unable to attain such speeds and computer modelling was rudimentary. But the role of an engineering test flight was to determine the performance of the vehicle, and this empirical data was applied to future missions.

As they descended towards 50,000ft, Gus Grissom was primed to pull his "D" ring to activate the ejector seats if the drogue parachute failed to deploy. The surprise came after the pilot chute pulled out the main parachute below 10,000ft. Grissom threw a switch to transition from a single point of attachment with the capsule's nose straight up to a two-point configuration in which the nose was angled slightly above the horizontal. This transition was so violent that Grissom's head was thrown forward and his faceplate was cracked when it struck the frame of his window.

After the capsule hit the surface, the chute dragged it underwater before a switch was thrown to jettison it. Then as it pitched and

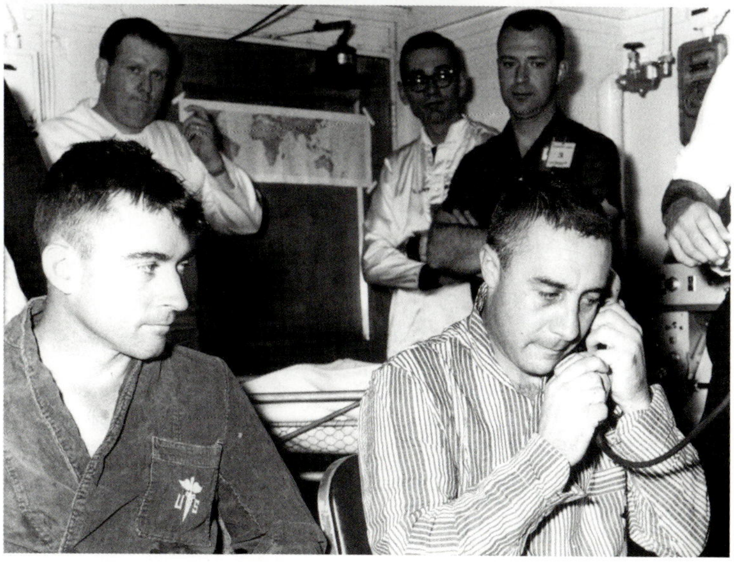

ABOVE **John Young and Gus Grissom on board the USS *Intrepid* after their recovery.** *(NASA)*

ABOVE Gemini 4 in the water with a flotation collar attached. The HF antenna for this spacecraft was positioned under the water but the descent and recovery antennae are visible where they popped up in the bridle trough between the hatches. *(NASA)*

rolled in the 5ft seas, swimmers, delivered by a helicopter, attached a U-shaped flotation collar. Since the ship was so far away, the astronauts opted for a helicopter pickup. By then, both men had vomited. As John Young wryly noted later, "Gemini may be a good spacecraft, but she's no boat."

RIGHT Jim McDivitt and, behind him, Ed White step onto the deck of the USS *Wasp* after being picked up from their spacecraft. *(NASA)*

Ballistic re-entry

From time to time during the flight of Gemini 4, its commander, Jim McDivitt, would power up his spacecraft's computer to allow the ground to update its data. It had become routine. But then the on/off switch failed in the off position. Without a computer to navigate re-entry, they would have to perform the same type of re-entry as in the Mercury program, where the capsule was set rolling around its axis for a ballistic, no-lift return.

Upon McDivitt's recommendation, this would be the last mission to undertake the fail safe maneuver, and after it had been executed he began the retrofire sequence one second late. Although this does not sound like very much, their orbital speed of 28,000km/hr meant they would be a little "long."

As the capsule penetrated the atmosphere, McDivitt used the thrusters on the nose to initiate a roll rate of 15°/sec in order to cancel out the lift which its shape would otherwise generate. The steep descent increased the deceleration load to 8*g*. Mindful of their predecessors, shortly prior to transitioning to the two-point suspension on the main parachute the two men raised their arms to prevent their helmets from striking the window frames. The capsule splashed down very heavily 530nmi southwest of Bermuda. As the USS *Wasp* was 36nmi away, the astronauts requested a helicopter pickup.

Navigation error

In the case of Gemini 5, the first three retros fired in their normal rapid sequence but there was a lengthy pause before the fourth one triggered. At the entry interface at 400,000ft Gordon Cooper initiated a series of roll maneuvers, first banking one way and then the other in an effort to both refine the length of the trajectory and correct any cross-range error. When the computer indicated they were too high and would overshoot, he increased the magnitude of his banking to reduce the lift and thereby shorten the trajectory, in the process increasing the deceleration almost to that of a ballistic re-entry, which was stressful after being weightless for eight days. Although their computer continued to show them coming

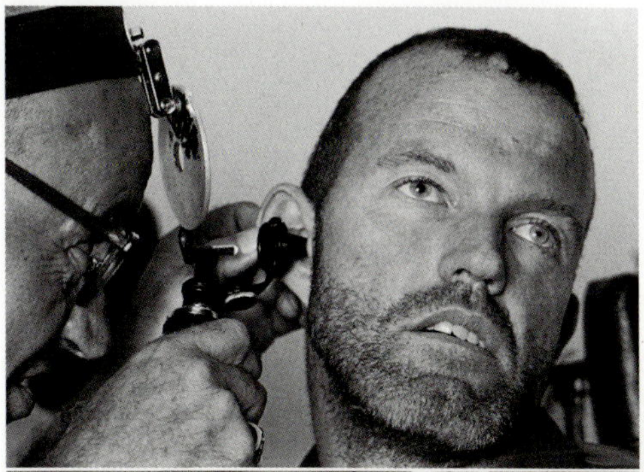

FAR LEFT Gordon Cooper is hoisted away from his Gemini 5 spacecraft. *(NASA)*

LEFT As NASA's longest space flight yet, medics were keen to check the health of its crew. Gordon Cooper gets his ears examined and a stethoscope listens to Pete Conrad's heartbeat. *(NASA)*

in "long," when they splashed down they were 70nmi short!

An investigation discovered a flaw in the calculations used for the de-orbit burn; the onboard computer had been misled, with the result that Cooper's efforts to correct its false indication served only to progressively draw them short of the target. The USS *Lake Champlain* was 80nmi farther east, but the destroyer USS *Du Pont*, having been stationed 72nmi up-range of the prime recovery ship, was close by. However, it was 45 minutes before a helicopter from the carrier arrived and dropped swimmers to attach the flotation collar. The sea state was calm, but the astronauts were recovered by helicopter.

Nearing the ships

After performing the first rendezvous in space, Wally Schirra, the commander of Gemini 6, set out to clinch a bet he had made with Gemini 7 commander Frank Borman, regarding which of them would make the most accurate descent. Once the retrograde section of the adapter module had been jettisoned, Schirra rotated the spacecraft heads down to enable him to monitor the horizon during the early phase of re-entry. At 60nmi altitude he banked 55° left and held this angle until down to 50nmi, at which time he began to follow the computer's steering cues. The capsule splashed down just over 7nmi from the target point in

BELOW Tom Stafford (left) and Wally Schirra, still with their helmets on, chat with frogmen as they await recovery. *(NASA)*

LEFT Gemini 7 descends to the ocean under its main parachute. *(NASA)*

the prime recovery zone, about 500nmi southwest of Bermuda. Once the flotation collar was on, he and Tom Stafford opened their hatches and chatted with the swimmers. Being so near the USS *Wasp*, they remained in their capsule and rode the crane onto the deck of the ship.

Although there was a slight pause before the fourth solid rocket ignited for Gemini 7's de-orbit burn, to Borman's delight the computer was able to trim half a mile off Gemini 6's recently set record. Nevertheless, once the swimmers had attached the flotation collar he and Jim Lovell opted for retrieval by helicopter.

Geminis 6 and 7 had shown that the computer could accurately measure an atmospheric entry trajectory and provide cues to enable the pilots to steer to within visual range of the recovery force. If the next few missions could repeat this, the computer would be allowed to bring the final missions home "closed loop."

An early landing

As events transpired, Gemini 8 was obliged to make an emergency return when a problem involving the OAMS meant that Neil Armstrong had to activate the thrusters in the nose which were intended for re-entry. Rather than wait for an opportunity to aim for the primary recovery site in the Atlantic, a backup site in the Pacific was selected where, instead of a flotilla of ships based on an aircraft carrier, there was a solitary destroyer.

Although the USS *Leonard F. Mason* was ordered to steam 160nmi to the aim point, it would not arrive until several hours after the spacecraft landed. To provide immediate assistance, a pair of HC-54 aircraft flew in,

LEFT Side-by-side, the re-entry modules of Gemini 6 and Gemini 7 on the deck of the USS *Wasp*. Note that the skin panels of the re-entry control sections, made from highly toxic beryllium, have been removed. *(NASA)*

ABOVE Neil Armstrong and David Scott on board the USS *Leonard F. Mason* after their pickup in the Pacific Ocean. *(NASA)*

ABOVE Gemini 8 is hoisted aboard the USS *Leonard F. Mason*. Note the section of parachute bridle still attached to the nose of the spacecraft. *(NASA)*

one from the Japanese mainland and the other from Okinawa, to deliver swimmers with a flotation collar. In addition, an amphibious aircraft was sent in case it became necessary to make an emergency pickup.

The good news was that the weather was excellent and the sea state was calm. The de-orbit burn was made over central Africa in darkness, with all four retros firing in sequence. The spacecraft entered the atmosphere over China, still in darkness. Armstrong managed to use Sirius to verify their orientation prior to devoting his attention to "flying the needles:" to endeavor to land at the designated point. As they neared the dawn terminator he asked Dave Scott whether he could see the ocean behind them. He could. So they were confident they would not come down on land.

As soon as they splashed down, the two HC-54s began to circle. One dropped swimmers into the 15ft swell to attach the flotation collar. This done, the astronauts opened the hatches and chatted with their rescuers. After the *Mason* eventually drew alongside, they scrambled up a rope ladder onto the deck and watched as a crane lifted the capsule aboard. When the *Mason* tied up in port on the island of Okinawa, the astronauts were ferried by helicopter to the local airport to begin their long trip home. As Armstrong wryly told reporters, it had been a magnificent flight for the first seven hours.

Closed-loop re-entry

Tom Stafford steered his craft to a splashdown within 2,000 yards of the USS *Wasp*. Once the swimmers had fitted the flotation collar he opted to ride the crane onto the carrier's deck.

After John Young steered Gemini 10 to a splashdown only 4nmi from the USS *Guadalcanal*, NASA was willing to try a "closed-loop" re-entry; the computer would issue steering commands to bring a spacecraft in without human intervention. So for Gemini 11, instead of following the computer's steering cues by "flying the needles," Pete Conrad was to monitor its performance and be ready to intervene if it strayed off course. The computer placed the capsule within 3nmi of the USS

RIGHT Gemini 9 splashes down within sight of the main recovery ship, USS ***Wasp***. *(NASA)*

FAR RIGHT A frogman works underwater beneath the Gemini 10 spacecraft to attach a flotation collar. This helps stabilize the spacecraft in the water and prevents the possibility of it sinking. *(NASA)*

RIGHT Gemini 11 descends in two-point suspension near the recovery ship USS ***Guam***. *(NASA)*

Guam. Although the splashdown was not as close to the ship as Gemini 9, this was the most accurate descent to date in terms of the trajectory flown.

On the final mission, Gemini 12, the computer was again allowed to fly the re-entry with Jim Lovell monitoring its performance. It clipped several hundred feet off the "closed loop" record. The sea state made the splashdown a little rough, but within 30 minutes a helicopter delivered the astronauts to the USS *Wasp*.

The achievement of controlled re-entry to splash down at a specific target for rapid recovery illustrated the program's methodology. On the early missions, the issues were worked out. Astronauts then

RIGHT With personalized "Dick" and "Pete" caps, Gordon and Conrad pose in front of the recovery helicopter. *(NASA)*

LEFT **Gemini 12 approaches and then splashes down in the Atlantic Ocean 170nmi northeast of the Turks and Caicos Islands.** *(NASA)*

BELOW **A frogman leaps from a helicopter to begin the recovery of the Gemini 12 spacecraft. Its long HF antenna has been fully deployed.** *(NASA)*

showed that they could "fly the needles" and follow the computer's cues to make accurate splashdowns. Only then was the computer allowed to operate autonomously, but even then the crew monitored its performance, ready to intervene if necessary.

The development of controlled re-entry increased NASA's confidence in the atmospheric maneuvering that was to be used by an Apollo spacecraft returning from the Moon. The first mission to do this was Apollo 8 in December 1968, which splashed down within 2.4nmi of its target.

BELOW RIGHT **Buzz Aldrin and Jim Lovell with their Gemini 12 spacecraft on board the USS *Wasp*.** *(NASA)*

Conclusion

As Robert Gilruth, head of the Manned Spacecraft Center, observed after the program ended: "To go to the Moon, we had to learn how to operate in space. We had to learn how to maneuver with precision to rendezvous and to dock; to work outside in the hard vacuum of space; to endure long duration in the weightless environment; and to learn how to make precise landings from orbital flight; that is where the Gemini program came in."

Appendix

Acronyms

ACME Attitude Control and Maneuver Electronics
AMU Astronaut Maneuvering Unit
ATDA Augmented Target Docking Adapter
ATMU Auxiliary Tape Memory Unit
BEF Blunt End Forward
CapCom Capsule Communicator
CIA Central Intelligence Agency
CUVMS Chemical Urine Volume Measuring System
ECS Environmental Control System
EEG Electroencephalogram
ELSS Extravehicular Life Support System
EOR Earth Orbit Rendezvous
ESP Extravehicular Support Pack
EVA Extravehicular Activity
FLSC Flexible Lnear Shaped Charge
G&C Guidance and Control
GATV Gemini-Agena Target Vehicle
GLV Gemini Launch Vehicle
HF High Frequency
HHMU Hand-Held Maneuvering Unit
ICBM Intercontinental Ballistic Missile
IMU Inertial Measurement Unit
IRFNA Inhibited Red Fuming Nitric Acid
IVAR Insertion Velocity Adjustment Routine
IVI Incremental Velocity Indicator
LOR Lunar Orbit Rendezvous
MDIU Manual Data Insertion Unit
MDS Malfunction Detection System
MMH Monomethylhydrazine
MODS Manned Orbital Development System
MOL Manned Orbiting Laboratory
MON Mixed Oxides of Nitrogen
NASA National Aeronautics and Space Administration
OAMS Orbit Attitude and Maneuver System
PEM Proton Exchange Membrane
PPS Primary Propulsion System
PTFE Polytetrafluoroethylene
R&R Rendezvous & Recovery
RCS Re-entry Control System
REP Radar Evaluation Pod
RRS Retrograde Rocket System
SCS Secondary Propulsion System
SEF Sharp End Forward
STG Space Task Group
TPI Terminal Phase Initiation
UDMH Unsymmetrical Dimethylhydrazine
UHF Ultra-High Frequency
USA United States of America
USAF US Air Force
USB Unified S-Band
USSR Union of Soviet Socialist Republics
VCC Voice Control Center
VCM Ventilation Control Module
VHF Very-High Frequency
VOX Voice Activation "

Gemini Chronology

Spacecraft	Launched	Crew	Duration	Revs
Gemini 1	April 8, 1964	-	-*	3
Gemini 2	January 19, 1965	-	18min 16sec	0
Gemini 3	March 23, 1965	Gus Grissom and John Young	4hr 53min	3
Gemini 4	June 3, 1965	Jim McDivitt and Ed White	97hr 56min	62
Gemini 5	August 21, 1965	Gordon Cooper and Pete Conrad	190hr 56min	120
Gemini 7	December 4, 1965	Frank Borman and Jim Lovell	330hr 35min	206
Gemini 6	December 15, 1965	Wally Schirra and Tom Stafford	25hr 51min	16
Gemini 8	March 16, 1966	Neil Armstrong and Dave Scott	10hr 42min	7
Gemini 9	June 3, 1966	Tom Stafford and Gene Cernan	72hr 21min	45
Gemini 10	July 18, 1966	John Young and Mike Collins	70hr 47min	43
Gemini 11	September 12, 1966	Pete Conrad and Dick Gordon	71hr 17min	44
Gemini 12	November 11, 1966	Jim Lovell and Buzz Aldrin	94hr 35min	59

*Planned mission duration of Gemini 1 was 4hr 50min but once complete, the spacecraft was left to naturally re-enter, and was destroyed after almost 4 days.

Units

Force	
N	newton
kN	kilonewton
MN	meganewton
Time	
hr	hour
min	minute
sec	second
Distance	
ft	foot
m	meter
cm	centimeter
mm	millimeter
km	kilometer
nmi	nautical mile
Speed	
ft/sec	feet per second
m/sec	meters per second
km/hr	kilometers per hour
Electricity	
V	volt
A	ampere
Ah	ampere-hour
W	watt
kW	kilowatt
Force	
g	acceleration load
lbf	pounds force
Radio	
MHz	megahertz
Angles	
°	degree
arc-min	minute of arc
Temperature	
°C	degree Celsius
Pressure	
psi	pounds per square inch
Mass	
lb	pound
kg	kilogram

Conversion Factors

Distance		
feet	0.3048	meters
meters	3.281	feet
kilometers	0.6214	statute miles
statute miles	1.609	kilometers
kilometers	0.54	nautical miles
nautical miles	1.852	kilometers
nautical miles	1.1508	statute miles
statute miles	0.86898	nautical miles
Velocity		
feet/sec	0.3048	meters/sec
meters/sec	3.281	feet/sec
kilometers/hr	0.6214	statute mph
statute mph	1.609	kilometers/hr
Volume		
US gallons	3.785	liters
liters	0.2642	US gallons
imperial gallons	4.546	liters
liters	0.22	imperial gallons
cubic feet	0.02832	cubic meter
cubic meter	35.315	cubic feet
Mass		
pounds	0.4536	kilograms
kilograms	2.205	pounds
Pressure		
pounds/sq inch	70.31	grams/sq cm
grams/sq cm	0.0142	pounds/sq inch
Force		
pounds force	4.4482	newtons
newtons	0.2248	pounds force

Glossary

actuator A mechanism that transmits energy for the operation of another mechanism or system.
attitude A spacecraft's orientation in relation to its direction of travel.
augment To increase or make something greater by adding to it.
ballistic Of or relating to projectiles.
capsule A small part of a spacecraft that contains the instruments or crew.
Cold War The state of political hostility that existed between the Soviet bloc countries and the US-led Western powers from 1945 to 1990.
dock To join with another spacecraft in space.
hypergolic The spontaneous ignition of rocket propellant on mixing with another substance.
lunar Relating to the moon.
maneuver The skillful movement of a spacecraft.
orbit The path of a celestial body or spacecraft around a star, planet, or moon.
oxidize To combine chemically with oxygen.
pressurize To produce artificially high pressure in a cabin.
propellant A substance that allows something to move.
propulsion The action of pushing a spacecraft forward.
pyrotechnic A brilliant display.
rendezvous An arranged meeting.
retrograde Moving backward relative to another object's position.
transponder A device for receiving a radio signal and transmitting a different signal.

For More Information

Jet Propulsion Laboratory
4800 Oak Grove Drive
Pasadena, CA 91109
(818) 354-4321
Website: http://www.jpl.nasa.gov
The Jet Propulsion Laboratory is a national research facility that carries out robotic space and Earth science missions. JPL also developed and manages NASA's Deep Space Network, a worldwide system of antennas that communicates with interplanetary spacecraft.

John H. Chapman Space Centre
6767 Route de l'Aéroport
Saint-Hubert, Quebec J3Y 8Y9
Canada
(450) 926-4800
Website: http://www.asc-csa.gc.ca
The Canadian Space Agency is committed to leading the development and application of space knowledge for the benefit of Canadians and humanity.

National Aeronautics and Space Agency (NASA)
300 E. Street SW, Suite 5R30
Washington, DC 20546
(202) 358-0001
Website: http://www.nasa.gov
NASA is the space agency of the United States. Its mission is to "reach for new heights and reveal the unknown for the benefit of humankind."

National Air and Space Museum
Independence Ave at 6th St, SW
Washington, DC 20560
(202) 633-2214
Website: https://airandspace.si.edu
The Smithsonian's National Air and Space Museum maintains the world's largest and most significant collection of aviation and space artifacts. It welcome more than eight

million visitors a year, making it the most-visited museum in the country. It also is home to the Center for Earth and Planetary Studies.

Websites

Because of the changing nature of internet links, Rosen Publishing has developed an online list of websites related to the subject of this book. This site is updated regularly. Please use this link to access the list:

http://www.rosenlinks.com/GGTS/gemini

For Further Reading

Adamson, Thomas K. *Apollo 11 Moon Landing: An Interactive Space Exploration Adventure.* North Mankato, MN: Capstone Press, 2017.

Bisney, John, and J. L. *Pickering. Moonshots and Snapshots of Project Apollo: A Rare Photographic History.* Albuquerque, NM: University of New Mexico Press, 2015.

Cadbury, Deborah. *Space Race: The Epic Battle Between America and the Soviet Union for Dominion of Space.* New York: NY: Harper Perennial, 2007.

Chaikin, Andrew, and Tom Hanks. *A Man on the Moon: The Voyages of the Apollo Astronauts*. New York, NY: Penguin Books, 2007.

Holden, Henry M. *Space Shuttle Disaster: The Tragic Mission of the Challenger.* Berkeley Heights, NJ: Enslow Publishers, 2013.

Holt, Nathalia. *Rise of the Rocket Girls: The Women Who Propelled Us, from Missiles to the Moon to Mars.* New York: NY: Little, Brown and Company, 2016.

Lewis, John S., and David Gump. *Asteroid Mining 101: Wealth for the New Space Economy.* Moffett Field, CA: Deep Space Industries, Inc, 2015.

Mailer, Norman. *Moonfire: The Epic Journey of Apollo 11.* Cologne, Germany: Taschen, 2015.

Regas, Dean. *Facts from Space!: From Orbiting Urine to Outer Space Volcanoes, Extraterrestrial Facts to Blow Your Mind.* Avon, MA: Adams Media Corporation, 2016.

Reynolds, David W. *Apollo: The Epic Journey to the Moon, 1963–1972*. Minneapolis, MN: Zenith Press, 2013.

Roach, Mary. *Packing for Mars: The Curious Science of Life in the Void.* New York, NY: W.W. Norton & Company, 2011.

Scott, David R., A. A. Leonov, and Christine Toomey. *Two Sides of the Moon: Our Story of the Cold War Space Race.* New York: NY: Thomas Dunne Books, 2006.

Seedhouse, Erik. *Mars via the Moon: The Next Giant Leap.* Chichester, England: Springer, published in association with Praxis Publishing, 2016.

Seedhouse, Erik. *SpaceX's Dragon: America's Next Generation Spacecraft.* Chichester, England: Springer, published in association with Praxis Publishing, 2016.

Seedhouse, Erik. *XCOR, Developing the Next Generation Spaceplane.* Chichester, England: Springer, published in association with Praxis Publishing, 2016.

Shetterly, Margot. *Hidden Figures: The American Dream and the Untold Story of the Black Women Mathematicians Who Helped Win the Space Race.* New York, NY: William Morrow, 2016.

Stefoff, Rebecca. *Space Race: An Interactive Space Exploration Adventure.* North Mankato, MN: Capstone Press, 2017.

Tyson, Neil, Michael A. Strauss, and J. R. Gott. *Welcome to the Universe: An Astrophysical Tour.* Princeton, NJ: Princeton University Press, 2016.

Waldman, Ariel, and Brian Standeford. *What's It Like in Space? Stories from Astronauts Who've Been There.* San Francisco, CA: Chronicle Books, 2016.

Index

actuator, 56–57
adapter module, 15, 41, 42, 48, 49–50, 55, 56, 58, 64, 75, 78, 79, 82, 83, 88, 95, 96, 99, 116, 130, 145, 148–149, 151, 155–156, 157, 160, 165, 167–168
Agena, 14, 57, 65, 66, 115, 119, 122, 126–130, 131, 132, 133, 134, 135, 136, 138, 151–152–153, 154, 157, 159, 161
  target vehicle, 31–39, 54–55, 64, 113, 145
Apollo, 6, 11, 14, 42, 76, 96, 99, 122, 138
  Apollo 1, 43
  Apollo 8, 54–55
  Apollo 11, 78
  Apollo 13, 74
  crews of, 33–34
  and the lunar goal, 11–12, 33, 74, 109
  manufacturer, 44
  spacecraft, 23, 69–70, 87, 107, 126, 130, 141, 171
Armstrong, Neil, 56, 58, 119, 121, 168, 169
astronaut maneuvering system (AMU), 17, 95, 96, 147, 149, 150, 151, 153, 155, 156, 161
Atlas, 6, 14, 22–23, 25, 105
  boosters, 33, 122
attitude, 10, 39, 54, 60, 61, 64, 66, 67, 68, 69, 7--71, 86, 96, 99, 122, 165
attitude control, 34, 36, 39, 43, 54, 95–96, 123
  system, 38, 119, 124, 138
attitude control and maneuver electronics (ACME), 57
attitude indicator, 119
augmented target docking adapter (ATDA), 39, 122

ballistic arcs, 148, 164
ballistic flights, 10
ballistic re-entry, 47, 166
Braun, Wernher von, 12

Chamberlin, James, 13
Cold War, 21
Cooper, Gordon, 10, 106, 109, 112, 166
  efforts of, 167

docking, 6, 11, 33, 39, 44, 54, 66, 121–122, 124, 127, 133, 136, 138, 141, 145, 156, 171
  adapter, 128–129, 153, 154, 159
  apparatus, 14, 119
  bar, 149, 150, 155
  collar, 124
  equipment, 65
  gear, 15
  lamp, 129
  maneuvers, 99, 126, 132
  system, 123

Earth orbit rendezvous (EOR), 12
Eisenhower, Dwight, 16
encoder controller, 38
equipment section, 15, 43, 49, 50, 58, 76, 77, 78, 82, 165

Faget, Maxime, 13

Gagarin, Yuri, 6, 10, 16
gas generator, 27–28, 35, 36, 105

heatshield, 10, 11, 15, 17, 42–43, 47, 48–49, 50, 58, 60, 86, 163, 165
Houbolt, John, 12

inhibited red fuming nitric acid (IRFNA), 34
intercontinental ballistic missiles (ICBM), 22
interstage, 26, 28–29, 103

Kennedy, John F., 6, 11
  Moon challenge of, 16

landing, accurate, 6, 47
Langley Research Center, 10, 18
  engineers at, 12
long duration flight, 6, 15, 64, 94
LR-87-7 engine, 26–28
lunar landing, 6
  vehicle, 11
lunar orbiter probes, 33
lunar orbit rendezvous (LOR), 6, 12

malfunction detection system (MDS), 25, 102, 105, 106
manned orbital development system (MODS), 17
manned orbiting laboratory (MOL), 17
  space station, 24, 95, 146
Manned Spacecraft Center, 10, 93–94, 171
Marshall Space Flight Center, 12
McDonnell Aircraft Corporation, 9, 13, 15, 37, 39, 41
McNamara, Robert, 17
Mercury, 6, 9, 10–11, 16, 18, 22, 42, 46, 49, 53, 56, 87, 96, 105, 106, 164, 166
Mercury Mark II, 12–13, 14, 15
monomethylhydrazine (MMH), 56

Nagy, Alex, 14
National Aeronautics and Space Administration (NASA), 6, 10, 11, 12, 13, 14, 15, 16, 17–18, 24, 33–34, 36, 39, 55, 63, 64, 74, 76, 77, 88, 95, 96, 104, 105, 106, 107–108, 115, 119, 126, 135, 138, 142, 145, 147, 151, 153, 156, 169, 171
  creation of, 16
  headquarters, 164
  satellites, 131
  spacecraft, 42
Nikolayev, Adrian, 16

orbit attitude, 55–57
oxidizer, 23, 24–26, 34, 36, 37, 56, 105
  tank, 28, 29, 35, 82

pogo, 24, 25
polytetrafluoroethylene (PTFE), 58
Popovich, Pavel, 16
primary propulsion system (PPS), 33–34, 126
propellants, 23, 24, 26, 27, 28, 34–35, 36, 56, 57–58, 60, 61, 95, 96, 103, 112, 117, 119, 121, 123, 125, 126, 128, 129–130, 132, 138, 145
  hypergolic, 23, 83
  tanks, 37, 38, 55, 58, 82, 128
propulsion, 11, 32–33, 38, 39, 43, 49, 53–61, 95–96, 122, 130
pyrotechnics, 58, 74, 76, 102, 103, 104, 106, 165
  systems, 81–89, 105

re-entry control system (RCS), 15, 39, 42, 60–61, 121–122, 154, 165
re-entry module, 15, 41, 42, 43–46, 47, 48, 49, 50, 58, 61, 77, 79, 83, 84, 85, 86, 98, 164, 165
rendezvous, 6, 11, 12–13, 14, 16, 33, 39, 44, 54, 63, 64, 70, 96–97, 111, 112, 113, 114, 115–116, 119, 122, 123, 124, 125, 126, 128, 129, 136, 138, 167, 171
  in one, 130–135
rendezvous & recovery (R&R), 15, 42, 84–85
retrograde attitude, 60
retrograde burn, 134. 163
retrograde rocket system (RRS), 58
retrograde section, 15, 42–43, 49, 50, 79, 82, 83, 84, 130, 165, 167–168
Rogallo wing, 18

Saturn V launch vehicle, 12, 28
Scott, Dave, 58
secondary propulsion system (SPS), 36–37, 129, 138
Shepard, Alan, 6, 16
skin, of spacecraft, 25, 26, 45–46, 47–48, 49, 50, 58, 63, 78, 79

Soviet Union, 6, 10, 15, 16, 22, 31, 107
satellites of, 146
space race, 10, 14, 15–16, 18, 22, 32
Space Task Group, 10, 12
chief spacecraft designer, 13
spacewalking, 6, 13–14, 16, 17, 43, 78, 93–94, 95, 129, 130, 132, 138, 141–161

target docking adapter, 37–38
Titan rocket, 6, 101, 103, 104, 106, 131
launch vehicle, 13–14, 21–29, 111–112
Titan II, 14, 15, 19, 49, 55, 60, 83
Titan III, 17
transponder, 33, 39, 65, 66, 98, 113, 115, 116, 123, 126, 129

ullage, 37

Vostok, 10, 16